The Battle of Kursk in the summer of 1943 was one of the greatest battles in military history, involving more than 3 million soldiers, 10,000 tanks and 8,000 aircraft. While numerous books have been written on what many consider to be the most decisive battle of the Second World War, many legends live on, not least of all due to the inaccurate information which continues to appear in a variety of publications – even in the most recent books. Based on almost twenty years' research, in reassessing the primary sources Roman Toeppel sheds new light on the pre-battle decision-making, the preparations on both sides and the actual course of the battle. He provides material on little-known events, presenting some remarkable new insights into a battle which continues to fascinate. This work aims to set the record straight, exposing the erroneous nature of many of the popular myths which have continued to be perpetuated decades after the battle.

Roman Toeppel was born in Bautzen, Germany, in 1976. He studied history and political science at the University of Dresden (1996-2001). He completed his Master's degree with a thesis on the Battle of Kursk. Subsequently, Toeppel received his doctoral degree for research on Saxony in the Age of Napoleon, which led to his book *Die Sachsen und Napoleon* (2008). He went on to work on the annotated edition (with a critical commentary) of Adolf Hitler's *Mein Kampf*, part of a research project based at the Institute for Contemporary History, Munich. He was one of the four editors of the publication, which created heated debate in Germany, also winning a major academic prize in 2016. Toeppel has been a freelance historian since 2015; his main fields of historical research are currently the Battle of Kursk, the history of the Waffen-SS and Nazi ideology.

KURSK 1943

THE GREATEST BATTLE OF THE SECOND WORLD WAR

Modern Military History

Series Editors

ALARIC SEARLE, Professor of Modern European History, University of Salford, UK

DONALD STOKER, Professor of Strategy and Policy, US Naval War College, Naval Postgraduate School, Monterey, CA, USA

This series is dedicated to making available, at a reasonable price, quality academic military history, based on innovative and thorough scholarly research. While the main emphasis is on the publication of single-authored monographs, there will be scope for edited collections which focus primarily on new perspectives and evidence, as well as occasional translations of important foreign-language studies. *Modern Military History* will be framed in an 'inclusive' fashion, so that it encompasses armies, navies and air forces. While the traditional core concerns of military history—such as tactics, combat experience, technology, strategy and officer education—remain important fields of consideration, the encouragement of new angles and original approaches, whether methodologically, geographically or thematically, form a significant part of the editors' agenda.

Titles

No 1 *Genesis, Employment, Aftermath: First World War Tanks and the New Warfare, 1900-1945* edited by Alaric Searle (ISBN 978-1-909982-22-2)

No 2 *Naval Advising and Assistance: History, Challenges, and Analysis* edited by Donald Stoker and Michael T. McMaster (ISBN 978-1-911512-82-0)

No 3 *Expeditionary Police Advising and Militarization: Building Security in a Fractured World* edited by Donald Stoker and Edward B. Westermann (ISBN 978-1-911512-86-8)

No 4 *Kursk 1943: The Greatest Battle of the Second World War* by Roman Töppel (hardback ISBN 978-1-912390-03-8, paperback 978-1-914059-62-9)

Kursk 1943

The Greatest Battle of the Second World War

Modern Military History No.4

Roman Töppel

Helion & Company

For Virginie

Helion & Company Limited
Unit 8 Amherst Business Centre
Budbrooke Road
Warwick
CV34 5WE
England
Tel. 01926 499 619
Email: info@helion.co.uk
Website: www.helion.co.uk
Twitter: @helionbooks
Visit our blog http://blog.helion.co.uk/

Published by Helion & Company 2018. Reprinted in paperback 2021
Designed and typeset by Mach 3 Solutions Ltd (www.mach3solutions.co.uk)
Cover designed by Paul Hewitt, Battlefield Design (www.battlefield-design.co.uk)

Translation by Katharina Straub, Bern, Switzerland

Front cover: Panzerkampfwagen IV of the *Leibstandarte's* Panzer Regiment advancing on Teterevino (North) on 6 July 1943. (Private Collection)

ISBN 978-1-914059-62-9

British Library Cataloguing-in-Publication Data.
A catalogue record for this book is available from the British Library.

Contents

List of Illustrations

In plate section

Additional images of German armour from private collections

List of Maps

In colour section

Preface

The first book I ever read on military technology was 'Panzers Yesterday and Today' by Vladimir Mostovenko.[1] That was back in 1984, I was eight years old. Even then I was fascinated by the history of the Second World War – not least of all because of the glorification of the 'friendly sister nation', the Soviet Union, which was an integral part of the culture of remembrance in the German Democratic Republic, just as remembering the heroic deeds of the Red Army was part of the school curriculum. Soviet heroic epics, such as the five-part drama 'Liberation', were regularly shown on television in the German Democratic Republic. The first part, 'The Bulge of Fire', was a dramatisation of the tank battle of Kursk in 1943. Apart from feature films, documentaries on the Second World War were also regularly broadcast on grand anniversaries. It might therefore not be solely by chance that the Battle of Kursk has always been the focus of my interest, especially since, from the Soviet perspective, this battle is considered the very essence of armoured warfare, the 'biggest tank battle of the Second World War.' Even though I have been working on different historical events during my research – the interest in the Battle of Kursk has stayed with me.

But do we really need new studies on this battle, when especially in recent years numerous books have been published on the subject in the United States, Great Britain and the Russian Federation? Most certainly! Not only because many questions are still unanswered, but also because many historians have based their research primarily on previously published works and remain prejudiced by what various memoirs taught about the battle. Despite the vast number of studies on crucial decisions taken prior to the battle and on the summer 1943 battles themselves, there are still surprisingly many gaps in research and incorrect information.

The aim of this book is not a comprehensive account of the Battle of Kursk, recounting all combat operations of the units involved. Instead I would like to outline those developments and events which have so far remained more or less unknown or gone unnoticed, presenting the reader with new, sometimes surprising, findings about the battle.

1 Wladimir D. Mostowenko, *Panzer gestern und heute: Abriss der Entstehung und Entwicklung der Panzertechnik* (East Berlin, 1961); Russian original, *Tanki: Ocherk iz istorii zarozhdeniya i razvitiya bronetankovoi tekhniki* (Moscow, 2nd edn, 1958).

The records from the estate of Field-Marshal Erich von Manstein have been invaluable for my research on the battle; I would like to thank Rüdiger von Manstein for having made his father's papers available to me. I would also like to thank Jens Mulzer for allowing me to read the letters and diaries of his father, Rainer Mulzer. I have obtained further information about the tactical, technical and organisational aspects of the battles in summer 1943 from the war veterans Adolf Albers, Otto Altmann, Kurt Arp, Ernst Barkmann, Wolfgang Barth, Heinz Becher, Hans Behrend, Heinz Berner, Hans-Ekkehard Bob, Georg Bose, Anton Bumüller, Günther Burdack, Peter Richard von Butler, Otto Carius, Rolf Diercks, Gerhard Dilling, Edmund Dreilich, Heinrich Engel, Julius Faulhammer, Ulrich Felden, Oswald Filla, Hans Findeisen, Hans Joachim Fischer, Hans-Gottfried Fischer, Hellmuth Franke, Johann Franz, Fritz Fuchs, Günther Gaul, Alfred Genath, Heinz Gentzsch, Joachim Glade, Werner Gösel, Heinz Günther Guderian, Erhard Gührs, Norbert Hartmann, Eberhard Heder, Hermann Hehn, Horst Hellner, Fritz Henke, Richard Henze, Hermann Herz, Carl Hupfeld, Clemens Graf Kageneck, Bruno Kahl, Werner Kindler, Rolf Kliemann, Ernst Knauff, Werner Kortenhaus, Fritz Kosmehl, Horst Krönke, Willi Kubik, Rudolf Kuntzsch, Fritz Langanke, Günther Lange, Martin Lange, Heinz Lorenz, Heinrich Marenbach, Hubert Meyer, Günter Möbus, Helmut Mück, Horst Naumann, Heinrich Neff, Karl Neunert, Wilhelm Nußhag, Viktor Petermann, Hermann Pfitzner, Hellmuth Pock, Günther Polzin, Walter Pregetter, Rudolf Pufe, Hans-Dietrich Rade, Walter Rahn, Günther Rall, Alfred Regeniter, Günther Reichhelm, Rudolf von Ribbentrop, Gernot Richter, Werner Ritter, Wilhelm Roes, Hermann Röhm, Richard von Rosen, Alfred Rubbel, Kurt Sametreiter, Erich Schmidhäuser, Max Schmidt, Karl-Heinz Schnarr, Walter Schüle, Gerhard Schulze, Horst Schumann, Eibe Seebeck, Hans Siegel, Hans Siptrott, Kurt Söhrmann, Josef Steinbüchel, Ewald Stellmach, Alfred Stelter, Ralf Tiemann, Werner Völkner, Rupert Weiss, Werner Wendt and Waldemar Wienke.

I am much obliged to the staff of the archives and libraries which helped me with my research, above all Barbara Kiesow and Andrea Meier from the German Federal Archives, Military Archive Department in Freiburg im Breisgau, as well as Wolfgang Loof from the archive of the Verein Garnisongeschichte Jüterbog 'St. Barbara' e.V. I am indebted to Ulf Balke, who not only supplied me with material about the German Luftwaffe and taught me the basics of cartography but also time and again pointed out the importance of weather for the preparation of military operations. I am also grateful to Karl-Heinz Frieser for his valuable help and advice, even though we went separate paths after a time of fruitful exchanges of ideas. For their expertise and suggestions I would like to thank Christian Bauermeister, Jürgen Förster, Johannes Hürter, Peter Lieb, René Pfahlbusch, Markus Pöhlmann, Ralf Raths, Marco Sigg, Boris Sokolov, Sebastian Stopper, Philipp Vogler, Jürgen Wedemeyer, Adrian Wettstein, Mariya Solotarëva and Katharina Straub (who also translated the manuscript of this book from German to English). Many thanks!

My thanks also go to Alaric Searle (Series Editor) and Duncan Rogers (Helion & Co.) for accepting my book into the Modern Military History Series. I am most grateful to fellow historian Othmar Plöckinger, the authority on the early history of the NSDAP and most important expert for the history of Hitler's *Mein Kampf*, because he was one of the first people who, during a time when I was suffering a severe illness, motivated me, something for which he has earned my utmost gratitude. The same goes for my long-time and best friends Sarah K. Reader and Daniel Ristau. Special thanks for helping me through difficult times also go to Tomás Enrique Araya Díaz and his wife Sandra. Thank you very much, my friends. And don't ever let your anger interfere with your big smiles!

For her love, understanding and support my greatest thanks go to my wife, to whom I dedicate this book.

Roman Töppel,
Munich, Spring 2018

Introduction: 'Battle of Kursk' or 'Battle between Orel and Belgorod'?

On 22 July 1943, Lieutenant-General Nikolay Ivanovich Biryukov, member of the Military Council of the Armoured and Mechanized Forces of the Red Army, received a telegram from the Soviet 1st Tank Army. It read: 'The battles of the large armoured units which took place from 5 to 15 July 1943 demonstrated the improved military abilities of our commanding officers, tank commanders, drivers, artillerists, machine-gunners... [and] the *superiority* of Soviet technology over the enemy's [...].'[1] The telegram was signed by the commander of the 1st Tank Army, Lieutenant-General Mikhail Efimovich Katukov and by Major-General Nikolay Kirillovich Popel', member of the Military Council of Katukov's Army. Yet, in his memoirs, published in 1960, that same General Popel' quoted a 'party organizer' and Sergeant of the 1st Tank Army as follows: 'But the Germans again outmatched us with their tanks. For how long can this go on? It does not matter that they have more tanks. What matters is that our guns and tanks are no match for the 'Tiger'.'[2] This account contradicts both the statement in the above-mentioned telegram to Lieutenant-General Biryukov as well as official Soviet historiography. It also illustrated how difficult it apparently was in the Soviet Union to give an honest account of the Battle of Kursk. Instead of stating the undeniable truth of the superiority of German tanks himself, Popel' preferred to echo the opinion of a subordinate, who moreover had shown great bravery.

Such discrepancies mark the historiography of the Battle of Kursk. Soviet accounts usually give minute descriptions of the in-depth defensive positions the Red Army built in the Kursk salient in the months prior to the battle, yet why could these first two particularly strong and heavily mined lines of defence withstand the German attack for only a few days? And if the German panzer force was really destroyed in the

1 Tsentral'nyy Arkhiv Ministerstva Oborony Rossiskoy Federatsii, Podolsk (Central Archive of the Russian Ministry of Defence, hereafter, TsAMO), f. 38, op. 11353, d. 47, l. 2, telegram, communications centre of the People's Commissariat of Defence, report from the commander of the Soviet 1st Tank Army to the main department and the Military Council of the Armoured and Mechanized Forces, 22 July 1943; copy from the document collection ('Materialsammlung'), Centre for Military History and Social Science of the Federal German Armed Forces (*Zentrum für Militärgeschichte und Sozialwissenschaften der Bundeswehr*, hereafter, ZMSBw).

2 Nikolai N. Popjel, *Panzer greifen an* (East Berlin, 1964), p. 157.

Battle of Kursk, how is it possible that it could still launch strong counterattacks and 'remained an extremely aggressive and dangerous opponent until the very end of the war', as the Canadian military historian Gregory Liedtke put it a few years ago?[3] The list of such questions can be easily continued.

Unfortunately, many important German sources have been lost, such as most proceedings of Hitler's briefings, the war diary of Army Group Centre for spring 1943 and most Luftwaffe (German Air Force) records. These losses can barely be compensated by parallel sources. However, for the period of the actual battle the records from the armies which were engaged, the war diary of the Operations Section of the General Staff of the Army as well as reference files from the commander of Army Group South make up for the loss of the missing war diaries of Army Groups South and Centre.

With regards to the German side, it was possible to base the research for this study on the preparation phase and the attack itself almost solely on contemporary documents – largely thanks to the considerable quantity of records still accessible today. Post-war reports have also been taken into account, particularly the memoirs and numerous studies and essays of commanders who had been involved in the battle, though it should be noted that these reports, which always aim at justifying the actions of the respective author, mainly pass on myths. Thus, less credibility has been ascribed to the memoirs of leading military officers unless they can be checked against primary sources.

But, first of all, what exactly is meant by the 'Battle of Kursk'? German propaganda referred to the fighting at Kursk in summer 1943 as the 'battle between Orel and Belgorod.'[4] Even German Kursk veterans sometimes answer the question whether they took part in the Battle of Kursk with a 'No': They participated in the fighting at Khar'kov in spring 1943 and at Belgorod in summer 1943, but at Kursk? However, the operation at Belgorod *was* in fact Operation Citadel, that is, the first phase of the battle in the Kursk salient. The name Kursk, it seems, did not stick in their minds because it was not prevalent in German public awareness at that time.

By contrast, the Russians named the fighting in summer 1943 at Orël, Kursk and Khar'kov, 'Kurskaya bitva' (Battle of Kursk). They divided the battle into three phases: first, the phase of defence, which lasted from 5-11 July 1943 in the north of Kursk

3 Gregory Liedtke, 'Furor Teutonicus: German Offensives and Counter-Attacks on the Eastern Front, August 1943 to March 1945', *Journal of Slavic Military Studies*, 21 (2008), pp. 563-87, here, 564. Moreover, there are a number of German counterattacks Liedtke did not even take into account in his enumeration, such as the counterattacks at the Mius river in July/August 1943, at Breslau (Wrocław) in February 1945, at Lauban (Lubań) at the beginning of March 1945 and at Bautzen in April 1945.

4 The *Deutsche Wochenschau*, No. 672, 21 July 1943, stated: 'The battle between Orel and Belgorod is beginning to affect more and more front sectors.' See also *Die Wehrmachtberichte 1939-1945*, vol. 2: *1. Januar 1942 bis 31. Dezember 1943* (Cologne, 1989), p. 516.

and from 5-23 July 1943 in the south of Kursk, second, the counterattack at Orël from 12 July-18 August 1943; and, third, the counteroffensive at Khar'kov from 3-23 August 1943. This division of the Battle of Kursk has become widely accepted in modern historiography. Strictly speaking, however, it is incorrect because it suggests a continuous period of fighting when there was actually a gap between the three phases. According to the Soviet account of the battle there was a lull in the fighting in the southern sector of Kursk, which lasted from 23 July-3 August 1943. The war diaries reveal that this also is not true, as will be shown later. The matter of dividing the battle into phases becomes particularly important when calculating both sides' losses during the Battle of Kursk, since the Soviet losses from the three phases mentioned above are not equal to the total of losses the Red Army suffered in the battle – a fact which has gone unnoticed in the historiography until now.

The Battle of Kursk went down in history as the biggest tank battle of the Second World War. Indeed, the battle in the southern sector of the Kursk salient had, above all, the character of an enormous tank battle. The same is true for the Soviet counterattacks at Orël and Khar'kov. In the northern sector of the Kursk salient heavy tank battles took place during the defensive phase, too, but the fighting there was mainly characterized by a massive deployment of artillery. Moreover, Kursk was also one of the greatest air battles of the Second World War – another fact which so far has received only marginal attention by scholars.

Another battle which is almost forgotten today but which played a crucial role in the fighting in summer 1943 is the Soviet offensive in the Donets Basin, although the Soviet side did occasionally consider the engagements there as part of the Battle of Kursk. In the *History of the Art of War* edited by Ivan Khristoforovich Bagramyan, it is claimed that the 'defensive operation at Kursk was one of the biggest strategic operations. It involved troops of the Central and the Voronezh Front which collaborated with other fronts attacking in the direction of Orël and the *Donets Basin*.'[5] So far, historical research, including more recent Russian studies, has paid little attention to the battle which took place in the Donets Basin in July 1943. However, even if this battle is not considered as part of the Battle of Kursk, the actions at Kursk, Orël and Khar'kov in summer 1943 remain the biggest battle of the Second World War – and possibly even the 'biggest battle in history.'[6]

5 Iwan C. Bagramjan (ed.), *Geschichte der Kriegskunst* (East Berlin, 1973), p. 265 [emphasis added, RT]. The Soviet edition was first published in 1970 under the title *Istoriya voyn i voennogo iskusstva* [History of Wars and of the Art of War].

6 Karl-Heinz Frieser, 'Die Schlacht im Kursker Bogen', in Militärgeschichtliches Forschungsamt (ed.), *Das Deutsche Reich und der Zweite Weltkrieg*, vol. 8: *Die Ostfront 1943/44: Der Krieg im Osten und an den Nebenfronten* (Munich, 2007), pp. 81-208, here, 200.

1

The Strategic Context: The Preparations for the Summer Battle, 1943

The Strategic Situation of the German Reich in Spring 1943

For the German Reich, the year 1943 began with a series of catastrophic defeats. In February, the remainder of the Sixth Army capitulated in the Stalingrad pocket. The announcement of their surrender had 'a shock effect on the German people', as German propaganda minister Joseph Goebbels admitted in his diary on 4 February 1943.[1] The defeat at Stalingrad came as a shock not only to the home front, the front-line soldiers, too, were apprehensive of how things would turn out. The advancing Red Army seemed unstoppable; on 8 February Soviet troops recaptured Kursk and on 16 February the Germans had to evacuate Khar'kov. Two days later Joseph Goebbels called for 'total war' in his speech given at the Berlin Sport Palace. And when a platoon leader of an assault gun battery stationed on the Eastern Front, Lieutenant Ludwig Schön, wrote in a letter that the 'fall of Stalingrad and the total war really are a test of nerves. Peace at all cost?' he must have echoed the feelings of many other Germans.[2]

Yet Stalingrad was not the only portent indicating a change in the fortunes of war in favour of the Allies. After its defeats at Midway in June 1942 and on Guadalcanal and New Guinea at the beginning of 1943, Germany's most important ally Japan was now definitely forced into a position of strategic defence. On 21 January 1943, the Allied powers moreover agreed on the Casablanca directive, a joint approach to intensifying the strategic bombing of Germany. The nature of the subsequent phase of the air war, which also saw the introduction of new technical means, first manifested itself in the Battle of the Ruhr. This battle began during the night of 6 March 1943 with a heavy air raid on Essen; when it ended on 31 July 1943, over 15,000 people

1 Joseph Goebbels, *Die Tagebücher von Joseph Goebbels*, ed. Elke Fröhlich, pt. II: Diktate 1941-1945, 15 vols. (Munich, 1993-1996), vol. 7, p. 256.

2 Archive of the Verein Garnisongeschichte Jüterbog 'St. Barbara' e.V. (hereafter, Garnisongeschichte Jüterbog): [no signature] Beitrag zur Geschichte der Sturmgeschütz-Brigade 909, Zusammenstellung aus Briefen des damaligen Leutnants d. R. Ludwig Schön, p. 6.

in the Ruhr area had lost their lives. As Goebbels noted in his diary, Field-Marshal Erhard Milch, Chief of Aircraft Procurement and Supply, had told him on 9 April that it would probably take until November 1943 'to answer the English on a larger scale, and until next spring, that is a year from now, to pay them back in kind. [...] Until then the British can, if they are actually able to do it, lay a large part of the territory of the Reich in ashes.'[3] During the attack on Dortmund on 24 May 1943 alone the Royal Air Force dropped more than 2,500t of bombs – about as much as the Luftwaffe dropped over Britain in 1943 in total. Even towns outside of the Ruhr area were destroyed in heavy raids during the Battle of the Ruhr, such as the raid on Wuppertal in the night of 30 May 1943, which caused the first 'firestorm' and cost 3,500 lives.

In May 1943, the German Reich suffered two more bitter defeats: On 13 May Army Group Afrika surrendered; 270,000 German and Italian troops were taken prisoner by the Allies. Yet only two months earlier, the Commander-in-Chief of the German Kriegsmarine, Admiral of the Fleet Karl Dönitz, had told Hitler that Tunisia was a 'first-class strategic position.'[4] Now it was irrevocably lost and, as a consequence, the Allied invasion of Italy had become simply a matter of time. The same month went down as 'Black May' in the history of the Kriegsmarine. Through tactical and technical innovations the Allies finally managed to turn the tide of submarine warfare, even though in March 1943 the Allied merchant navy had still suffered significant losses in the North Atlantic due to German U-boats. In fact, on 2 April Goebbels triumphantly commented on this last success: 'The U-boat war really is our ultimate weapon, which gives the English a hard fight.'[5] The German leadership was all the more dismayed when in May successes could no longer be reported, while German U-boats were lost on a near daily basis – 40 boats in total until the end of the month. On 14 May, Admiral of the Fleet Dönitz reported to Adolf Hitler that the Germans were facing 'the most serious crisis of U-boat warfare' because the enemy not only inflicted heavy losses on the U-boats but actually kept them from fighting in the first place through the use of new tracking devices.[6]

In view of all these problems and of the very tense situation, Hitler reasoned that he had only one option – to bring about a military decision in the East. In a meeting on the Obersalzberg on 25 June 1943, he explained to Goebbels that whilst one would just have to patiently bear the current defensive phase, new weapons which would change the war in the air and at sea in favour of the German Reich would be ready within the next few weeks and months. The key front, Hitler stressed, was the Eastern Front. After all, the Wehrmacht had managed to bring the Soviet winter offensive to

3 Goebbels, *Tagebücher*, pt. II, vol. 8, p. 81.
4 Gerhard Wagner (ed.), *Lagevorträge des Oberbefehlshabers der Kriegsmarine vor Hitler 1939–1945* (Munich, 1972), p. 472.
5 Goebbels, *Tagebücher*, pt. II, vol. 8, p. 33.
6 Wagner, *Lagevorträge*, p. 505.

a halt and recapture Khar'kov in March 1943. This victory not only increased prestige and served to reassure Germany's wavering allies but also gave reason to hope that the war might not just yet be militarily lost. On 14 March 1943, Field-Marshal Erich von Manstein, commander of Army Group South, wrote to his wife in relief: 'So it seems that thanks to our success we have once more survived the crisis in the East. Well, one should not assume that it is the end just because things sometimes go wrong, as many people at home surely prophesied.'[7]

In view of this success Hitler thought that the war might not be lost – a political compromise with the Soviet Union was out of the question for him. In a speech to *Reichs-* and *Gauleiter* on 7 May 1943, he even talked about achieving his old goal of German world domination, as Joseph Goebbels noted: 'The *Führer* expresses his absolute certainty that the Reich will one day dominate all of Europe. We still have to fight a great many battles but they will doubtlessly lead to a spectacular success, from whence the path to world domination is all but predetermined. Whoever controls Europe will thereby seize the leadership of the world.'[8] In an address to commanders-in-chief and commanding generals of the *Ostheer* (the German Army in the East) on 1 July 1943, Hitler reiterated that for Germany the battle in the East was 'a battle for *Lebensraum*, without which the German Reich and the German nation cannot exist. Germany must become the hegemonic power in Europe.'[9] However, the German-occupied Soviet territories were more than future '*Lebensraum*' for the German people – in economic terms, Hitler considered the East as decisive for the outcome of the war. On the one hand, he believed that in the long run the war could not be continued without the rich natural resources of the Donets Basin, the coalfield in the southeast of Ukraine. On the other hand, the German economy was in constant need of new workers and largely relied on forced labourers from the occupied eastern territories. In fact, the shortage of labour began to play a crucial role even in military operational planning. Whilst in 1941/42 two million Soviet prisoners of war had been starved to death, it was an explicit objective of the German summer offensive in 1943 to capture as many soldiers of the Red Army as possible, so they could be used for forced labour. Furthermore, the eastern theatre of operations was of key importance for the German Reich also because it was here that in 1941/42 the mass murder of the European Jews had been taking place. News of this began to spread in Germany by mid-1942; the German population reacted to it mostly with a fear of retribution, a fear that was deliberately fuelled by German propaganda in order to strengthen the endurance of the *Volksgemeinschaft*. But their guilty conscience over the mass murder of Jews was not the only source of fear for the Germans.

7 Private Archive of Rüdiger von Manstein, Icking, estate of Erich von Manstein (hereafter, Private Archive of Rüdiger von Manstein), excerpts from Field-Marshal von Manstein's letters to his wife, March 1943, p. 4.

8 Goebbels, *Tagebücher*, pt. II, vol. 8, pp. 237-8, quote, 238.

9 Helmut Krausnick, 'Zu Hitlers Ostpolitik im Sommer 1943', *Vierteljahrshefte für Zeitgeschichte*, 2 (1954), pp. 305-12, 311.

The Red Army's victories gave new hope and confidence to the Soviet prisoners of war and civilians who were forced to work as *Ostarbeiter* in the German Reich. A report from the SS Security Service on the morale in Germany dated 25 February 1943 states that the changes in the military situation greatly affected the 'discipline and working morale' of the *Ostarbeiter*. Now, they openly spoke about retaliation against the Germans, confident that after the Soviets' entry into Germany they would torture and kill all Germans. Female *Ostarbeiter* who worked as domestic helpers for German families said they would 'show their gratitude for good treatment by making sure the respective families would die a quick death.'[10] The Germans' fear of defeat grew even worse in the following weeks. In early 1943, the bodies of about 4,500 Polish officers were found in mass graves in the Katyn forest, west of Smolensk, who had been murdered by the Soviet NKVD (*Narodnyy komissariat vnutrennykh del*, People's Commissariat for Internal Affairs) in spring 1940. In April 1943, Goebbels used this discovery for a major propaganda campaign aimed at fuelling the German population's fear of Soviet atrocities. At the same time, more and more Germans doubted that the war could actually still be won. Even old party members, such as the *Landeshauptmann* (State Governor) of the province of Westphalia, Karl-Friedrich Kolbow, became increasingly pessimistic. On 22 March 1943, Kolbow wrote in his diary that it 'all depends on whether we can deliver the *coup de grâce* to Russia this summer.'[11]

German Strategic Considerations on the Eastern Front, 1943

Due to the heavy losses suffered during the two major offensives on the Eastern Front in 1941 and 1942 and the heavy defeats they had to face in early 1943, the German leadership had to decide which strategy it should – and still could – adopt on the Eastern Front. Should the Wehrmacht launch an early attack on the Eastern Front in spring 1943 in order to forestall the expected Soviet offensives and thus maintain the initiative? This option offered the Germans the advantage of deciding on the main focus of the battle, or whether it would be better to remain on the defensive and waiting until the Red Army attacked. In this case, the Wehrmacht could – having repelled the Soviet troops, who would then be worn out – mount a counteroffensive and advance far beyond the original positions. Manstein and other German military officers called this latter concept a 'backhand blow' (*Schlagen aus der Nachhand*).[12] The Red Army

10 Heinz Boberach (ed.), *Meldungen aus dem Reich 1938-1945: Die geheimen Lageberichte des Sicherheitsdienstes der SS*, 17 vols. (Herrsching, 1984), vol. 12, pp. 4849-50.

11 Karl Friedrich Kolbow, *Die Tagebücher Karl Friedrich Kolbows (1899-1945): Nationalsozialist der ersten Stunde und Landeshauptmann der Provinz Westfalen*, ed. Martin Dröge (Paderborn, 2009), p. 564.

12 Manstein used this term for example in an estimate of the situation to the Chief of the General Staff of the Army, 21 March 1943, located in Private Archive of Rüdiger von

had successfully applied this concept at Stalingrad in November 1942, and Manstein had used it in February/March 1943 when he stopped the Soviet winter offensive at Khar'kov, cutting off and destroying the Soviet offensive forces. Such a 'backhand blow' on a large scale was what Manstein had in mind for the following spring and summer. On 3 February 1943 he sent a teletype message to General Kurt Zeitzler, Chief of the Army General Staff, with his estimate of the situation 'to be passed on to the *Führer*.' In his assessment Manstein suggested 'dragging the Russian southern flank along in battle to the Melitopol–Dnepropetrovsk line in order to first hit their northern front of attack and sever their northern and southern connections, taking advantage of the favourable railway network. Following this, turning to the southwest [sic!] and with cover from the north, the enemy should then be pushed towards the Sea of Azov. For this operation', Manstein continued, 'it is necessary that the Army Group [South] must be withdrawn in time to preserve combat strength, supply the needed personnel and to hold the area of Orël–Kursk (or at least of Bryansk–trainstation of Lgov [L'gov]).'[13]

However, the conditions for a massive strike as listed by Manstein were simply not there. First of all Hitler refused to pull out temporarily from the Donets Basin. Secondly, on 3 March 1943, the Red Army recaptured the important railway junction at L'gov – the junction which according to Manstein would have been vital for a German strike. Besides, Hitler did not want to launch another large-scale offensive on the Eastern Front in 1943 anyway, as he made clear in a briefing at the headquarters of Army Group South in Zaporozhe on 18 February 1943. 'We cannot mount any major operations this year', Hitler informed the officers present. 'We have to avoid any risk. I think we should just take minor evasive actions (*kleine Haken schlagen*).'[14] These actions should be carried out as initial strikes, that is, Hitler wanted to pre-empt the Red Army with minor offensive attacks to keep the initiative. In a briefing in the *Führer*'s Headquarters 'Werwolf' near Vinnitsa on 5 March, he argued that the panzer formations should be reinforced within the next few weeks so that they would be ready to attack right after the mud season; he claimed that this view was shared by Chief of Staff Zeitzler. What Hitler meant by mud season was the spring *rasputitsa* (literally the 'time without roads'), which transformed Soviet streets and roads into mud, making any large-scale troop movements impossible.

As Manstein had to give up his hope of carrying out a large-scale 'backhand blow', he adopted the idea of an initial strike. On 8 March 1943 he drew up an estimate of the

Manstein, Handakte des Oberbefehlshabers der Heeresgruppe Süd, no pagination.

13 Bundesarchiv-Militärarchiv, Freiburg i.Br. (hereafter, BA-MA), RH 19 VI/39, Kriegstagebuch der Heeresgruppe Don/Süd, 3.2.-15.2.1943, fol. 12-14, quote, fol. 14.

14 Private Archive of Rüdiger von Manstein, Handakte des Oberbefehlshabers der Heeresgruppe Don/Süd, Februar 1943, no pagination. The minutes of this briefing are also cited in Eberhard Schwarz, *Die Stabilisierung der Ostfront nach Stalingrad: Mansteins Gegenschlag zwischen Donez und Dnjepr im Frühjahr 1943* (Göttingen, 1986), pp. 254-6, but there the significant sentence from the original 'We have to avoid any risk' is omitted.

situation, in which for the first time he also elaborated on the time after the *rasputitsa*. Manstein recommended a joint attack of Army Groups Centre and South to forestall a Soviet offensive against Army Group South. Elements of Army Group South were to deploy from the area west of Khar'kov to the north, while units of the Second Army of Army Group Centre were to move from the area north of Sumy towards the southeast. This was the small version of a pincer attack south of Kursk (map 1). The larger version was first brought up for discussion two days later. However, it was not proposed by Manstein or Hitler, but by a general whose role in this matter has so far gone unnoticed in historical scholarship. On 10 March 1943, the commander of Army Group Centre, Field-Marshal Hans Günther von Kluge, made a phone call to the commander of the subordinate Second Panzer Army, Colonel-General Rudolf Schmidt. At that time, the Second Panzer Army was positioned south of Orël. Between this army and its neighbour, the Second Army, there was a huge gap in the front line where the Red Army had broken through to the river Desna. Kluge urged Schmidt to close the gap between the two armies before the beginning of the *rasputitsa*. To achieve this, Kluge planned to bring up another assault group: the Ninth Army, commanded by Colonel-General Walter Model, which had just become available after having pulled out from the Rzhev salient. Model's army was to strike from the south of Orël towards Kursk.

In a written comment on Kluge's suggestion, Schmidt argued that the Second Panzer Army was currently engaged in a fierce defensive battle and fully occupied with preventing the Soviet thrust towards Bryansk. Even with the newly brought-up forces from the Ninth Army the front line could only just be held. But it would be impossible to form an offensive group south of Orël before the *rasputitsa* began. Instead one should 'refrain from offensive schemes and economise forces' for the moment. Schmidt suggested 'forming [a] stronger [group of] operational forces …, whose deployment from the area south of Orël towards Kursk, combined with a northbound attack by another group from the area of Khar'kov, would be conceivable' – though only after the mud season.[15] This is exactly the approach which was later applied in Operation Citadel. The originator of this plan was therefore Schmidt. Proof of this can also be found in Kluge's reaction when he called Schmidt in the late evening of 10 March and declared: 'I must say, your line of thought really has some merit.'[16] The Ninth Army, Kluge continued, would be deployed anyway, but it would not have to rush it. Indeed, that same evening, Kluge called Colonel-General Model to tell him that by now it was probably impossible to launch an offensive operation as it was already beginning to thaw. Model's Army would not, therefore, be transferred to the area south of Orël until later rather than immediately.

15 BA-MA, RH 21-2/433, Panzerarmee-Oberkommando 2, Sonderanlage A zum Kriegstagebuch 4.2.-6.8.1943, Akte Ia – Chefsachen ('Verschiedenes'), fol. 13.
16 BA-MA, RH 21-2/452, Kriegstagebuch des Panzerarmee-Oberkommandos 2, Ia, Anlagen vol. 9, 1.3.-15.3.1943, fol. 683.

On the following day, 11 March 1943, Hitler paid another visit to the headquarters of Army Group South in Zaporozhe. Manstein used the occasion to reiterate his wish of eliminating the salient at Kursk before the beginning of the *rasputitsa*. Hitler replied that the salient could not be removed because that way 'one would lose the option for smaller offensive pushes.' Hitler proceeded to explain that it was actually impossible to launch any major operations in the near future: 'Through continuous raids we have to keep the initiative and maintain losses at a ratio of about 1:10. The Russian has to be systematically weakened, not so much with divisions as with modern weapons. And then we have to hold and defend!'[17] Manstein was not convinced by this concept. On the same day, he made a note in his private war diary about the briefing and about Hitler: 'No clarity about his own agenda. We are moving on two different levels – I on the operational one, he on the level of material and numbers. This way we will never obtain a result.'[18]

At this time, Hitler himself was unsure where the offensive operations of the following spring and summer should be launched. The only thing he strongly and repeatedly insisted on was that the Donets Basin had to be held at all cost because it was of crucial economic importance for the future course of the war. He made his final decision two days later, on 13 March 1943, when visiting the headquarters of Army Group Centre in Smolensk. Apart from Hitler, Zeitzler and Kluge, who took part in the briefing, the armies' commanders were also present, including Colonel-General Schmidt, who now received the opportunity to present Hitler with his plan of attack. Hitler seems to have been impressed by it, for on the same day he issued Operations Order No. 5 ('Warfare directive for the next months'), which reads: 'On the northern flank of Army Group [South] the formation of a strong panzer army must be begun at once; its assembly must be complete by mid-April so that after the end of the spring thaw we can mount an offensive *before* the Russians do. The aim of this operation is the destruction of the enemy forces in front of [the] Second Army by a thrust north from the area of Khar'kov together with an offensive group from the area of the Second Panzer Army.'[19] Operation Citadel, the plan for the pincer attack on Kursk, was thus initiated. If the father of this child was Rudolf Schmidt, then its godfathers were Kluge and Hitler. Incidentally, it is a myth that in this briefing Schmidt insulted Hitler with the statement that 'your war experience can be carried off on a sparrow's tail.'[20] Hitler would never have put up with such insolence and would have promptly

17 Schwarz, *Stabilisierung*, pp. 261-2.

18 Private Archive of Rüdiger von Manstein, Erich von Manstein, persönliches Kriegstagebuch Nr. 4, 19.11.1942-14.3.1943, transcript, p. 37.

19 Ernst Klink, *Das Gesetz des Handelns: Die Operation 'Zitadelle' 1943* (Stuttgart, 1966), p. 277 [emphasis in original, RT].

20 This is what Fabian von Schlabrendorff claimed in his memoirs. Fabian von Schlabrendorff, *Begegnungen in fünf Jahrzehnten* (Tübingen, 1979), p. 264. At the beginning of 1943, Schlabrendorff was a lieutenant and aide-de-camp in the staff of Army Group Centre. His allegation has since been repeated frequently in the literature, even

rebuked Schmidt. Goebbel's diary also gives evidence to the contrary. Hitler, as is well known, would never tire of affronting his generals among old party comrades when he was dissatisfied with them. An insult such as Hitler had allegedly suffered by Schmidt in Smolensk would undoubtedly have resulted in one of his feared sudden bursts of anger. But on 15 March 1943, Goebbels wrote in his diary: 'The *Führer* has concluded his flight to the Central Front. He has found conditions to be excellent there. The situation in the centre is portrayed very positively. The *Führer* also had the best impression of the leadership there.'[21]

It is true that Colonel-General Schmidt was forced to take leave in April 1943, relieved as commander of the Second Panzer Army and eventually discharged from the Wehrmacht on 30 September 1943. But the reason for this were the letters to his brother Hans-Thilo, who had become a target of German counterintelligence, which suspected him of treason, and who was arrested on 2 April 1943. After Hitler had complained bitterly to him about the generals, Goebbels noted in his diary on 10 May 1943: 'For example, when they had to arrest Colonel-General Schmidt's brother for treason, they found a whole series of letters from the colonel-general himself, sharply attacking the *Führer*. That was only one of the generals the *Führer* had strongly relied on – and once more he was bitterly disappointed.'[22] Nevertheless, Schmidt's plan of attack was not scrapped because of this, even though the counterproposals Hitler made during the following weeks reveal that he was by no means as convinced of the plan as has often been suggested.

German Operational Planning, Spring 1943

Operations Order No. 5, issued on 13 March 1943, specified that the pincer attack on Kursk should begin only after the spring *rasputitsa*. Manstein, however, did not want to give in and kept urging the Army General Staff to remove the Kursk salient at once. On 18 March, he telephoned the Chief of Staff Zeitzler and told him: '[The] Russian in front of our left wing and in front of [the] right wing of [Army Group] Centre is

though his reminiscences are verifiably erroneous and unreliable and should not be given credence.

21 Goebbels, *Tagebücher*, pt. II, vol. 7, p. 554. Evidence for the fact that Schmidt did not insult Hitler on this occasion is also provided by the personal diaries and letters of Colonel-General Gotthard Heinrici, the commander of the German Fourth Army, and Colonel-General Hans-Georg Reinhardt, commander of Third Panzer Army. Both were present at the meeting with Hitler in Smolensk on 13 March 1943, and neither of them mentioned Schmidt's alleged insult. BA-MA, N265/13, Nachlass Gotthard Heinrici, Persönliches Tagebuch, Januar bis März 1943, BA-MA, N245/2, Nachlass Hans-Georg Reinhardt, Auszugsweise Abschriften von Briefen des Generals an seine Frau, 1939 bis Januar 1945, fol. 24, N245/3, Persönliches Kriegstagebuch, 17.6.1941 bis Ende 1945, fol. 40.

22 Goebbels, *Tagebücher*, pt. II, vol. 8, p. 266.

not capable of doing much anymore. I think that Army Group Centre could now take Kursk without difficulty.' Zeitzler replied that 'the *Führer* would like an operation from Chuguev towards Izyum.'[23] The two towns of Chuguev and Izyum southeast of Khar'kov were situated in a salient in the north of the Donets Basin, which reached into the front of Army Group South (map 1). Hitler feared that the Red Army might launch an offensive towards Dnepr in the southwest to cut off the Donets Basin, which for him was the neuralgic point of the whole Eastern Front.

Manstein refused the idea of an offensive at Chuguev and Izyum before the beginning of the spring thaw because he was convinced his forces were not strong enough. Two days later, on 20 March, he called Lieutenant-General Adolf Heusinger, Chief of the Operations Section of the General Staff , explaining that now was a good opportunity for an advance on Kursk – though not without the participation of Army Group Centre. Heusinger, however, pointed out that Hitler favoured an immediate push on Izyum. Manstein declined, reiterating that he preferred an operation at Kursk in order to remove the wide open northern flank of his Army Group, west of Khar'kov. He restated his opinion the following day, on 21 March, in a telephone call with Zeitzler: If the attack on Kursk was launched immediately, Izyum could still be attacked afterwards. Zeitzler brought up Manstein's request during the noon briefing on the Obersalzberg on the same day, but Hitler was against the idea and argued that if an advance before the spring thaw was at all still feasible 'it will be an advance at Izyum.' By contrast, it 'makes no sense for the Army Group South continue its offensive in the direction of Kursk.'[24] Zeitzler therefore had to inform Manstein in the evening that Hitler had given the order to discontinue Army Group South's preparations for the operation against Kursk and instead start preparing one from Khar'kov towards the southeast.

Yet Manstein would not give up so easily. Without delaying, he gave his opinion to Zeitzler regarding Hitler's planned operation at Chuguev and Izyum, emphasizing that at the moment this operation could only be detrimental. First, the units were too weakened to carry out the attack before the beginning of the thaw. Second, the panzer divisions needed urgent rest and refitting. Finally, the planned new front line would not help economizing forces – on the contrary: the threat on the northern flank of Army Group South at Khar'kov would not only remain but actually increase as the Germans would be forced to withdraw troops.

The next day, on 22 March, Manstein once again told Zeitzler about his objections to the operation. His estimate of the situation was furthermore shared by his panzer commanders, who also advised against an operation at Chuguev and Izyum. In spite of this, Hitler ignored Manstein's opposition and that same day issued the '1st

23 BA-MA, RH 19 VI/43, Anlagen zum Kriegstagebuch Nr. 1 der Heeresgruppe Süd, Ferngespräche (Gespräche des Oberbefehlshabers), vol. 2: 4.2.-23.3.1943, fol. 42.

24 Helmut Heiber, et al. (eds.), *Hitler and His Generals: Military Conferences 1942-1945* (London, 2002), pp. 115-6.

addition to Operations Order No. 5', in which he ordered that the planned offensive on Kursk should be preceded by an attack over the Donets in order to destroy the enemy forces west of Kupyansk. The attack on Kursk should commence only after this operation. At least Manstein had managed to postpone the offensive from Chuguev and Izyum to Kupyansk until after the spring thaw.

In the end, however, Manstein had to yield. On 23 March he ordered the High Commands of the First Panzer Army and Army Detachment Kempf, the latter being named after its commander, *General der Panzertruppe* Werner Kempf, to begin preparing for an operation against the Soviet forces at the Donets in the Chuguev–Izyum–Kupyansk triangle. This operation was due to be launched in the middle of April and was given the code name *Habicht* (Hawk) (Map 1). On the following day, Army Group Centre ordered the Second Army, the Second Panzer Army and the Ninth Army to prepare for the push on Kursk, which would be launched in cooperation with forces of Army Group South immediately after Operation *Habicht*. It was in this order that the code name for the planned operation was mentioned for the first time: Operation Citadel.[25] The date set for it was 1 May 1943.

Now, however, broad resistance against Operation *Habicht* began to stir. On 24 March, the chiefs of staff of the First Panzer Army and Army Detachment Kempf – the two armies assigned to carry out *Habicht* – agreed that it was wrong to launch smaller, successive attacks because 'that way the troops would again not be given a chance to rest and refit this year.' Instead, 'one should better mount one larger attack at a later time.'[26] In fact, Hitler had shown with the '1st addition to Operations Order No. 5', issued on 22 March, that his intentions for an attack on Kupyansk actually went beyond what had been planned for *Habicht*. The attacking formations were to take a longer way around and so destroy more enemy forces, and the new front line would then run from Volchansk via Kupyansk to Lisichansk. This larger version of Operation *Habicht* received the code name *Panther* (Map 2). On 25 March, the High Command of the First Panzer Army presented Army Group South with a first proposition for Operation *Panther*, which stated that it could begin only around 1 May 1943 – this, however, was the date which had already been set for Citadel. It was thus clear that the bigger Operation *Panther* could not be launched before the attack on Kursk since it was actually an alternative to Citadel. When Manstein visited the First Panzer Army on 27 March, he agreed with its commander *General der Kavallerie* Eberhard von Mackensen that Operation *Panther* was more promising than *Habicht*. Yet the decision as to which operation would be chosen now lay with the Army High Command – and therefore ultimately with Hitler. That same evening, Manstein tried

25 BA-MA, RH 20-9/142, Oberkommando der Heeresgruppe Mitte, 24.3.1943, Befehl für die Vorbereitung der Operation 'Zitadelle', Anlage zum Kriegstagebuch Nr. 8, Armee-Oberkommando 9, Ia, vol. V, Befehle übergeordneter Stellen (Auswahl), Berichtszeit: 26.3.-18.8.1943, no pagination.

26 BA-MA, RH 21-1/89, Nachträge zum Kriegstagebuch Nr. 10 des Panzerarmee-Oberkommandos 1, Ia, 1.1.-30.4.1943, Chefsachen, fol. 3.

to achieve clarification in a telephone call with Zeitzler, who told him that Hitler favoured Operation *Panther*; and, when Manstein visited Army Detachment Kempf the next day, he was told that they, too, favoured Operation *Panther* over Operation *Habicht*.

But the operational situation now began to change. In an estimate of the situation written on 29 March, Manstein explained to Zeitzler that the Red Army was moving more and more troops into the area south of Kursk. Therefore, Manstein continued, it might 'first be necessary to strike towards Kursk and eastwards in cooperation with Army Group Centre' – that is Operation Citadel.[27] On 2 April 1943, the Army High Command ordered that all three operations should be prepared for as a precautionary measure: If Operation *Habicht* could not be 'launched on time due to weather conditions, Operation *Panther* should be prepared for as well. Furthermore, Army Group [South] must be ready to join Operation Citadel should a changed enemy situation require it.'[28]

Citadel was the operation the commanders of the armies of Army Group South clearly favoured over Hitler's offensive plans *Habicht* and *Panther*. This is what the Chief of Staff of the First Panzer Army, Major-General Walther Wenck, told the Operations Officer of Army Group South, Colonel Georg Schulze-Büttger, at a briefing on the situation which took place on 4 April. On the same day, Colonel-General Model visited the Fourth Panzer Army. He was temporarily in charge of Army Group South because Manstein had to undergo tonsillectomy and was on leave. Model learned from the commander of the Fourth Panzer Army, Colonel-General Hermann Hoth, that the goals of Operation *Panther* could not be achieved with the available forces. Besides, the Fourth Panzer Army did not expect the operation to become a 'resounding success, as the goal of the attack – the destruction of the attacking enemy forces – could not be achieved, since these were outside the operational area.'[29] Hoth, too, preferred Operation Citadel, considering it the most promising scheme of manoeuvre.

In the meantime, the limited Operation *Habicht*, which was to precede Operation Citadel, had become redundant: on 5 April, Army Group South sent a report from its military meteorologists to the Army High Command which made clear that even with favourable weather conditions it was not possible to build any bridges over the Donets before the beginning of May 1943. None of the three operations could thus be launched before the beginning of May, as Army Group South informed the Army High Command once more on 8 April. It also pointed out that the preconditions for both *Habicht* and *Panther* were no longer given since Operation *Habicht* had to be

27 Private Archive of Rüdiger von Manstein, Handakte des Oberbefehlshabers der Heeresgruppe Süd, März 1943, no pagination; BA-MA, RH 19 VI/45, Kriegstagebuch der Heeresgruppe Süd, Ia, 24.3.-4.7.1943, fol. 14.

28 BA-MA, RH 2/3060, Kriegstagebuch der Operationsabteilung des Generalstabs des Heeres, 9.3.-31.7.1943, fol. 63.

29 BA-MA, RH 19 VI/45, Kriegstagebuch der Heeresgruppe Süd, Ia, 24.3.-4.7.1943, fol. 23.

carried out before the other operations began, which was not now possible. Operation *Panther*, on the other hand, could not achieve the objective of destroying strong enemy forces because the situation had changed. Considering that these two operations were therefore practically pointless, the High Command of Army Group South was in favour of Operation Citadel. In his private war diary, Manstein summed up the month of March 1943 as follows: 'My plan to advance on Kursk [before the beginning of the spring thaw] in order to cut off [the] salient between us and [Army Group] Centre, has been rejected because [Army Group] Centre is unable to join in right away.' Due to the 'delay until the second half of April due to weather conditions and condition of our troops', Manstein continued, 'the *O.K.H.* [*Oberkommando des Heeres*, Army High Command] decided upon request of Army Group [South] and [Army Group] Centre to first cut off the Kursk salient and defeat the surrounding reserves, which had become a prerequisite for an offensive in the Donets salient.'[30] This diary entry makes very clear who the driving force behind the realisation of Operation Citadel was: the two commanders of Army Groups South and Centre – not Hitler, as has been claimed repeatedly.[31]

Subsequently, Hitler approved the requests from Army Group South; in Operations Order No. 6, dated 15 April, he decided that 'the first of this year's attacks, as soon as the weather permits, is Operation Citadel.'[32] In spite of this decision, Hitler had not yet given up Operation *Panther*. The same order states that, provided Operation Citadel went according to plan, Hitler reserved the right to launch Operation *Panther* as soon as possible so as to take advantage of the enemy's confusion.

The commanders of the army groups and armies greeted Hitler's decision in favour of Operation Citadel with relief. On 19 April, the commander of Army Detachment Kempf, General Werner Kempf, for example, expressed his optimism in a phone call to the operations officer of Army Group South, reckoning that the success of Operation Citadel is 'not uncertain. All the more, we can and have to reinforce the Donets Front to counter any attempt to unhinge the operation.'[33]

Hitler himself was not as convinced of Operation Citadel, in particular of the deployment of forces of the Ninth Army in the area south of Orël. On 19 April he asked the Chief of Transportation of Army Group Centre, Colonel Hermann Teske, whether it would be possible to transfer the attacking formations of the Ninth Army

30 Private Archive of Rüdiger von Manstein, Erich von Manstein, persönliches Kriegstagebuch Nr. 5, März 1943-1.4.1944, no pagination.

31 See, for example: Günther Reichhelm, *Verantwortung und Gewissensnot: Erinnerungen* (Würzburg, 2003), p. 140; Mark Healy, *Zitadelle: The German Offensive against the Kursk Salient 4–17 July 1943* (Stroud, 2008), p. 32; and, Anthony Tucker-Jones, *Kursk 1943: Hitler's Bitter Harvest* (Stroud, 2018), p. 80.

32 Walter Hubatsch, *Hitlers Weisungen für die Kriegführung 1939–1945: Dokumente des Oberkommandos der Wehrmacht* (Erlangen, 4th edn, 1999), p. 312.

33 BA-MA, RH 20-8/81, Armee-Oberkommando 8, Anlagen zum Kriegstagebuch, Chefsachen, Panther, Habicht, Zitadelle, Löwe, 1.2.-30.6.1943, Annex 38, no pagination.

at short notice to Vorozhba so they could attack the Kursk salient frontally from the west (map 2). Teske reported that the shift posed little problem technically since the traffic junction of Vorozhba allowed for a rapid movement of large troop formations. On the following day, the 20 April 1943, the Chief of Staff of Army Group South, Major-General Theodor Busse, learned in a meeting with Zeitzler that Hitler considered 'launching the attack from Army Group Centre from the area of the Second Army (not the Second Panzer Army).'[34] Present at this meeting also were the Chief of the Operations Section of the General Staff, Lieutenant-General Heusinger, and the Chief of Staff of Army Group Centre, Lieutenant-General Hans Krebs.

Busse, as well as Heusinger and Krebs, spoke out against Hitler's alternative plan of attack, arguing that the assembly in the area of Vorozhba would take too much time, the terrain was unfavourable and the success questionable since the enemy would be pushed out of, rather than be surrounded, in the area of Kursk. Zeitzler agreed with them and managed to talk Hitler out of this idea, especially since the Headquarters of the Second Army in the area of Vorozhba was also against this alternative. Except for Hitler, almost everyone was against the plan of rolling up the Kursk salient frontally. This fact has to be clearly emphasized here because until today the alternative has been presented as a missed opportunity in German memoirs as well as in military historiography – an opportunity the military officers would in fact have liked to seize had Hitler not been against it. In truth, it was actually Hitler's idea since, on 10 July 1943, during the climax of Operation Citadel, he took it up once more. As the attack of the Ninth Army had by this point become bogged down, he suggested shifting the remaining Panzer reserves of Army Group Centre to the front of the Kursk salient, so they could attack frontally. Manstein, however, was opposed to this and argued that, 'The pocket must be rolled up from the *east*.'[35]

In the spring and summer 1943, Hitler, who has often been described as 'obstinate' in memoirs, was apparently willing on occasions to listen to his generals and let himself be convinced by their counter-arguments. He not only stuck to launching Citadel as the first offensive after the spring thaw but also followed the commanders of Army Groups Centre and South on their plan of attack for the Kursk salient, contrary to his own reservations. Only when the attack was postponed repeatedly, and it became apparent that the attacking forces were too weak to break through swiftly into the deeply echeloned Soviet defensive system north and south of Kursk, were alternative plans brought up once again. On the evening of 7 May 1943, Hitler arrived in Berlin from Munich to meet Goebbels, who later wrote of the meeting: 'In the east the *Führer* will soon begin a limited offensive, namely on Kursk. If need be

34 BA-MA, RH 19 VI/45, Kriegstagebuch der Heeresgruppe Süd, Ia, 24.3.-4.7.1943, fol. 41-2.

35 Private Archive of Rüdiger von Manstein, Handakte des Oberbefehlshabers der Heeresgruppe Süd, Juli 1943, Kriegstagebuch-Notiz vom 10.07.1943, no pagination [emphasis in original, RT].

he might wait to see if the Bolsheviks try to beat us to it – that would present us with an even better opportunity than if we took the initiative.'[36] On 23 May, Goebbels again noted in his diary that Hitler intended to let the Red Army attack first before launching a backhand blow.

Yet Hitler was not the only one who was sceptical about the success of Operation Citadel. On 1 June 1943, Manstein expressed his doubts in a letter to the Army High Command whether it still made sense to launch Operation Citadel. Instead, Manstein suggested, it would be better to attack with a broader scope and by doing so to advance past the strongest Soviet defensive positions towards Kastornoe (map 2). Alternatively, Manstein proposed to abandon any offensive plans and wait for the Red Army to attack and then launch a counter-offensive. Zeitzler was not averse to Manstein's suggestion of attempting a larger push on Kastornoe, but he wanted to make sure first if Army Group Centre would be able to contribute to such a large-scale attack – which it was not. On 19 June 1943, however, Army Group Centre provided an estimate of the situation, which finally swung the decision in favour of Operation Citadel. In this document, Kluge came to the conclusion that a Soviet offensive had to be expected in any case; the best countermeasure would be to beat them to it with Operation Citadel, which should be launched as soon as possible. The following day, Army Groups South and Centre received a message from the High Command of the Army, informing them that, 'the *Führer* has decided to launch Operation Citadel.'[37] On 25 June, Hitler set the final date of the offensive for 5 July 1943.

But why was the attack launched so late? Was it, as has often been claimed in historiography, simply Hitler's wish to wait for the new tanks and self-propelled guns, which he hoped would play a decisive role? Or were there, in fact, other reasons for the postponement?

The Postponement of the Attack

It was initially planned to launch Operation Citadel on 1 May 1943 but this date was soon called into question. As early as 12 April, the High Command of Army Group Centre had come to the conclusion that the earliest possible date for an attack on Kursk would be 10 May, explaining that 'any deterioration of the weather, even a temporary one, will delay preparations for the attack, especially the maintenance of tanks. As far as can be seen, the delivery of the needed weapons, in particular tanks, as well as the deployment of reserves could not be fully completed by this date.

36 Goebbels, *Tagebücher*, pt. II, vol. 8, p. 225.
37 BA-MA, RH 20-9/142, Anlage zum Kriegstagebuch Nr. 8, Armee-Oberkommando 9, Ia, vol. V, Befehle übergeordneter Stellen (Auswahl), Berichtszeit: 26.3.-18.8.1943, no pagination.

It is therefore *desired* to plan the attack for 15 May.'[38] The Army High Command, however, rejected the postponement until mid-May and told Army Group Centre that the attack would begin on 1 May as scheduled. On 14 April, Lieutenant-General Krebs, chief of the general staff of Army Group Centre, called the Chief of General Staff of the Ninth Army, Colonel Harald von Elverfeldt, informing him of this decision. Elverfeldt, whose staff had devised the operation, argued that a date as early as 1 May would lead to 'absolutely insurmountable problems.'[39] In order to replenish troops and supplies, 10 May would have to be maintained as the earliest possible date for the attack. Even if it was decided to forego proper training of the replacements and sufficient replenishment of the troops, it would be impossible to launch the attack before 5 May. On the same day, 14 April, a meeting was held between General Kempf and several commanding generals of his army detachment in Khar'kov, during which Kempf remarked that in the area of Army Group South, too, Operation Citadel could not possibly be mounted before 10 May.

Yet Hitler dismissed the doubts of his commanders, setting the 'earliest date' for Operation Citadel at 3 May 1943 in Operations Order No. 6 dated 15 April 1943.[40] The deferment he granted was thus a mere two days – which was unacceptable for the commanders of the army groups and armies and their general staff officers. They had one more chance to voice their concerns on 20 April 1943, when a conference took place at the headquarters of the Army High Command between Zeitzler, Heusinger and the chiefs of the general staffs of Army Groups Centre and South, Generals Krebs and Busse. Both Krebs and Busse asked for a longer postponement of Operation Citadel because it would be impossible to complete preparations until the scheduled date. Zeitzler assured the two generals that he would convey their request to Hitler, but Hitler again refused to postpone the attack. On that same evening Krebs called the commander of the Ninth Army, Colonel-General Model, and told him that the Army High Command could neither satisfy the allocations requested by Model nor defer the attack. Upon hearing this, Model had one of his notorious fits of anger and replied that he was not willing to carry out the attack under these circumstances. If the early date was indeed maintained, the goals of the attack would have to be reduced. If, however, the attack was to be carried out as planned, it would have to be postponed until 15 May, and the supply of weapons would have to be increased. It would be irresponsible to carry out Operation Citadel otherwise, Model declared – and threatened that if the attack was to be launched prematurely the Army Group would have to find someone else to command the Ninth Army. Model promptly drafted a corresponding teletype, which Army Group Centre forwarded to the Army High Command. For

38 Klink, *Gesetz*, p. 288 [emphasis in original, RT].

39 National Archives and Records Administration, Archives II, College Park, Maryland (hereafter, NARA), T312/317/7886035, Kriegstagebuch Nr. 8, Armee-Oberkommando 9, Führungsabteilung, 26.3.-18.8.1943.

40 Klink, *Gesetz*, p. 293.

the time being, he did not achieve a postponement of the attack, but on 23 April Model received a call from Zeitzler, who informed him that more reinforcements would be sent in the following days, including 135 tanks and assault guns. While this news reassured Model, who now awaited Operation Citadel with confidence, Army Group South again objected to the scheduled date of attack, which they thought was premature. On 24 April, the Army Group thus asked the Army High Command to defer Citadel until 5 May, as it was not possible to bring up all attack forces. This time Hitler gave in and on, 26 April, he postponed Operation Citadel until 5 May.

Up to that point, operational and tactical reasons as well as unfavourable weather conditions had led to the postponement of the attack. But, at this point, one strategic dimension came to the fore, the importance of which has so far been underestimated in literature on the Battle of Kursk. It has been overlooked that the generals were primarily focused on the operational situation in their own sector of the front, while Hitler's reasoning was based on the wider situation. His concerns were therefore not always a sign of rigid insistence, but rather can also be understood as valid strategic considerations, particularly since the German-Italian defeat in North Africa had been looming since April. Hitler feared that after their victory in North Africa, the Western Allies might be strong enough to land both in Italy and in the Balkans. For this reason, Hitler wanted to carry out the offensive on the Eastern Front as soon as possible, hoping that a quick success in the East would free reserves for the other theatres of war. It is also the reason why Hitler refused to comply with his commanding officers who asked for a postponement of Citadel until mid-May, convinced it was imperative that the offensive be launched at the beginning of May – and, hence, finished before the decisive defeat in North Africa.

It was, in fact, Colonel-General Model who interfered with Hitler's plans, when, on 27 April, Model arrived at the Obersalzberg to receive the Knight's Cross of the Iron Cross with Oak Leaves and Swords. Following the ceremony, he had the chance to present Hitler with his own ideas of how the Ninth Army should be deployed for Operation Citadel. Based on aerial photographs of the Soviet defensive system opposite the Ninth Army, which showed heavily fortified Soviet positions to a depth of 20 kilometres, Model made it clear that a swift breakthrough through the Soviet line could not be achieved. Even though it was possible to carry out the attack, it would take six days alone to push through the defensive lines. Six days, however, is what Army Group Centre had scheduled for the whole of Operation Citadel: two days to push through the Soviet defensive front and four more days to reach the city of Kursk.

Hitler was impressed by Model's presentation and began to have doubts whether the attacking forces of the Ninth Army would be able to break through the Soviet deeply echeloned defensive positions at all. Moreover, if the breakthrough was to take nearly a week, as Model predicted, the Red Army units in the Kursk salient would have enough time to pull out and avoid encirclement. A quick success would therefore be as unlikely as a big victory at Kursk, while the risk that the offensive might not be finished before Anglo-American troops landed in Italy or the Balkans increased. So, Hitler decided to postpone Operation Citadel until 12 June 1943, which according to him offered two advantages. In the first instance, an estimate of the weapons delivery times showed that by 10 June numerous new tanks, assault guns and heavy anti-tank guns would be available: this suggested a considerable reinforcement of the Ninth Army and a significant increase of their chances of success. Second, postponing the operation would allow for a substantial reinforcement of the German troops in Italy and the Balkans until June. That way an Allied landing in these areas would no longer necessitate a withdrawal of forces from the Eastern Front, and Operation Citadel could thus be carried out, even if the Western Allies landed in the Mediterranean area. On 26 July, one day after the toppling of the Italian dictator Benito Mussolini, Hitler expressed his views on this situation very clearly:

> Actually, I have always feared this development. That was the whole reason why I was afraid to start in the East too early [in spring 1943], since I always thought that everything would happen immediately in the South: the British would exploit it, the Russians would roar, the British would land, and with the Italians – I'd like to say – betrayal was in the air. Under these circumstances, I thought it best to wait [with the offensive on the Eastern Front] at least until several units were ready [as operational reserves for the Italian theatre]. We do have [reserve] units in the West. Because I am determined to strike like lightning [in Italy], of course, just as I did in Yugoslavia.[41]

The Chief of Staff Zeitzler was, however, by now opposed to postponing the attack until 12 June. He managed to convince Hitler to hear the opinion of the commanders of Army Groups Centre and South, before announcing the new date of attack. Zeitzler was certain that Kluge and Manstein would speak against such a long delay of the attack. On 4 May 1943 a briefing took place in Munich; apart from Hitler and Zeitzler, Field-Marshals von Kluge and Manstein attended, as did the Inspector General of Panzer Troops, Colonel-General Heinz Guderian, the Chief of Staff of the Luftwaffe, Hans Jeschonnek, as well as other officers. Just like Zeitzler had hoped, Kluge and Manstein both supported his standpoint and declared themselves against a deferment of the attack. Even though Kluge was in favour of postponing the attack for a few days until 11 or 12 May, he strongly objected to a delay until June and explained that he thought Model was overly pessimistic, to which Hitler replied that the pessimist was not Model but he, Hitler, himself. Guderian supported Hitler's position, arguing in favour of the proposed deferment of Operation Citadel. Moreover, he proposed deploying the panzer formations all together, either with Army Group Centre or Army Group South, to attack the Kursk salient with combined forces from one direction only. Albeit supported by Colonel-General Jeschonnek, Guderian's suggestion was not taken up. Jeschonnek pointed out, though, that the Luftwaffe could not be substantially reinforced even if the operation was postponed. Except for

41 Heiber, *Conferences*, pp. 252-3.

Hitler and Guderian no one present at the meeting thus spoke out in favour of postponing Citadel until June. Still, Hitler was not deterred: On the following day, 5 May, he announced that Operation Citadel would be launched on 12 June 1943.

Among the army commanders-in-chief, only Model was happy about the postponement of the attack until June. He had been informed about the deferment one day earlier, when, on the evening of 4 May the Chief of Staff of Army Group Centre, Lieutenant-General Krebs, informed him that Citadel was likely to be postponed by several weeks, though the exact date was not yet confirmed. Model saw this as a welcome opportunity for further troop training, which increased the operation's chances of success. By contrast, General Kempf expressed grave concerns about the postponement of Operation Citadel in a phone call with Zeitzler on 7 May. Kempf stressed that preparations were already complete, the troops were in good spirits, and a considerable force had been assembled. It would be detrimental from both the operational and a psychological viewpoint to postpone the attack, all the more because the delay helped the defenders more than the attackers. Additionally, there was an increased danger that the Red Army would launch an offensive first, placing the Wehrmacht at a disadvantage. Zeitzler agreed with Kempf, but said that he had been unable to convince Hitler.

The fact is that Operation Citadel quite possibly could not have been carried out in May 1943 anyway, even if Hitler had wanted it. The reason for this is a factor which has been ignored in literature until now: the weather. Because of the poor infrastructure on the Eastern Front, the German troops were heavily dependent on favourable weather conditions. Yet from mid-May to the end of the month it rained almost every day in the area of Model's Ninth Army; as a result, the mostly unpaved roads were in such a deplorable condition that they temporarily had to be closed for all vehicles.[42] Under these circumstances, no major military offensive could possibly be launched. It was not until June that weather conditions improved and streets and roads became passable again.

Army Group Centre used the time of rest before the beginning of the attack not just for troop training and the intensified construction of field fortifications in the Orël salient, but also for several anti-partisan operations, the largest of which, Operation *Zigeunerbaron* (Gypsy Baron), took place south of Bryansk. A number of divisions scheduled to take part in Operation Citadel, namely the 4th Panzer Division, the 18th Panzer Division, the 10th Motorized Infantry Division, the 7th Infantry Division and the 292nd Infantry Division, were involved in this anti-partisan operation. The deployment of these formations shows how dangerous the Germans considered the partisans in the rear of Army Group Centre to be, particularly because the Bryansk railway junction was vital for the supply of Army Group Centre. At the same time,

42 The author would like to thank Ulf Balke (Freiburg im Breisgau), who provided him with a table of the weather and road conditions in the area of the German Ninth Army, compiled from the army's war diaries.

Operation *Zigeunerbaron* also illustrates how weak the German forces on the Eastern Front really were, as even panzer and motorized divisions had to be used in anti-partisan warfare. During the operation, which began on 17 May 1943 and lasted three weeks, it became evident how well the partisans were equipped: on 27 May, the 7th Infantry Division captured a T-34 tank which partisans had used. The final report from Army Group Centre dated 8 June 1943 listed the following enemy losses: 3,152 killed, 569 deserters, 24 guns, three tanks, 14 anti-tank guns, 55 mortars, two aeroplanes and infantry weapons in large numbers. What is striking is the comparison with the report that the Second Panzer Army Headquarters – in whose area *Zigeunerbaron* took place – had delivered the previous day. It gave a number of 1,584 dead and 1,568 prisoners; in accordance with the orders regarding the treatment of captured 'bandits', all partisans who were taken prisoner during Operation *Zigeunerbaron* were shot.

Operation *Freischütz* (Marksman), an anti-partisan operation which took place from 21 to 28 May, saw the deployment of another division taking part in Operation Citadel, namely the 6th Infantry Division. Both of these anti-partisan operations led to a further delay of Operation Citadel, because the Ninth Army needed additional time to reassemble the divisions involved in the offensive, as it reported to Army Group Centre on 29 May. Besides, the anti-partisan warfare had also taken a toll on the German formations. The 7th Infantry Division alone lost 859 men during Operation *Zigeunerbaron*: four officers and 33 non-commissioned officers and enlisted men were killed or missing, 183 officers and 639 non-commissioned officers and enlisted men were wounded.

Meanwhile, the difficult strategic situation was exacerbated when on 13 May the last Axis forces surrendered in North Africa. At least for the time being, Operation Citadel was therefore out of question for Hitler. In a briefing on 19 May he stated that there was no relying on the Italians. 'If some sort of mess were to develop' in Italy, that is if she should surrender, he first of all wanted to send three SS divisions to Italy because 'they are most familiar with Fascism.'[43] What Hitler meant were the three SS Panzergrenadier Divisions *Leibstandarte SS Adolf Hitler*, *Das Reich* and *Totenkopf* – the three divisions which were designated to be the spearhead of the offensive in Operation Citadel. The following day Hitler once more expressed his concern about Italy, convinced that a crisis might occur at any moment. Three days later, the German military attaché issued a report on the state of the Italian Army which came to the conclusion that it had 'failed miserably because the officer corps is inadequately trained' while 'most soldiers lack inner readiness. … The core of the Italian Army has been destroyed in Africa, Greece and Russia. What remains of the air force is technically outdated and only partly ready for combat. The armament of the costal defences is insufficient. … A major enemy attack on Italy can only be repulsed with strong German support.'[44]

43 Heiber, *Conferences*, p. 121.
44 Werner Rahn and Gerhard Schreiber (eds.), *Kriegstagebuch der Seekriegsleitung 1939-1945*, pt. A, 68 vols. (Herford, 1988-1997), vol. 45, p. 412.

This became apparent on 11 June 1943, when the Italians surrendered Pantelleria to the Allies without a fight. This island, also known as 'Italian Malta', later became an important base for the Allied landing on Sicily. Lampedusa and Linosa, Pantelleria's neighbouring islands, surrendered within the following 24 hours. The war diary of the German Naval Command commented on the loss of Pantelleria: 'The surrender of this base, which is of vital importance for the obstruction of enemy navigation in the Strait of Sicily, is a true and devastating defeat for the cause of the Axis powers. … Pantelleria is certainly not a glorious chapter for the Italians and hopefully no portent of how they will fare in future battles for the islands.'[45] A similar view on the situation presents itself in Goebbels's diary: 'The surrender of Pantelleria seems to refute the theory that the Italians would fight more fiercely on their own ground than in Africa. It also illustrates that [in battle] against the Italians one can achieve something with just the support of the air force [...] without having to launch a ground assault. This is the first time that the air force has captured a fortress.'[46]

It would take until the end of June to convince Hitler that the deployment of German divisions from the west had sufficiently stabilized the situation in Italy, so that even if Italy quit the war it would not be necessary to withdraw troops from the Eastern Front. In view of this development the offensive in the East could now finally be launched. The date set for Operation Citadel had accordingly to be postponed; as early as 11 May the Army High Command had informed Army Group South that the date that was announced last for the beginning of the attack, 12 June, was not the final effective date but rather the earliest possible day for the start of Citadel. On 1 June, the Army High Command informed Army Groups Centre and South that Operation Citadel would not start before 25 June. Four days later, on 5 June, the Army High Command announced a new provisional date for the attack, namely 20 June. At the same time it notified the Army Groups that a decision on the final date should be reached by the following week. Yet the decision was long in coming. It was not until 16 June that the Army Groups Centre and South received word that from 18 June they could expect the announcement of the final date for Citadel.

Yet the repeated postponements were not only the result of Hitler's intention of strengthening the defensive power in the Mediterranean and supplying the formations on the Eastern Front with new tanks. He also would have preferred that the decision for a strike in the East had been brought about by a Soviet offensive, as Goebbels noted in his diary on 23 May: 'With regards to the offensive in the east both sides adhere to the policy of 'Hannemann, you go first, you have the largest boots!'… The *Führer* intends to let the Bolsheviks attack first.'[47] On 6 June, Goebbels had a meeting with Guderian, about which he wrote: 'Guderian is happy that the *Führer* has cancelled the May offensive. He obviously views military operations only from the

45 Rahn and Schreiber, *Kriegstagebuch*, pt. A, vol. 46, p. 184-5.
46 Goebbels, *Tagebücher*, pt. II, vol. 8, p. 466.
47 Goebbels, *Tagebücher*, pt. II, vol. 8, p. 351.

perspective of the panzer force. At least he is right in his statement that each month we gain is equal to a thousand new tanks. So if we wait a little longer, we can only profit from it. The *Führer* expressed his concern to Guderian that one might think him a coward because he does not attack now. Guderian managed to allay his fears.'[48]

In the meantime the commanders of the army groups and armies on the Eastern Front urged that Operation Citadel be launched as soon as possible – or be cancelled altogether. They repeatedly pointed out that a delay was beneficial only to the Red Army; even though postponing the attack would permit the Germans to reinforce their troops the Soviet Forces would still gain considerably more strength in the same time. On 15 June Manstein sent a teletype message to Zeitzler in which he explained that the longer Citadel was deferred, the smaller the operational chances of success would become, even if the tactical chances would be enhanced through the arrival of new tanks. Three days later, Army Group South reported to the Army High Command that all along the front line of Army Group South the enemy had been reinforced and had formed operational combat groups; an enemy offensive against the area of Khar'kov seemed likely. On the same day, 18 June, the Armed Forces Operations Staff (*Wehrmachtführungsstab*) compiled an assessment of the situation for Hitler, suggesting that Operation Citadel should be postponed until the strategic overall situation was fully clear and that large operational reserves should be accumulated on the Eastern Front and in Germany instead.

But Hitler did not want to wait any longer for the Red Army to attack first. On 18 June he ordered that Operation Citadel should be launched. In a briefing on 24 June he remarked that the impression the 'catastrophe of Tunis' had left could only be dispelled by achievements and deeds, not by propaganda. On the following day he fixed the definite date of the attack, which was disclosed in code to Army Groups Centre and South on 27 June 1943. In the war diary of the Fourth Panzer Army Headquarters it was noted in code: '*Erntefest für 'Zitadelle' Blumenduft Karl minus 9.* 5 July is therefore set as the attack date for Operation Citadel.'[49]

48 Goebbels, *Tagebücher*, pt. II, vol. 8, pp. 431-2.

49 BA-MA, RH 21-4/104, Kriegstagebuch des Oberkommandos der 4. Panzerarmee, Ia, 25.3.-31.7.1943, fol. 105. Here a mistake must be pointed out in the – otherwise still commendable – study by Ernst Klink on the preparation phase of Operation Citadel. In Klink, *Gesetz*, p. 144, it is noted, 'On 17 June, 3 July was announced as the definitive date for the beginning of the attack.' This is incorrect in two respects. Checking the document Klink cited in the reference, it can be determined that on 17 June 1943 there was only mention of a period of forewarning for Citadel, but a date for the attack is not given. The other document used by Klink, which is found in the same file, is not dated 17 June but 27 June 1943. In this document, the date of attack is given as 5 July 1943. See BA-MA, RH 20-8/81, Armee-Oberkommando 8, Anlagen zum Kriegstagebuch, Chefsachen, Panther, Habicht, Zitadelle, Löwe, 1.2.-30.6.1943, no pagination. The date of 3 July 1943, which is given as tentative date of attack in other studies as well, was mentioned by Hitler on 21 June 1943 according to the war diary of the Armed Forces Operations Staff. This date,

The Struggle for Qualitative Superiority on the Battlefield

Operation Citadel has gone down in history primarily as a tank battle. And it was in fact the new tanks and assault guns in which Hitler placed high hopes for the summer offensive in 1943. As early as the briefing, which was held at Manstein's headquarters in Zaporozhe on 18 February 1943, Hitler declared: 'At the beginning of May we are going to have 98 heavy assault guns constructed by Porsche. We are furthermore going to have 150 new *Tiger* tanks in addition to 200/250 *Panther* tanks, 50 heavy self-propelled infantry guns, 100 flamethrower tanks as well as a number of Panzer IV tanks. Most of these new weapons are indestructible, their firepower is unmatched. [Porsche's] assault gun is able to put any enemy tank out of action at a distance of 2,000 metres. With this gigantic amassing of the latest offensive weapons it must be possible to regain the initiative.'[50]

Which armoured vehicles was Hitler actually referring to? The 98 heavy assault guns were the new heavy tank destroyer *Ferdinand*, a self-propelled gun designed by Ferdinand Porsche, whose development had begun at the end of 1942. Its box-like, non-rotating superstructure was fitted with an 8.8cm cannon with a tube length of nearly 6.3 metres – the most effective gun any tank or tank destroyer was equipped with at that time. Its standard ammunition penetrated an armour plate more than 13cm thick at a distance of 2,000 metres; it could therefore knock out practically any enemy tank at any battle range. The *Ferdinand*, named after its designer Ferdinand Porsche, had frontal armour of 20cm and was thus more or less invulnerable. However, it had a combat weight of over 68 tonnes and a fuel consumption of roughly 1,200 litres per 100km, which posed considerable logistical problems for the troops.

In the spring of 1943, 91 (not 98) heavy *Ferdinand* tank destroyers were produced in total, two of which were delivered to the Army Experimental Station (*Heeresversuchsstelle*), Kummersdorf, for testing and remained in Germany. Of the 89 *Ferdinands* that were sent to the front, the 654th Heavy Tank Destroyer Battalion (*schwere Panzerjäger-Abteilung* 654) received 45, while 44 were sent to the 653rd, its sister battalion. Together with the 216th *Sturmpanzer* Battalion, the two battalions formed the 656th Heavy Tank Destroyer Regiment (*schweres Panzerjäger-Regiment* 656), which was assigned to Model's Ninth Army for the attack on Kursk. The *Ferdinand* had originally been designated as assault gun, which was changed to tank destroyer in spring 1943; however, both terms still appear in contemporary documents dating from summer 1943. In 1944, its name was changed from *Ferdinand* to *Elefant*, which did not help the confusion about the vehicle's designation.

however, was never communicated to the troops, not least of all as Hitler specified the definite date for the attack as 5 July 1943 only four days later.

50 Private Archive of Rüdiger von Manstein, Handakte des Oberbefehlshabers der Heeresgruppe Don/Süd, Februar 1943, no pagination; Schwarz, *Stabilisierung*, p. 255.

The heavy *Panzerkampfwagen* (armoured fighting vehicle) *Tiger* which Hitler mentioned second was not actually a new tank; it had been used on the Eastern Front since September 1942 and in North Africa since December 1942. The *Tiger* was also not developed as a response to the Soviet T-34 tank, as is sometimes assumed.[51] In reality, its development had begun as early as 1937 as a breakthrough tank (*Durchbruchswagen*). After several reconfigurations of the original design, tests and delays, its production as a heavy *Panzerkampfwagen* commenced in August 1942. When the *Tiger* was introduced to the troops, they were first disappointed by it, as they had hoped for a tank of modern design, with a sloped armour plate similar to the feared Soviet T-34. Sloped armour provides better protection not only because projectiles are more likely to bounce off, but likewise because they have to travel a greater distance to penetrate the plate. A third, often underestimated fact is that a projectile entering a sloped armour plate does not travel through the plate in a straight line but is in fact 'pushed away' by opposing forces, resulting in an even longer path through the armour. In some circumstances, heavily sloped armour can thus offer three times as much protection – in this case, an armour plate with a thickness of 4cm provides the same protection as a vertical plate 12cm thick. Or, using the words of the '*Nachrichtenblatt der Panzertruppen*' dating from September 1943: 'As a rule of thumb one can say that given a constant distance, [a projectile] impacting at an angle of 30 degrees will penetrate only a third of the thickness of a plate than [one] impacting at an angle of 90 degrees.'[52]

In spite of this knowledge, the construction of the *Tiger* featured mainly vertical armour plates, which gave it a box-like look. Nonetheless, its crews would soon come to appreciate the advantages of their vehicle: with a thickness of 10-12cm, the front armour could withstand hits from nearly all tanks and anti-tank guns the Soviets used in summer 1943. The armour of the turret side and the upper hull was 8cm thick and offered good protection against the 7.6cm gun F-34 of the T-34 tank. A report from the Military Council of the Armoured and Mechanized Forces of the Red Army on a ballistic test carried out with a captured *Tiger* dating from 4 May 1943 concluded: 'A direct hit on the 82mm side armour of the T-VI tank [*Tiger*] fired from a 76mm gun F-34 at a distance of 200 metres has shown that the armour-piercing rounds of this gun are too weak to penetrate the armour plate.'[53] A T-34 could only penetrate the side armour of a *Tiger* using either special sub-calibre shells or at a very short range and at a good angle of impact of the projectile. The same report stated that, on the other hand, the 8.8cm gun of the *Tiger* could penetrate even the thickest armour plates of

51 See, for example, Walther K. Nehring, *Die Geschichte der deutschen Panzerwaffe 1916-1945* (Stuttgart, 1974), p. 122.

52 NARA, T78/623/H16/295, Nachrichtenblatt der Panzertruppen, herausgegeben vom Generalinspekteur der Panzertruppen, Vorschriftenstelle, Nachrichtenblatt Nr. 3, September 1943, p. 11.

53 Sergey A. Mel'chin, '"Obespechit' prevoskhodstvo sovetskikh tankov:" Dokladnye zapiski I.V. Stalinu', *Istoricheskiy arkhiv*, 1 (1993), pp. 105-15, quote, 109.

the T-34, the frontal ones, at a distance of 1,500 metres – and the *Tiger* was not even equipped with the *Ferdinand*'s new 8.8cm gun but with an older version with a barrel length of 4.9 metres and a smaller propellant charge. Nevertheless, in summer 1943, the 8.8cm gun of the *Tiger* could destroy any enemy tank at long ranges.

But the *Tiger* was highly popular with the crews not only because of its superior armour and firepower, it was also fairly spacious and offered the crew a relatively comfortable fighting compartment. Apart from that the *Tiger*, unlike previous prototypes, had a semi-automatic gearshift transmission and a steering gear which allowed the driver to operate the tank with a steering wheel instead of levers. The driver could also turn the *Tiger* on the spot without having to fully decelerate one set of treads. The driving experience was therefore exceptionally good, and former tank drivers recall that operating the *Tiger* was as easy as driving a lorry.

Despite these considerations, the *Tiger*'s fighting power and high comfort for its crew made it a complex and expensive vehicle unsuitable for mass production. It was thus employed mostly in independent formations of the Army, so-called 'heavy panzer battalions' (*schwere Panzerabteilungen*). In summer 1943, only five such heavy panzer battalions existed – and only three of these were deployed on the Eastern Front. Two of these, the 503rd and the 505th Heavy Panzer Battalion, both with an authorized strength of 45 *Tigers*, took part in the attack on Kursk. The 505th Battalion was deployed with Model's Ninth Army, though it began Operation Citadel with two companies and 31 *Tigers*; the third company, equipped with 14 *Tigers*, did not join the battalion at the front until three days after the beginning of the attack, on 8 July. The 503rd Heavy Panzer Battalion served with Army Detachment Kempf in the southern sector. When it joined the attack on Kursk, the battalion was at full strength of 45 *Tigers*, but on General Kempf's orders, the battalion's individual companies were subordinated to the three panzer divisions of the III Panzer Corps respectively: The 1st Company was assigned to the 6th Panzer Division, the 2nd Company to the 19th Panzer Division and the 3rd Company to the 7th Panzer Division. By splitting the battalion and deploying the three *Tiger* companies separately, Kempf hoped to balance out the weakness of the three divisions and their lack of modern tanks.

The four elite Panzergrenadier Divisions *Großdeutschland*, *Leibstandarte SS Adolf Hitler*, *Das Reich* and *Totenkopf* each had one company of *Tigers*, which increased the total number of tanks of this type for Operation Citadel to 147. This small quantity is particularly noteworthy because no other weapon system shaped the perception of the Battle of Kursk as much as the *Tiger*. In Soviet combat reports, books and war films about the Battle of Kursk, there are usually hundreds of *Tiger* tanks, most of which are then destroyed by the Soviet troops. Reality, however, was quite different: no more than 340 *Tigers* in total were produced from the beginning of manufacture in August 1942 until the end of June 1943, 65 more were built in July and 60 in August 1943. On all fronts, only 73 *Tigers* were lost between July and August 1943, and 307 in the year 1943 – another indicator of the quality of this weapon system, which was always deployed to the points of main effort and used as a 'battering ram' in offensive operations time and again.

The third armoured vehicle mentioned by Hitler on 18 February 1943 was the *Panther*. This was indeed a brand-new type of tank, whose development had begun around the end of 1941 as an answer to the Soviet T-34. It had initially been constructed as a medium tank with a weight of 30-35t. However, due to additional reinforcing of its armour during the development phase, the *Panther* eventually reached a combat weight of 45t, which made it a heavy tank rather than a medium one. It had the same weight as the heavy Soviet KV-1 tank and the IS-2 introduced in 1944, which in German sources is sometimes called a super-heavy tank (*überschwerer Panzer*), even though it was not heavier than the *Panther*. Tactically the *Panther* was not a heavy 'breakthrough tank' (*Durchbruchspanzer*); it was scheduled to be deployed to the 'medium Panzer companies' (*mittlere Panzerkompanien*) and replace the medium Panzer IV tank. From the beginning of the manufacture in January 1943 until the end of June 1943, approximately 500 *Panthers* were produced, 190 more in July and about 120 in August 1943. Yet serious technical difficulties delayed their deployment to the front, and a few days before Operation Citadel was launched, only 200 *Panthers* had actually reached the front. They were pooled in the 39th Panzer Regiment, which consisted of the 51st and the 52nd Panzer Battalion and was subordinated to Army Group South. Even before the attack on Kursk began, two *Panthers* were destroyed by engine fires, so the 39th Panzer Regiment had to begin the operation with 198 *Panther* tanks. It soon became obvious that the deployment of the 51st and 52nd Panzer Battalion had been precipitous – not only were its crews insufficiently trained, the vehicles themselves had apparently not been tested properly. The *Panther* had various technical defects which would sometimes bring the crews to the verge of despair. The tankers above all complained about the faulty final drive, which transfers the rotation speed of the gear to the drive wheels. They also criticized the poor fuel pump, the leaking seals of the fuel and oil lines, the inadequate mounting of the carburettors and the insufficient motor cooling. 'We were sent into combat with these cripples – with a very predictable result', a member of the I. Battalion of the 2nd SS-Panzer Regiment later wrote.[54] This battalion, equipped with the first version of the *Panther* like the 39th Panzer Regiment, took part in the last phase of the Battle of Kursk in late August 1943. As early as one week after its first deployment, 40 of the battalion's 71 *Panthers* were already in need of repair.

In conclusion, all these technical deficiencies of the vehicle itself, as well as the poor level of training of its crews, greatly reduced the efficiency of the 198 *Panthers* deployed for Operation Citadel. Hitler had high hopes for this tank type, often described as one of the most successful tank constructions of the Second World War. At Kursk, however, his expectations were not met. In fact, the *Panther* tanks suffered proportionally the highest rate of losses in the Battle of Kursk, compared to all other German tank types deployed in the battle. Of the 200 *Panthers* which arrived at the

54 Letter from Fritz Langanke to the author, 16 April 2009.

front in early July 1943, 83 had to be written off as completely destroyed by the end of the month.

Another vehicle Hitler had talked about in the briefing on 18 February 1943 is more difficult to identify, because '50 heavy self-propelled infantry guns' might refer to the vehicle type *Grille* (cricket), a lightly armoured self-propelled gun armed with the reliable 15cm calibre heavy infantry gun 33. However, this cannot be the vehicle Hitler had in mind. First of all, by summer 1943, not 50 but 100 vehicles of this type had been delivered to the front. Secondly, the lightly armoured and open-top *Grille* self-propelled gun could hardly be considered an 'indestructible' vehicle. What Hitler actually referred to was another armoured fighting vehicle with a 15cm gun, namely the *Sturmpanzer*, a self-propelled howitzer whose heavily armoured non-rotating superstructure was equipped with a 15cm howitzer which used the same ammunition as the heavy infantry gun 33. In the historiography this vehicle is often labelled as the '*Brummbär*' (grouch, literally 'grumbling bear') – which is incorrect, because even though this designation appears in contemporary Allied documents it was never used by the Germans themselves. 60 *Sturmpanzers* were produced in spring 1943, 45 of which had been sent to the 216th Sturmpanzer Battalion on the Eastern Front by the beginning of July 1943. Ten additional *Sturmpanzers* were delivered to the frontline troops as replacement vehicles in July 1943.

As the name implies, the *Sturmpanzers* were employed as 'battering rams' by the Ninth Army – just like the *Ferdinand* assault guns – to destroy well-fortified pockets of resistance with direct fire. The 216th Sturmpanzer Battalion constituted the III. Battalion of the 656th Heavy Tank Destroyer Battalion (*schwere Panzerjäger-Abteilung* 656), which during Operation Citadel was subordinate to the XXXXI Panzer Corps and the XXIII Army Corps, supporting the 86th Infantry Division, the 292nd Infantry Division as well as the 78th Assault Division (*Sturmdivision*). Of the 55 *Sturmpanzers* deployed on the Eastern Front in July 1943, 17 were lost in total that same month.

As reported by Hitler at the discussion of the situation, 100 flamethrower tanks were produced in total in spring 1943. The tank type in question here was the *Panzerkampfwagen* III, which instead of the usual 5cm gun was equipped with a flamethrower with a range of nearly 60 metres. The divisions taking part in Operation Citadel, however, received only 41 of these flamethrower tanks: 14 tanks were attached to the 6th Panzer Division, 13 to the 11th Panzer Division and 14 to the Panzergrenadier Division *Großdeutschland*; the remaining ones were sent to panzer divisions not engaged on the Eastern Front.

Another of Hitler's statements at the said briefing is also slightly misleading, namely 'a number of Panzer IV tanks' in addition to the various new types of tanks and self-propelled guns, as the medium Panzer IV was produced in high numbers and had been in action since the first day of the Second World War. It saw various technical upgrades in the early years of the war, especially a reinforcement of the armour plating from 1.5 to 5cm at the front and 3cm on the sides. Its armament, however, remained a weak point: until the beginning of 1942, the Panzer IV was equipped with a 7.5cm gun, whose barrel length was a mere 1.8m and was hence called a 'stub gun' (*Stummelkanone*) by the soldiers. Besides, due to its low muzzle velocity, the penetrating power of the armour-piercing projectile was rather low: at a distance of 100 to 500 metres, it could just penetrate an armour plate 4cm thick – on the frontal armour of the T-34, 4-5cm thick and heavily sloped, it had no effect. In contrast, the 7.6cm gun of the T-34 could easily pierce the light armour of the German Panzer IV at any battle range.

The G version of the Panzer IV, introduced in 1942, remedied this weakness. The first vital improvement was the 7.5cm gun with a barrel length of 3.2m mounted in this new version. Additionally, the propellant of the shell cartridge was increased substantially, more than doubling its armour piercing capacity: At a distance of 500 metres, the standard projectile could penetrate 9cm of armour steel, and 8cm at a distance of 1,000 metres. Now the T-34 could be effectively combated. In early 1943, the thickness of the hull front plate was increased from 5 to 8cm, whereas structural reasons prevented an improvement of the turret armour, which was just 5cm thick and remained the Panzer IV's weak point until the end of the war. The tank was upgraded again in April 1943, when a new gun with a barrel length of 3.6m was mounted, which slightly increased both the muzzle velocity and armour piercing capacity of the projectile. At the same time, so-called tank skirts (*Panzerschürzen*) were introduced for the Panzer III and IV and for the assault guns and *Sturmpanzers* – large steel plates which were installed on the sides of the vehicle, covering almost all of the turret and the hull. Contrary to what is commonly believed, these plates, about 0.5 to 0.8cm thick, were made of soft steel rather than armour steel. They still increased protection though, since the side armour of the Panzer IV measured only 3cm and, just like the turret, could not be reinforced. Without skirts, the Panzer IV's side was vulnerable even to light Soviet anti-tank weapons, such as the 14.5mm calibre anti-tank rifle. These were used on a large scale by the Red Army in summer 1943 – 36,000 were available on the three Soviet fronts in the Kursk salient alone. They were easy to use and, under favourable conditions, could penetrate 5 to 6cm of armour steel. However, when the projectiles passed through an object before hitting the actual target, they lost much impact energy, even if that object was just a relatively thin steel plate protecting the side armour of the tank. On 14 May 1943, a ballistic test was carried out on the hull of a Panzer IV with mounted skirts at the Army Experimental Station Kummersdorf. It turned out that the skirts offered protection not only against the Soviet 14.5 mm calibre anti-tank rifle but also against 7.5cm high explosive shells.

The tank crews were not very enthusiastic about the tank skirts at first. A report drawn up by the 20th Panzer Division on 27 May 1943 offered only negative comments. The mounting of the skirts was so weak that it deformed even from slight bumps against the plate. When driving through mud, the mud was clogged between the hull of the tank and the skirts and increased the resistance, while in dry weather the skirts resulted in blown up dust and dirt to pass directly to the air intake flaps into the engine compartment, resulting in clogged cooling air intakes of the engine cooling system. Furthermore, the skirts not only complicated refuelling but also made working on the tank's running gears much more difficult. On top of that they covered the machine pistol hatches, so that in close combat enemy soldiers could approach the tank undetected. When it came to explosive charges, the skirts functioned like a basket, while the insulation amplified the force of the blast. During an exercise, an exploding hand grenade actually pierced the top of a tank's hull, causing material damage. Last but not least, the weight of the steel plates put additional stress on the chassis and the engine. 'According to the division's experiences so far', the report concluded, 'the disadvantages outweigh the advantages. The extra amount of work and material does therefore not seem justifiable.'[55]

The Battle of Kursk, however, taught the tank crews a different lesson; various reports reflect their change of opinion. An officer of the General Staff of the Army who visited Army Group Centre in August 1943 noted: 'At first, the tank crews strongly opposed the tank skirts, in some cases even removing them. However, they soon proved to be indispensable and were mounted again quickly. It often happened that a tank received more than 100 hits on the skirts.'[56] What remained a problem was the insufficient mounting of the skirts, a flaw many veterans of the panzer troops recall to this day. The skirts were frequently torn off the mounting brackets when a tank was driving past obstacles such as bushes or trees. Some crews remedied this problem by welding the skirts onto the mounting brackets – that way they could no longer be lost, but problems arose when a tank needed fixing or when the skirts had to be removed for rail transport, in which case the soldiers often used brute force to remove the plates, knocking them off with sledgehammers.

The new and more powerful gun, reinforced armour and the additional protection offered by the tank skirts were all vital improvements for the Panzer IV, so much in fact that the tank could now fully meet the requirements of tank warfare in summer 1943. To this day, the four most important criteria for the combat strength of a tank are command and control capability, firepower, mobility and protection/armour.[57] In 1941, the T-34 was far superior to the Panzer IV with regards to firepower, manoeuvrability and armour, but it was no match for the German tank when it came to command and control. Above all, the T-34 lacked a fifth crew member to allocate tasks efficiently; as the tank commander also had to double up as gunner, it was very difficult for him to keep track of things in the heat of battle. To make things worse, many Soviet tanks were not equipped with radios. By contrast, the German medium and heavy tanks all had a five-man crew (driver, radio operator, commander, gunner and loader), were equipped with a radio and an intercom system – and had optimally designed turrets. Unlike the German ones, Soviet tanks also did not have a turret

55 BA-MA, RH 10/48, 20. Panzerdivision, Erfahrungsbericht über Panzer-Schürzen, 27.5.1943, fol. 14-5, quote, fol. 15.

56 BA-MA, RH 10/54, Reisebericht des Majors i.G. von Busse zur Heeresgruppe Mitte, 17.8.1943, fol. 86.

57 Karl-Theo Schleicher and Wolfgang Schneider, 'Gedanken zur Weiterentwicklung des Kampfpanzers', *Das schwarze Barett*, 14 (1995), pp. 8-14, here, 9.

platform on which the tank crew worked and which rotated with the turret. Instead, the commander and the loader of a T-34 had each just a seat attached to the turret but otherwise had to stand on the floor of the hull, where the ammunition was stored, covered by a neoprene mat. In order to access the ammunition, the loader first had to roll the mat aside and open the ammunition boxes beneath it. In 1943, moreover, most Soviet tanks did not have a commander's cupola, which made it easier to observe the battlefield, but a periscope with a limited field of view. And when in 1942/43 the G and H versions of the Panzer IV were equipped with the new guns, the German tank now outclassed the T-34 in terms of firepower as well, the more so as it also had a much better sighting mechanism. Although its mobility and armour both remained inferior to the T-34, the improved armour still considerably increased the Panzer IV's survivability on the battlefield.

In total, 1,278 Panzer IVs were produced in the first half of 1943. Taken together, the Panzer and Panzergrenadier Divisions which took part in Operation Citadel on 5 July 1943 had 685 Panzer IV version G and H, as well as 50 outdated Panzer IV with 'stub guns', which since the introduction of high-explosive anti-tank (HEAT) rounds at the end of 1941 actually did stand a chance against the T-34 on the battlefield. The shaped charges could penetrate more than 7cm of armour, but they were unreliable. The target had to be hit at a favourable impact angle to create any effect, otherwise the projectile would simply bounce off the armour without exploding. When detonating on the armour plate, the effect of the shell depended on the impact angle, just like a conventional shell. A German anti-tank company, which on 6 June 1943 conducted a test firing on a captured T-34 with their 7.5cm anti-tank gun reported: 'The [HEAT] round 38 HL/B is supposed to have the same penetrating power at any distance (up to about 1,200 metres), i.e. 75mm. The test did not confirm this at all, however. The penetrating power of the round 38 HL/B depends above all on the impact angle.' The troops accordingly had 'little faith' in the HEAT rounds, the report concluded.[58] Another anti-tank company had had similar experiences earlier when conducting a test firing on a captured heavy KV-1 tank on 18 May 1943. The performance of the HEAT rounds turned out to be 'totally unsatisfactory.' According to the company's report, 'the crews no longer had any confidence in the HL round and thus in their guns after the shooting.'[59] Such experiences were not limited to the crews of anti-tank guns but were shared by those of tanks, tank destroyers and assault guns. Those tanks and assault guns which in summer 1943 were still equipped with short barrelled guns were, therefore, hardly suitable for armoured warfare.

Apart from the Panzer IV version G and H, the *Tiger*, *Panther* and heavy tank destroyer *Ferdinand*, the Germans had a large number of modern assault guns and

58 BA-MA, RH 10/58, 1./Schnelle Abteilung 329, 7.6.1943, Versuchsschießen mit der s. Pak 7,5 cm 40 am 6.6.1943, fol. 55-8, quote, fol. 58.

59 BA-MA, RH 10/58, Schnelle Abteilung 123, 18.5.1943, Erfahrungsbericht über ein Schulgefechtsschießen mit der s. Pak 7,5 cm (40), fol. 52-4, quotes, fol. 52-3.

light tank destroyers in summer 1943, which were also superior to the Soviet tanks in terms of firepower. Assault guns were especially popular with the troops. These self-propelled guns, mounted on a Panzer III chassis, were equipped with a fixed super-structure and a potent 7.5cm gun, which offered the same ballistic performance as the 7.5cm gun of the Panzer IV version G and H, instead of the usual rotating turret with its 5cm tank gun. A distinct advantage of the assault gun was the low profile of its structure. Compared to the Panzer IV (height 2.7 metres) and the *Tiger* and *Panther* (height 3 metres), the assault gun, less than 2.2 metres in height, made a more difficult target. Apart from that, its 8cm thick front armour offered more protection than the frontal armour plate of the Panzer IV's turret. Another advantage was that in addition to the usual commander's cupola, the gun commander also had a binocular periscope, which made it easy for him to observe targets at a greater distance.

Even though the assault gun had originally been designed for direct infantry support mainly against unarmoured targets, they eventually became one of the most important anti-tank weapons of the Wehrmacht. A record dating from 6 December 1943 kept by the tank officer at the General Staff of the Army indicates that assault guns were the most efficient German fighting vehicles at that time. First of all, they achieved the best ratio of the production output, friendly-to-enemy losses, as well as the number of fully operational vehicles compared to those under repair. Secondly, they were easier and less expensive to produce than tanks: the price for an assault gun was about 87,000 *Reichsmark*, whereas a Panzer III cost about 103,000, a Panzer IV 117,000, a *Panther* 130,000 and a *Tiger* 300,000 *Reichsmark*. In the first half of 1943, 1,230 assault guns were produced – and more than 3,000 in total throughout the year 1943. The formations which started the attack on Kursk on 5 July 1943 had 432 assault guns equipped with 7.5cm long-barrelled guns at their disposal, as well as 42 assault howitzers, which were equipped with a 10.5cm howitzer instead of the 7.5cm gun, and four obsolete assault guns with 7.5cm short-barrelled guns.

What is often underestimated and ignored in strength reports in literature is the light tank destroyer type *Marder* (marten), a 7.5cm or captured Soviet 7.6cm anti-tank gun mounted on a tank chassis, which allowed for a more mobile anti-tank defence. A *Marder*'s firepower was equal to that of a Panzer IV or a long-barrelled assault gun; however, it only had an open and lightly armoured crew compartment; and, because of its height of 2.5 metres it was much easier to spot in open terrain than a standard anti-tank gun. The crews therefore had to find good cover and frequently change position so as not draw fire from Soviet tanks. A field report from the tank destroyer battalion of the 6th Panzer Division dating from February 1943 stated: 'In a duel between T-34 and self-propelled gun at a distance, which corresponds to the penetrating power of both weapons, the self-propelled gun is, due to its weak armour, in any case inferior to the T-34.'[60]

60 BA-MA, RH 10/56, Panzerjäger-Abteilung 41, Erfahrungsbericht, 6.2.1943, fol. 258-62, quote, fol. 260.

In comparison to normal anti-tank guns, which were towed by lorries or prime movers, the self-propelled guns had the advantage of being able to evade enemy fire by quick changes of position. According to reports delivered by frontline officers from Army Group Centre in August 1943, the self-propelled anti-tank guns were very popular with the troops in spite of their disadvantages because they were able to actively 'hunt' enemy tanks.[61] This was not possible with the towed anti-tank guns: the standard German anti-tank gun, the heavy 7.5cm Pak (*Panzerabwehrkanone*, anti-tank gun) 40, weighed nearly 1.5 tonnes in action. The gun crews could not simply manhandle the heavy gun into a new firing position; in battle, the heavy anti-tank guns thus usually remained static. A report on the Battle of Kursk in the area of the Ninth Army, dated 20 August 1943, concluded: '*Towed* anti-tank guns could rarely repel tank attacks, but self-propelled tank destroyers, tanks and assault guns always could, even when the number of attacking tanks was *far greater*. The only effective anti-tank gun is the *self-propelled gun*, either as a tank, assault gun or as self-propelled tank destroyer. For one thing, *towed anti-tank guns* are too exposed to enemy artillery and air strike preparation, and for another thing they are too immobile to achieve any notable success.'[62]

Apart from the new tanks, assault guns, assault tanks and the *Ferdinand* and *Marder* tank destroyers, which played an important role in the fighting for Kursk, the German units received a number of other new vehicles in summer 1943. These included self-propelled artillery, that is, the 10.5cm howitzer *Wespe* (wasp) and the 15cm howitzer *Hummel* (bumblebee), as well as the *Hornisse* (hornet) tank destroyer, with the new 8.8cm Pak 43/1 gun mounted on a lightly armoured and open-top crew compartment. Adding to the arsenal of new weapon systems were demolition carriers – small remote-controlled tracked vehicles used against minefields, fortified positions and bunkers. Two versions of these were deployed in the attack on Kursk. One was the light carrier *Goliath*, an unmanned tracked vehicle made of soft steel which weighed about 400 kilos, was 1.5 metres long and 60cm in height, and looked almost like a miniature version of the British tanks of the First World War. It could carry a load of 60-75kg of explosives. The *Goliath* carriers were used by two panzer engineer companies which supported the attack of the 78th Assault Division (*Sturmdivision*) and the 383rd Infantry Division in the area of the XXIII Army Corps. The second remote-controlled demolition vehicle was the heavy *Sonderschlepper* B IV manufactured by Borgward. The lightly armoured vehicle measured 3.7m in length and 1.2m in height, weighed 3.6t and carried 500kg of explosives. It was operated by a driver, who steered the carrier to its initial position from where it was driven to the target

61 BA-MA, RH 10/54, Reisebericht des Majors i.G. von Busse zur Heeresgruppe Mitte, 17.8.1943, fol. 87.

62 BA-MA, RH 10/58, Panzer-Artillerie-Regiment 103, II. Abteilung, Kommandeur, Taktische und artilleristische Erfahrungen in den Angriffs- und Abwehrkämpfen südlich Orel vom 5.7.-18.8.43, fol. 278-302, quote, fol. 279 [emphasis in original, RT].

by remote control. The explosive charges were then dropped and, once the carrier had returned to safety, detonated. Only when the remote control for releasing the charges did not work, or when the B IV could not be removed from the target area for other reasons, was the carrier itself also blown up. During the Battle of Kursk, the B IV was employed in particular to blast gaps in the Soviet minefields. All in all, three remote control panzer companies were attached to Model's Ninth Army, each of which were issued with 36 heavy Borgward B IV carriers at their disposal. The 312th Remote Control Panzer Company were subordinate to the XXXXVII Panzer Corps, supporting the *Tiger* tanks of the 505th Heavy Panzer Battalion, while the 313th and 314th Company were to pave the way for the *Ferdinand* assault guns and the *Sturmpanzers* of the 656th Heavy Tank Destroyer Regiment as part of the XXXXI Panzer Corps.

The Red Army had little to counter these various new weapon systems which the Germans employed during the Battle of Kursk. The T-34, the Soviet standard tank, had not been significantly improved since 1941. A new version, the T-34/85, equipped with a potent 8.5cm gun and a five-man crew, was not deployed until the beginning of 1944. Almost two thirds of the Soviet tanks taking part in the Battle of Kursk were T-34/76. The second main tank of the Soviet forces was the light T-70 tank. It weighed about 10 tonnes, had a two-man crew and was equipped with a 4.5cm gun, whose projectiles could penetrate four centimetres of armour steel at a distance of 100m – and hence did not stand the slightest chance against any medium and heavy German tank. Apart from the T-34/76 and the T-70, the Red Army formations which were to defend the Kursk salient also had a few hundred other tanks of different types, though in terms of fighting power, these were no match for the new German tanks either: the heavy KV-1 tank, which, even though heavily armoured, was armed only with the obsolete 7.6cm gun, the light T-60 tank with a 2cm machine gun as main armament, as well as British and American tanks delivered to the Soviet Union. The 'lend-lease tanks' included the light American M3 Stuart, the medium American Grant and Lee, and British tanks such as the Churchill, the Matilda and the Valentine, whose fighting power was rated rather poorly by both the Soviets and the Germans.

In summer 1943, the Red Army had three types of self-propelled guns: the SU-76, the SU-122 and the SU-152. The light SU-76 tank destroyer, mounted on a T-70 chassis, resembled the German *Marder*. Its 7.6cm gun had the same ballistic properties as the gun of the T-34 and was inadequate against the heavy German tanks and self-propelled guns. The medium SU-122 was based on the T-34 chassis and armed with a 12.2cm howitzer, which could undoubtedly acquit itself well in combat against the heavy German tanks, albeit at short distances, or with special ammunition only. According to a report by Vyacheslav Aleksandrovich Malyshev, the People's Commissar of the Tank Industry, from 10 April 1943, the armour-piercing standard ammunition of the 12.2cm howitzer could not penetrate the side armour of a *Tiger* at a distance of more than 400 to 500 metres, or the frontal armour at a distance of more than 200 to 300 metres. But it has to be accepted that such reports were often fairly optimistic, especially when directed to Stalin personally, as in this case.[63] Ballistic tests were carried out under favourable conditions, in other words, with an ideal angle of impact, and therefore did not reflect the realities of tank combat on the battlefield.

The only Soviet combat vehicle which could successfully engage the heavy German tanks frontally in summer 1943 was the SU-152 self-propelled gun, a heavy assault gun built on the chassis of the KV-1 and equipped with a 15.2cm howitzer. The maximum penetration capacity of this gun's armour-piercing shells was 13-14cm, but only at very short distances and a vertical impact angle. In theory, all German tanks except the *Ferdinand* could thus be penetrated frontally. At a distance of 1000 metres and an ideal impact angle, the projectile would go through 11-12cm of armour steel, or 9-10cm if the impact angle deviated from the perpendicular by 30 degrees, which was the German standard for ballistic tests. Under combat conditions, the crews of the *Tiger* and the *Panther* therefore still stood a chance of surviving frontal hits from a SU-152 unscathed, even though in reality the effect of the almost 50kg heavy 15.2cm armour-piercing shell was far more destructive than the theoretical penetration values suggest. In a field report dating from 10 October 1943, the 503rd Heavy Panzer Battalion pointed out that 'hits from assault guns on the *Tiger*' caused 'large fractures in the hull and frontal plate even from a distance of more than 1,500 metres.'[64] The shock of the hits also resulted in all kinds of mountings in the crew compartment falling off.

For the crews of the Soviet self-propelled guns, things became dangerous when they were spotted by German tanks, because the 6-7.5cm thick frontal armour plate of the SU-152 could be penetrated by the guns of the *Tiger* and the *Panther* at any range. Also, due to the large calibre, there were no cartridges for the guns of the SU-122 and the SU-152, which meant that the projectile and the cartridge case had to be loaded separately. The SU-152 could only carry 20 shells, not all of which could even be used against tanks as high explosive shells had also to be carried on board. Furthermore, the fumes released by firing the 15.2cm howitzer were not only a hazard to the crew in their badly ventilated fighting compartment but also gave away the vehicle's position, which was one more reason why the SU-152 had to hit its target with the first shot as its reload time was quite long, giving its target ample time to fire several rounds before the SU-152 could return fire.

The main problem for the Soviets in summer 1943 was that they had by far too few of those self-propelled guns which could match heavy German tanks. The formations of the Central Front, which were tasked with stopping the advance of Model's Ninth Army, had only 25 SU-152 and 32 SU-122 AFVs at their disposal. The Voronezh Front, defending the southern sector of the Kursk salient against Hoth's Fourth Panzer Army and against Army Detachment Kempf, was supported by only

63 Mel'chin, 'Obespechit', pp. 107-8.
64 BA-MA, RH 10/56, Schwere Panzer-Abteilung 503, Abteilung Ia, Erfahrungen, 10.10.1943, fol. 71-3, quote, fol. 73.

one heavy self-propelled artillery regiment with 12 SU-152s, along with 24 medium SU-122s. The Steppe Front, which stood by as reserve for the Voronezh Front, at least had 72 SU-122s available, but no SU-152s. It was therefore the regular towed anti-tank guns which had to bear the main burden of the Soviet anti-tank defence. For the most part, these were 7.6cm and 4.5cm guns. The 7.6cm divisional gun ZiS-3 had the same ballistic properties as the 7.6cm F-34 gun mounted on the T-34 and the KV-1 and could not penetrate the frontal armour of the new German tank models. Two versions existed of the other standard Soviet anti-tank gun, a 4.5cm calibre gun: the older 1937 version and the 1942 model, which had a higher penetration capacity, though it was still inferior to the 7.6cm gun. When a ballistic test was carried out on a captured *Tiger* in April 1943 it was shown that at least the special ammunition of both of these guns could pierce the side armour – the sub-calibre shell of the 1937 model at a distance up to 200 metres, the sub-calibre shell of the newer 1942 model up to 350 metres. However, these results were obtained under ideal conditions, that is, at an exact vertical impact angle, and hardly reflect the actual penetration performance under battle conditions.

One weapon which really did pose a threat to the heavy German tanks was the Soviet 5.7cm anti-tank gun ZiS-2. It had been developed as early as 1940 and the Red Army had received the first of these guns in summer 1941. But its production was ceased in favour of the 7.6cm divisional gun ZiS-3 in December 1941. The latter was preferred by the Red Army because its high explosive shells had a greater splinter effect than the 5.7cm shells, and the penetrating power of the 7.6cm gun was sufficient to combat the German tanks, which at that time were only relatively lightly armoured. When the Red Army captured the first *Tiger* and tests showed that the armour-piercing rounds of both the 4.5cm and the 7.6cm gun were not effective, it was decided to take up the production of the 5.7cm gun ZiS-2 again. On 15 June 1943 this type of gun was once more introduced in the Red Army – too late, however, to play a crucial role in the Battle of Kursk. If a significant number of these guns had been available to the Soviet formations defending the Kursk salient in early July 1943, the German tank losses would undoubtedly have been considerably higher. This is also indicated by a field report from the 503rd Heavy Panzer Battalion drafted on 10 October 1943, which reflected on the threat of the 5.7cm anti-tank gun: 'At a battle range of 800 to 1,000 metres, its steel-core projectile went right through the *Tiger*'s vertical plates of the turret and the upper hull – even at a slanted angle of impact.'[65] The report does, however, refer to the 5.7cm gun as an American anti-tank gun, so it is possible that this was a reference to the British 5.7cm calibre 6 pounder gun, which was also used by the Americans and delivered to the Soviet Union in large numbers. Still, as the 6 pounder had about the same penetrative capacity as the 5.7cm anti-tank

65 BA-MA, RH 10/56, Schwere Panzer-Abteilung 503, Abteilung Ia, Erfahrungen, 10.10.1943, fol. 71-3, quote, fol. 73.

gun ZiS-2, it is ultimately irrelevant which gun the German field report was actually referring to.

At Kursk, the Red Army formations only had very few 5.7cm guns at their disposal in July 1943; potent anti-tank guns were thus scarce. This is why Soviet soldiers resorted to a method the Germans had employed since the campaign against France in 1940 when encountering superior enemy tanks: they used their heavy anti-aircraft guns against the tanks. The famous German 8.8cm anti-aircraft gun soon acquired a fearsome reputation as an anti-tank gun. Its Soviet counterpart was the 8.5cm 52-K anti-aircraft gun, albeit with a much lower penetrative capacity than the German gun. On 4 May 1943, the Military Council of the Armoured and Mechanized Forces of the Red Army reported to Stalin that the 10cm thick frontal armour of the *Tiger*'s front hull could be penetrated by the armour-piercing rounds of the Soviet 8.5cm anti-aircraft gun at a distance of 1,000 metres. This assessment, however, was optimistic at best because the penetration capacity of 10cm could only be achieved at a precisely vertical impact angle; at an angle deviating from the perpendicular by 30 degrees, the distance had to be 100 metres or less in order to achieve similar penetration results. Together with the 15.2cm howitzer, the 8.5cm anti-aircraft gun was nevertheless one of the most effective anti-tank guns of the Red Army in summer 1943, even though only relatively few of these guns were available to the Soviet forces for anti-tank defence.

In summer 1943, the Red Army was at a considerable qualitative disadvantage against the Germans in terms of both tanks and anti-tank guns – which is what Hitler based his hopes on, feeling certain that the attack on Kursk could be a success, despite the massive numerical superiority of the Red Army and the Soviet in-depth defensive positions.

German Operational Planning for Citadel

The spring *rasputitsa* in 1943 provided a much-needed period of rest for both sides. The claim occasionally made in literature on the Battle of Kursk, that Operation Citadel could have been launched as early as April 1943[66], is a gross misjudgement of the actual situation at the time. In fact, the weather conditions would not have allowed for any major operations, and the troops were too exhausted to carry out another offensive following the conclusion of the winter operations of 1942/43. The war diary of the Ninth Army Headquarters records that a large part of the attacking

66 See, for example: Alfred Zins, *Die Operation Zitadelle: Die militärgeschichtliche Diskussion und ihr Niederschlag im öffentlichen Bewusstsein als didaktisches Problem* (Frankfurt/M., 1986), p. 20; Wolfgang Fleischer, *Die größte Panzerschlacht des Zweiten Weltkrieges: Operation 'Zitadelle'* (Wölfersheim-Berstadt, 1997), p. 12; and, Jean Restayn and Nicole Moller, *Operation Citadel: A Text and Photo Album*, vol. 2 (Winnipeg (Manitoba), 2006), p. 2.

forces, especially the panzer formations, were unable to attack in April 1943 'due to the strain of the winter fighting.'[67]

The repeated postponements of Operation Citadel offered the troops the opportunity to prepare intensely for the battles that were about to take place in the Kursk salient. Three German armies with a total of 33 divisions were to join the attack on Kursk, comprised of 17 infantry divisions, five panzergrenadier and 11 panzer divisions. Adding to this was a large number of GHQ troops (*Heerestruppen*), that is, formations which were independent from the divisions and which the senior command staffs temporarily allocated to certain formations, in order to form spearheads. Apart from artillery formations, these GHQ troops included numerous panzer, tank destroyer and assault gun battalions.

The Ninth Army was to attack from the area of Orël to the north of Kursk. It was commanded by Colonel-General Walter Model; 17 of its 22 divisions joined the attack on Kursk, nine of which were infantry divisions (the 6th, 7th, 31st, 36th, 86th, 216th, 258th, 292nd and 383rd), one was a reinforced infantry division (the 78th Assault Division), one a panzergrenadier division (the 10th) and six were panzer divisions (the 2nd, 4th, 9th, 12th, 18th and 20th).

Stationed to the south of Kursk, in the area of Belgorod, were the Fourth Panzer Army and Army Detachment Kempf. Of the nine divisions of Army Detachment Kempf, six participated in Operation Citadel – three infantry divisions (the 106th, 168th and 320th) and three panzer divisions (6th, 7th, 19th). Another infantry division, the 198th, was brought up a few days after the beginning of the attack to reinforce Army Detachment Kempf. These forces had the order to cover the thrust of the Fourth Panzer Army from the east and protect it against Soviet flank attacks (Map 3).

The Fourth Panzer Army was commanded by Colonel-General Hermann Hoth. It was allocated the most vital task of the southern attack forces, namely to break through the Soviet defensive positions, echeloned in depth, south of Kursk as quickly as possible, push towards the north and link up with Model's Ninth Army to close the ring around the Soviet forces in the Kursk salient. For the duration of Operation Citadel, 10 divisions were subordinate to the Fourth Panzer Army Headquarters in total, nine of which joined the attack on Kursk. Among them were the most powerful formations the Germans could muster: the four elite Panzergrenadier Divisions *Großdeutschland*, *Leibstandarte SS Adolf Hitler*, *Das Reich* and *Totenkopf*. In addition to these, two panzer divisions (the 3rd and the 11th), as well as three infantry divisions (the 167th, the 255th and the 332nd), of the Fourth Panzer Army also participated in the attack on Kursk. What is striking is the small number of infantry divisions, an issue that Manstein raised repeatedly with Zeitzler and Hitler before the beginning of Operation Citadel. Infantry divisions were not only needed to occupy and mop up occupied areas, but also to protect the flanks of the panzer formations. Manstein's

67 NARA, T312/317/7886028, Kriegstagebuch Nr. 8, Armee-Oberkommando 9, Führungsabteilung, 26.3.-18.8.1943.

warnings, however, were in vain. Instead, Hitler emphasized that infantry forces had to be replaced with additional panzer forces.

The Second Army under the command of *General der Infanterie* Walter Weiß, which was positioned to the west of the Kursk salient, was originally intended to join the offensive, too. However, this army only had eight infantry divisions and a few tank destroyer and assault gun battalions and was, therefore, too weak to carry out the initially planned holding attacks at the beginning of Operation Citadel. Instead, the leaders of the Second Army had to deal with the question of whether their formations would even be able to withstand a possible Soviet attack aimed at a breakthrough to the west and a link-up with the strong partisan units at Bryansk. It was decided that the Second Army would not join the attack until the danger to its front had been dealt with and, after the successful breakthrough of the Ninth Army and the Fourth Panzer Army, the enemy had disengaged from the front of the Second Army in order to break out towards to east.

Due to their lack of strength, the Germans were forced to thin out considerably all armies and corps which did not participate in Operation Citadel to free up troops and allocate them to the attacking formations; they also had to divert reinforcements and supplies to the units that were to take part in the attack. Even the Second Panzer Army, which was tasked with defending the Orël salient against Soviet counterattacks, had to transfer nearly all its panzer formations to the Ninth Army for Operation Citadel.

The principal focus of the German leadership in 1943 was on three attacking armies: the Ninth Army, the Fourth Panzer Army and Army Detachment Kempf. On 1 April 1943, the Kempf formation presented a first draft of Operation Citadel, at that time still called *Operationsvorschlag K*. Even though the corps' structure and the allocation of tasks were different than in the final operations plan, the course planned for Operation Citadel was already apparent in the proposal from Army Detachment Kempf: the SS Panzer Corps, which included the Panzergrenadier Divisions *Leibstandarte SS Adolf Hitler*, *Das Reich* and *Totenkopf*, was to form the main spearhead of the offensive. The aim of the assault was to encircle and destroy the strong Soviet forces in the Kursk salient and to eliminate it, thereby shortening the front line by 330 kilometres, thus freeing a large number of troops for redeployment. In addition to this, the new front line would run through terrain which seemed well suited to fend off Soviet counterattacks. Another important aspect was the capture of the railway and road hub Belgorod–Kursk–Orël. Finally, the Red Army would no longer be able to use the Kursk salient as a springboard for offensives against the flanks of Army Groups Centre and South.

On 3 April 1943, Army Group South notified the Army High Command that the final goal of Operation Citadel was to advance as far as Korocha–Skorodnoe–Tim (map 3). Six days were scheduled for the offensive: within three days the attack forces of Army Group South were to break through the Soviet positions and reach Oboyan and Skorodnoe. In the ensuing three days they were to push onward to Kursk and Tim and link up with the formations of Army Group Centre attacking from north, to then destroy the Soviet forces encircled in the Kursk salient.

On 8 April, the Ninth Army presented its plans for Operation Citadel, which in turn formed the basis for the initial plan Army Group Centre was to send to Army High Command four days later. It was planned that the XXXXVII Panzer Corps (2nd, 9th and 20th Panzer Division) as the main combat group would advance into the area east of Kursk, capture the city and then link up with the forces of Army Group South attacking from the south. Ninth Army Headquarters considered it particularly important to occupy the high ground east of Kursk as quickly as possible, since it was viewed as a key position for all east–west transport. The importance of this area becomes obvious when one looks at a map: the railway line L'gov–Kursk–Shchigry was the only rail connection leading into the Kursk salient from the east and westwards out of it. Once in German hands, it would have been much more difficult for the Red Army rapidly to bring up both strong reserves and swiftly withdraw the forces threatened by encirclement.

Both Army Groups (Centre and South) saw a swift conclusion of the operation as crucial. On 25 April 1943, the Chief of Staff of Army Group South, Major-General Busse, reiterated in a letter to the commanders of the Fourth Panzer Army and Army Detachment Kempf that it was vital 'to crack and break through the enemy's defensive front so fast that the mass of his reserves cannot intervene in time in this phase of the operation.' It was essential, Busse continued, 'that our rapid advance will force the enemy to bring up his reserves hastily and in dribs and drabs so we can defeat them in quick succession.' Speed was also necessary to prevent the Soviet forces in the Kursk salient from escaping eastwards – a manoeuvre that was to be expected as soon as a German success became foreseeable, as Busse pointed out: 'In the last few battles, the Russians have demonstrated that they are now trying to avoid being annihilated in hopeless situations.'[68]

Three days later, Busse reiterated his view to Field-Marshal Wolfram von Richthofen, whose *Luftflotte* was to support the assault forces of Army Group South, that the main goal of Operation Citadel was the rapid breakthrough to Kursk. On the same day, Busse told Zeitzler that further panzer forces were needed for the planned advance on Kursk, namely the XXIV Panzer Corps with the 23rd Panzer Division and the SS Panzergrenadier Division *Wiking*. Yet Hitler was adamant about keeping this corps in the Donets Basin, serving as an operational reserve in case the Russians should launch a counterattack in the Donbas. Even though Busse was more in favour of Army Group South risking bringing up the XXIV Corps for Citadel, Hitler would not change his mind and continued to retain the corps.

In view of the increasing delay to Operation Citadel, the Fourth Panzer Army expressed its doubts about the operations plan in late June 1943. In an estimate of the situation on 20 June, the Headquarters of the Fourth Panzer Army accordingly

68 BA-MA, RH 21-4/121, Panzerarmee-Oberkommando 4, Ia, Anlagenband 19 (Chefsachen), Operation 'Zitadelle', 2.4.-19.6.1943, quote on unnumbered page following fol. 113.

proposed the following changes: as Army Detachment Kempf was considered too weak to defend the flank of the Fourth Panzer Army from the expected strong Soviet counterattacks from the east on its own, Fourth Panzer Army Headquarters thought it better not to continue the push north towards Kursk after having broken through the Soviet positions. Rather, both panzer corps of the Fourth Panzer Army (the SS Panzer Corps and the XXXXVIII Panzer Corps) should at first turn eastwards in order to defeat the Soviet forces brought in from the east. Once as many enemy forces as possible had been destroyed on its eastern flank, the Fourth Panzer Army should push on towards the north and complete its advance until it linked up with the Ninth Army. This plan, however, was rejected by Army Group South. Thus, when presenting its operations plan for Operation Citadel on 28 June 1943, it adopted the original plan according to which Army Detachment Kempf had orders to protect the eastern flank of the Fourth Panzer Army, whereas the latter was to concentrate on the assault on Kursk.

The most important change in the attack plan for Citadel was again instigated by Colonel-General Model, commander of the Ninth Army. In his presentation on 27 April 1943, he had already been able to convince Hitler to postpone Operation Citadel by several weeks. Subsequently, however, it became more and more obvious that the Red Army would react to the German attack with offensives against the Orël salient, so, on 11 June, Model requested from Army Group Centre that the forces of the Ninth Army be regrouped for Operation Citadel. He suggested pulling out all panzer divisions from the frontline and forming an operational reserve from these formations. By doing so, Model at least took the latest developments on the German side into account, as Hitler had not yet set the definite date for the attack. It therefore remained unclear whether Citadel was planned as an initial strike or whether Army Group Centre would have to repel the expected Soviet attacks against the Orël salient – or even be forced to remain on the defensive. Model argued that the frontlines of the Second Panzer Army in the salient of Orël had been so weakened by the transfer of troops to the Ninth Army and that reserves were so depleted that the panzer divisions of the Ninth Army must be available as operational reserve for counterattacks.

Army Group Centre and the Army High Command agreed to Model's demands for the most part, and three days later, on 14 June, the Ninth Army issued a new operations order for Operation Citadel. Instead of the 2nd and 9th Panzer Division originally intended for the initial strike, the 6th Infantry Division, and instead of the 12th Panzer Division, the 31st Infantry Division, were tasked with breaking through the enemy defensive positions. For the time being, only the 20th Panzer Division remained part of the first assault wave, whereas the other panzer divisions were to follow the infantry in the second and third phase of the attack, which meant that the operational push on Kursk would come after the successful tactical breakthrough of the infantry. On 20 June 1943, however, Model stated in his estimate of the situation: 'The newly brought up 31st Infantry Division, which for the past three months has been used almost solely for the construction of field fortifications, needs replenishment and intensive training for the new task, as does the 6th Infantry Division.'[69]

In spite of the long waiting period, the German forces were thin and therefore had to be divided prior to deployment, as the example of the 12th Panzer Division demonstrates. On 28 June, Army Group Centre agreed to Model's request for employing at least one tank company and one self-propelled anti-tank company of the 12th Panzer Division being used in the first assault wave, whereas the bulk of the already weakened division was scheduled for the third phase of the attack; until its planned commitment it remained an army group reserve, over which Model had no jurisdiction.

Considering the severe lack of forces, the training to prepare the troops for the attack had to be all the more thorough. The 4th Panzer Division, the strongest offensive formation in Model's Ninth Army, conducted no less than 12 battalion exercises in the last weeks before the attack. One of these exercises was overseen by none other than Colonel-General Model himself, and the 4th Panzer Division reported: 'He [Model] takes an active involvement in all attack preparations, from the formation and camouflaging of the supply columns and their loading, which are checked by a delegated general, to the screening of the troops, which is checked from the air, to the camouflage painting, the use of spades and the combat formations of the panzergrenadiers.'[70]

The assault forces of Army Group South also conducted intensive preparations for the operation. The 240th Infantry Regiment of the 106th Infantry Division, for instance, formed an assault company, in which soldiers from all companies of the regiment – most of them volunteers – were thoroughly trained for special tasks such as raids and unarmed close combat. The three panzergrenadier divisions of the Waffen-SS, which were to form the main effort of the attack in the south, also carried out various training courses and exercises. A member of the *Totenkopf* Division wrote about these: 'Sometimes we [shook] our heads about the rigour of the training and the fussy preparations. But later we got proof that all this [was] necessary.'[71]

By the end of June and beginning of July 1943, the level of training of many German formations was nevertheless still rather poor, not least of all because the troops were regularly assigned ancillary tasks, such as combating partisans or preparing defensive positions. Since both Army Group South and Army Group Centre were expecting Soviet counteroffensives against their fronts, the construction of field fortifications was considered vital; and because suitable workers were scarce, these tasks fell to the troops themselves – to the detriment of their training. To the German leadership, it seemed obvious where these Soviet counterattacks would be launched: they would be

69 Klink, *Gesetz*, p. 327.

70 Joachim Neumann, *Die 4. Panzerdivision 1938–1945*, 2 vols. (Bonn, 2nd edn, 1989), vol. 1, pp. 641–2.

71 Hugo Zährl, *Vier Jahre in vorderster Front: Kriegstagebuch eines Trägers der Ehrenblattspange in der 3. SS-Panzerdivision 'Totenkopf'* (Trier, 2007), p. 54.

primarily aimed at the Donets basin and Khar'kov in the sector of Army Group South, and at the Orël salient in the area of Army Group Centre. As early as 17 March 1943, the High Command of Army Group Centre was thus ordered to intensify the fortification of its defensive positions, against which the enemy, it was hoped, would be bled white. The Germans consequently began building positions with several lines of defence. The entry for 21 May 1943 in the war diary of the Ninth Army Headquarters reported that setting up the second line of defence was being carried out with vigour because it had to be expected that the enemy would not remain on the defensive. Two days later, the same war diary stated: 'The enemy's artillery strength and the reserves he holds back at a distance, ready to use them against a German attack in any direction, make it seem possible that the enemy will be the one to launch an attack to bring about the collapse of the Orël salient.'[72] Then, on 12 June 1943, the war diary noted that a Soviet offensive against the whole Orël salient could begin at any time. In order to ensure a consistent chain of command for the German forces in the salient, Colonel-General Model was designated commander of all German formations at Orël, including the Second Panzer Army, as soon as the Soviets mounted their offensive. Model seemed particularly suitable for this task because of his forceful style of leadership; besides, Hitler thought very highly of him – which soon earned Model the reputation of being Hitler's favourite general.

Some formations of Army Group South, too, had problems preparing properly for the attack. Unlike Army Group Centre, Army Group South did not have to deal with strong partisan activities; therefore, no major anti-partisan operations were carried out in its area. But its troops had to prepare their defences against possible Soviet offensives just the same, even more so as in spring 1943 it long remained unclear whether one's own attack would be an initial strike or a 'backhand blow.' On 10 May 1943, the commander of the Fourth Panzer Army issued a key order for the defensive operations, tasking the LII Army Corps (57th, 255th and 332nd Infantry Division) and the 167th Infantry Division to make their defensive positions as deep and strong as possible. The 167th Infantry Division was the only infantry division available to the XXXXVIII Panzer Corps and the SS Panzer Corps; for the attack on Kursk, it had to be divided up between the two corps. Instead of preparing thoroughly for the offensive, this important division was now additionally tasked with building entrenchments.

Apart from the deficiencies in training there was also a shortage of materiel, which affected even the panzer and panzergrenadier divisions. In 1943, every panzer division should in theory have been allocated one panzer regiment with two panzer battalions. This also held true for the army's Panzergrenadier Division *Großdeutschland* and the SS Panzergrenadier Divisions *Leibstandarte SS Adolf Hitler*, *Das Reich* and *Totenkopf*. Considering their strength and order of battle, these four divisions were not actually

72 NARA, T312/317/7886099, Kriegstagebuch Nr. 8, Armee-Oberkommando 9, Führungsabteilung, 26.3.-18.8.1943.

panzergrenadier divisions anymore; in fact, they were subsequently re-designated 'Panzer Divisions' in autumn 1943.

In essence, every panzer battalion had an authorized strength of 96 tanks; a panzer regiment with two battalions was therefore equipped with 192 tanks. Additionally, there was the regimental staff with an authorized strength of eight tanks. In total, this added up to a theoretical strength of 200 tanks per panzer division. Yet not one of the German panzer divisions actually reached this strength in summer 1943. Most of them did not even have two panzer battalions at their disposal: Eight of the 11 panzer divisions and two of the four elite panzergrenadier divisions joined the attack on Kursk with panzer regiments which were allocated one instead of two panzer battalions. Only the 7th, the 11th and the 19th Panzer Division as well as the Panzergrenadier Divisions *Großdeutschland* and *Totenkopf* contained panzer regiments with two battalions each. In terms of their numerical strength, however, they missed the normal allocation of 200 tanks by a considerable margin. The 19th Panzer Division was actually one of the weakest panzer divisions; its panzer regiments could only muster 87 tanks at the beginning of Operation Citadel. The 11th Panzer Division was at least fitted out with 114 tanks, although 89 of these were obsolete. The 7th Panzer Division, which had proved itself in the previous campaigns and was considered one of the best panzer divisions of the Wehrmacht, only had 112 tanks at its disposal for the offensive at Kursk – 75 of which, moreover, were obsolescent. The best-equipped panzer formation was the Division *Großdeutschland*, even though its panzer regiment with 135 tanks did not reach the authorized strength either. The same holds true for the SS Division *Totenkopf*, which had 139 tanks in total, but 80 of which were obsolete and no match for the Soviet T-34 tank.

On paper, the increase in materiel received by the panzer formations of Army Groups Centre and South in spring 1943 seems massive. Even before the initial date of the attack, the Army High Command had assured both army groups they would be supplied with so many tanks that, by 10 May 1943, they would have 1,000 medium tanks and 66 heavy *Tiger* tanks at their disposal. Indeed, these numbers were even exceeded: on 10 May, both army groups were equipped with 1,008 medium tanks and 87 *Tigers* in total, 29 more than had been projected. Still, a large number of the medium tanks were outdated Panzer IIIs, which were still being produced at that time. Furthermore, a number of these did not come from new production but were repaired machines. On 2 May 1943, Army Group South reported that by 10 May, 50 Panzer IIIs, 24 Panzer IVs and 14 assault guns would be delivered to the troops for Operation Citadel from the large repair shops and maintenance units. Even though the Red Army, too, had a range of obsolete tanks in summer 1943, it was quantitatively vastly superior to the German Army; the German *Ostheer*, therefore, was dependent on tanks that could easily outperform the Soviet machines.

By postponing Operation Citadel, it was hoped that the panzer formations could be reinforced with a large number of modern tanks. Considering the total numbers of tanks deployed to the Eastern Front in May and June 1943, the increase appears considerable. However, if one also takes the concurrent reinforcements on the Soviet side into account, it does not seem very impressive at all – and the commanders of the German army groups and armies as well as the Chief of Staff Zeitzler repeatedly pointed out this alarming fact.

From mid-May until the beginning of July 1943, the number of German tanks on the Eastern Front increased by 19 command tanks, 124 Panzer IIIs equipped with the 5cm long-barrelled or the 7.5cm short-barrelled gun, 291 Panzer IVs, 200 *Panthers*, 41 *Tigers* and 45 *Sturmpanzers*. But 150 of these 720 tanks were obsolete or barely suitable for tank combat, namely the 19 command tanks, the 124 Panzer IIIs and seven of the 291 Panzer IVs – old versions armed with the 7.5cm short-barrelled gun mounted on them. As for the 200 *Panthers*, they had not yet been tested in battle and proved to still be technically flawed. In addition to these 570 modern tanks, 179 assault guns and 415 tank destroyers and self-propelled artillery pieces were sent to the Eastern Front. On the German side, this meant an increase of 1,314 tanks and self-propelled guns for the entire Eastern Front. In contrast, the three Soviet fronts defending the Kursk salient alone received 3,790 tanks and self-propelled guns from mid-April to early July 1943.

Hitler's repeated promises to equip the troops with a large number of superior tanks and assault guns in order to compensate for the increase of strength on the Soviet side was left unfulfilled. On the contrary, the lack of modern tanks made their uneven – and unfair, as far as the troops were concerned – distribution necessary, privileging some of the assault formations. While the SS Panzer Corps and the Division *Großdeutschland* received the most up-to-date tanks in spring 1943, the remaining panzer and panzergrenadier divisions found themselves at a distinct disadvantage. Even though the commanders of the armies and army groups as well as the tank officer at the General Staff of the Army again and again insisted on an even distribution of the various tank types to the divisions, in reality this never happened. At the beginning of July 1943, there was a very uneven distribution of tanks.

When Hitler issued his order of the day on 5 July 1943, as Operation Citadel was launched, he told his soldiers that they now finally had better tanks than 'the Russian.' Yet to the members of those panzer divisions which for the most part were equipped with obsolete machines, this must have seemed like cheap propaganda. In a report drawn up by an officer of the General Staff of the Army about a trip to Army Group South in August 1943, it was stated: 'On the radio and in the newspapers there is talk of an immense number of the most modern weapons – what the soldier sees, however, is that his old weapons are not being replaced.'[73]

But the soldiers of the Red Army had likewise to face a serious problem: while their tanks and anti-tank guns were superior to the majority of German tanks, they were no match at all for the new generation of tanks and assault guns of the Wehrmacht. In summer 1943, as in previous battles, the Red Army thus had to rely on quantity – and

73 BA-MA, RH 10/54, Reisebericht des Majors i. G. von Busse zur Heeresgruppe Mitte, 17.8.1943, fol. 87.

Tanks and SP Guns Allocated to Panzer and PzGren Divs in Operation Citadel (as of 30 June 1943)

Division	Latest Tanks	*Tigers*	Obsolete Tanks	Assault Guns	Tank Destroyers (self-propelled)	Artillery (self-propelled)	Total
Großdeutschland	81	15	54	35	28	34	232
Das Reich	73	14	73	34	13	30	223
Totenkopf	59	15	80	35	14	30	218
Leibstandarte	96	13	26	35	29	30	216
2nd Panzer Div.	65	–	51	–	34	30	180
4th Panzer Div.	79	–	22	–	26	30	157
9th Panzer Div.	56	–	53	–	28	18	155
11th Panzer Div.	25	–	89	–	14	18	146
7th Panzer Div.	37	–	75	–	14	12	138
6th Panzer Div.	32	–	85	–	12	6	135
20th Panzer Div.	40	–	42	–	28	6	116
3rd Panzer Div.	22	–	78	2	14	–	116
12th Panzer Div.	36	–	50	–	16	6	108
19th Panzer Div.	38	–	49	–	14	–	101
18th Panzer Div.	29	–	46	–	16	6	97
10th PzGren Div.	–	–	–	–	39	–	39

(Abbreviations: Div = Division; PzGren Div = Panzergrenadier Division)

on the enormous defensive works, which had turned the Kursk salient into a veritable fortress.

Soviet Preparations for the Battle of Kursk

The Kursk salient was of crucial importance not only for the German offensive plans in spring and summer 1943. The Soviet General Staff, too, soon recognized the possibilities the vast salient offered as a base of operations. It allowed for attacks against the flanks and the rear of Army Group Centre in the area of Orël, as well as for offensives against the formations of Army Group South at Belgorod and Khar'kov. Besides, from the end of March 1943, the *Stavka*, the Headquarters of the Supreme High Command, had been expecting the Germans to choose the Kursk salient as the objective for their own spring offensive. The *Stavka* thus decided that both fronts in the Kursk salient (the Central and the Voronezh Front) would remain on the defensive for the time being and build an in-depth defensive system. Each of these 'fronts' was about equivalent to a German army group. Furthermore, the formation of a whole reserve front was decided upon, which was named the Steppe Military District on 13 April, and re-designated the Steppe Front on 9 July. This new front had the task to help defend the Kursk salient against German attacks and, more importantly, to be available for offensives mounted from the area around Kursk.

On 27 March 1943, the Voronezh Front received the order to set up two defensive belts, which had to be completed by 15 April at the latest. In order to achieve this, the local population was put to work on the entrenchments on a large scale. On 31 March, the order was issued to establish and occupy a third, rearward defensive line. Yet both Stalin and General Nikolay Fëdorovich Vatutin, the commander of the Voronezh Front, harboured doubts whether it was sensible to wait for a German offensive. They suggested instead that an attack as soon as possible, pre-empting a German offensive, and destroying the enemy forces around Belgorod and Khar'kov, was advisable. Marshal Georgiy Konstantinovich Zhukov, the Deputy Commander-in-Chief of the Red Army, however, opposed this plan, as did Marshal Aleksandr Mikhaylovich Vasilevskiy, the Chief of the General Staff. On 8 April, Zhukov made an assessment of the situation, in which he concluded that the Germans would first carry out a pincer attack on Kursk. He suggested waiting for the enemy to attack, decimating the German forces in the Kursk salient, and then launching a large-scale offensive with fresh reserves. Two days later, the staff of the Central Front, which was under the command of General Konstatin Konstantinovich Rokossovskiy, also concluded that the Germans were going to attack the Kursk salient, albeit not before the second half of May. An assessment carried out by the staff of the Voronezh Front on 12 April shows that the commanders of this front had clearly recognized the intended German pincer attack on Kursk, as well, even though the Voronezh Front expected the German offensive to begin sooner than the Central Front had concluded, namely, at the beginning of May.

On the same day, 12 April, Zhukov and Vasilevskiy met with Stalin. They convinced him that their own planned offensives should not be devised as pre-emptive strikes but instead be launched only after the expected German attack against the Kursk salient had been repelled. Zhukov believed that the pincer attack on Kursk was just the beginning of a series of German operations, whose ultimate goal was to reach Moscow again. He was still confident that, for the first time in the 'Great Patriotic War', it would be possible to fend off a German summer offensive. The fortification of the three defensive lines in the front sector of the Kursk salient, so-called army defence belts, which reached as far as 40 kilometres into the salient, had to be pressed ahead with as energetically as possible. After completion of the defensive works, the local civilian population was to be evacuated. In addition to these three defensive sectors, the Soviet commanders ordered the construction of three so-called front defence belts. Four of the six defensive lines in total – the three army defence lines and the first front defence line – had already been manned before the beginning of the battle. For the Central Front this specifically meant that the defensive positions in the sector of the Soviet 13th Army, where the main effort of the German attack was thought most likely to be directed, were manned up to a depth of 30 kilometres. The manned defences of the Voronezh Front even reached as far as 60 kilometres in depth, as the Soviets expected a German attack on a broad front in this sector, whilst the axes of the main attacks were not as clearly defined as was the case with the Central Front. Furthermore, the Germans had more space here to shift the points of main effort, which is what the Voronezh Front tried to counter with an in-depth troop echelon.

Considering that Model and Hitler were worried when aerial photographs showed that the Soviet defences had reached a depth of 20 kilometres by the end of April 1943, they would have suffered nightmares if they had known the extent of the fortifications in the Kursk salient in early July 1943. In total, the Soviet defensive positions reached a depth of up to 110 kilometres. Furthermore, on 16 May 1943, the reserve front, that is the Steppe Military District, occupied another defensive line at the base of the Kursk salient, behind the rearmost front defence belt (Map 3). From 1 April to 1 July 1943, 4,240 kilometres of trenches in total were dug, roughly 500 kilometres of anti-tank obstacles were set up and 600,000 mines were laid in the sector of the Voronezh Front. In the area of the Central Front, the extent of trenches reached to about 5,000 kilometres; roughly 400,000 mines and demolition charges were planted. The first defensive belt, the so-called main defence line, was especially heavily mined: 2,043 mines were buried per kilometre in the sector of the Voronezh Front, and 1,130 per kilometre in the sector of the Central Front. The line was furthermore manned by 37 rifle divisions. By that time a rifle division and a guards rifle division had an authorized strength of 9,354 and 10,585 men respectively, even though their actual strength was usually lower, reaching 8,000 soldiers on average. Each of those divisions was assigned a sector of the front about 14 kilometres in length on average; the most important front sectors were about 6-12 kilometres long, the less important ones up to 25 kilometres.

The divisions manning the forward line had to defend an area to a depth of five to six kilometres. Each division had on average 66 kilometres of trenches and communication trenches – as many as four parallel trenches in the important sections. The first trench line was usually defended by machine guns and anti-tank weapons, while the mass of heavy infantry weapons was placed in the second trench line. Barbed-wire obstacles, minefields and tank barriers were placed not only before the first trench line but also between the trenches. In addition, both the main defensive sector and the second army defence line were laced with many anti-tank strongpoints. Such a strongpoint normally consisted of a company or a battalion of anti-tank riflemen, an engineer platoon with demolition charges, an anti-tank battery with four to six anti-tank guns, as well as two to three tanks or self-propelled guns. Some of these strongpoints were even more heavily armed and had 8-10 anti-tank guns each at their disposal. In the main defensive line of the Voronezh Front alone, almost 100 anti-tank strongpoints were established. The Germans had been able to spot these strongpoints thanks to their aerial reconnaissance and issued corresponding orders for combating them: 'The numerous anti-tank strongpoints (dug-in tanks, heavy anti-tank guns, infantry positions) detected on aerial photographs have to be dealt with as follows:

a) *Stuka* attack. Immediately exploit the opponent's shock, [when] the last bomb [has exploded], infantry assaults under covering fire from *Tiger* tanks. b) Concentrated artillery fire on the position. Blinding the anti-tank guns with artillery and tank guns of *Tigers*. Employment of assault detachments. Move in with the tanks. To make sure that the anti-tank emplacements are quickly put out of action, artillery has to closely follow the attacking armoured infantry so that as many batteries are ready to fire at any time.'[74]

The second Soviet army defence belt ran parallel behind the main defence line; the distance between the two lines was 10-15 kilometres on average and 20-25 kilometres in some areas. On the main axes, where the German attack was expected, the second defence belt was almost as strongly fortified as the main line of defence. It was not as heavily mined, though, and more thinly manned. Nevertheless, the density of fire, that is the number of weapons per kilometre of front, was hardly lower than in the main defensive line. In addition, tank regiments and brigades, directly subordinate to the armies, were assigned to reinforce the second line of defence. The authorized strength of an independent tank regiment was 39 tanks, 21 tanks for an independent heavy tank regiment and 65 for an independent tank brigade.

The third army defence belt followed the main defensive line at an average distance of 20-25 kilometres. In some areas, the third line was as far as 35-45 kilometres away from the main defensive line, and 10-23 from the second. Only operationally vital sectors were manned with troops. The bulk of front reserves were held in this rearward army defence line – and these reserves were substantial. Both fronts had their own tank army at their disposal for counterattacks: the 2nd Tank Army with 450 tanks was assigned to the Central Front, the Voronezh Front was supported by the 1st Tank Army with 645 tanks. To add to these, numerous independent reserve tank formations reinforced each front: for example, the 9th Tank Corps and the 19th Tank Corps were assigned to the Central Front, while the 2nd Guards Tank Corps and the 5th Guards Tank Corps were subordinate to the Voronezh Front. Each of these tank corps was equipped with around 200 tanks. In addition to these armoured forces, artillery, mortar and anti-tank formations were also kept ready as reserves.

In the area of the Voronezh Front, the river Psël constituted a significant natural obstacle as part of the third line of defence, while in the case of the Central Front the Ol'khovatka heights played a central role. From these heights, the terrain slopes down to Kursk, offering an unobstructed view in this direction. Due to their great operational importance, the Ol'khovatka heights were heavily fortified by the Red Army.

Behind the three defensive belts of the armies, the three defensive lines of the fronts were established. These formed a belt of 40-75 kilometres in depth, overall. The first two front defence lines were set up around Kursk, whereas the third was at the river

74 II. SS-Panzerkorps, Kampfanweisungen für den Angriff, 1.7.1943, reproduced in Silvester Stadler (ed.), *Die Offensive gegen Kursk 1943: II. SS-Panzerkorps als Stoßkeil im Großkampf* (Osnabrück, 1980), pp. 25-7, quote, 27.

Tim because the Soviet commanders assumed that the Germans would, if they were victorious at Kursk, launch further offensives from the Kursk salient towards the east – even though there were no such plans. Further defensive positions were built around the city of Kursk, so the German attackers had in any case to break through six lines of defence in order to reach Kursk (Map 3).

The *Stavka* believed that the strongest German offensive forces were assembled in Model's Ninth Army; accordingly, the fiercest battles were expected to take place in the front sector of the Central Front. The concentration of forces was thus highest in the area of the Soviet 13th Army, since this is where the main axis of attack of the Ninth Army was anticipated. The 13th Army, commanded by Lieutenant-General Nikolay Pavlovich Pukhov, had a strength of 114,000 men. It was equipped with 2,930 guns and mortars, 105 rocket launchers, as well as 270 tanks and self-propelled guns – this is excluding the front reserves, even though the sector it had to defend was only 32 kilometres long.

The Soviet 70th Army under the command of Lieutenant-General Ivan Vasil'evich Galanin was assembled west of the 13th Army and also in the attack sector of Model's Ninth Army. At the beginning of July 1943 it had a strength of 96,000 men, 1,660 guns and mortars and 125 tanks. Two other armies of the Central Front, the 60th and the 65th Army, were placed at the head of the Kursk salient, as was the 38th Army, which was subordinate to the Voronezh Front. Here the numerical difference between the Soviet and the German sides became most apparent. The German Second Army west of the Kursk salient, which had initially been tasked to assist Operation Citadel with holding attacks, consisted of about 130,000 men and had 940 guns and mortars at its disposal. It had no tanks, only 39 *Marder* tank destroyers and 31 assault guns. The three Soviet armies opposite the German Second Army on the other hand had a strength of 256,000 soldiers and were equipped with 4,410 guns, mortars and rocket launchers and 340 tanks and self-propelled guns.

The Voronezh Front had on average one division per 10 kilometres of frontage. In the sector of the 6th Guards Army and the 7th Guards Army, where the main German attacks were expected, a division had a frontage of only five kilometres. The 6th Guards Army, commanded by Lieutenant-General Ivan Mikhaylovich Chistyakov, had a strength of 79,900 men by the beginning of July 1943 and was equipped with 1,770 guns and rocket launchers and 155 tanks and self-propelled guns. The strength of the 7th Guards Army, which was led by Lieutenant-General Mikhail Stepanovich Shumilov, was 76,800 men, 1,620 guns, mortars and rocket launchers and 250 tanks and self-propelled guns. The reserves behind these two armies were the 1st Tank Army and the 69th Army under the command of Lieutenant-General Vasiliy Dmitrievich Kryuchënkin, the latter having a strength of 52,000 men and 890 guns and mortars. Another unit hit by the German offensive was General-Lieutenant Kirill Semënovich Moskalenko's 40th Army, which had 77,000 soldiers, 1,640 guns and 240 tanks.

Both the Central Front and the Voronezh Front each had six ground armies at their disposal. They also had their own air army: the 16th Air Army, equipped with 1,150 aeroplanes, was subordinate to the Central Front, and the Voronezh Front disposed of the 2nd Air Army with 1,030 planes. The first phase of the Battle of Kursk also saw the intervention of units of the 15th Air Army of the Bryansk Front (1,000 aircraft) and the 17th Air Army of the Southwestern Front (750 aircraft). Aside from these, more Soviet aerial formations joined the battle. For example, the long-range aviation with 320 planes, operating independently of the air armies, as well as the local air defence of Kursk with 210 aircraft also intervened.

The Red Army's 'strategic reserve' for the Battle of Kursk was Colonel-General Ivan Stepanovich Konev's Steppe Military District. Konev was also in command of six ground armies and one air army, whose total strength amounted to 573,200 men, 8,510 guns and mortars, 1,640 tanks and self-propelled guns as well as 520 aircraft.

The Soviet plan intended first to bring the German attack against the Central and the Voronezh Front to a halt in the defence belts, thereby critically weakening the enemy's attacking forces. Above all, it was hoped that the German panzer formations would be decimated during the defensive phase of the Battle of Kursk. The Soviet soldiers had a grudging respect of the German *Tiger* tanks and *Ferdinand* assault guns. In January 1943, the Red Army had captured an undamaged *Tiger*, which offered them the chance to test it thoroughly. It was not until April 1943, however, that the Soviets managed to gather information on the *Ferdinand* through their intelligence service, which is why in troop training special emphasis was placed on combating heavy tanks and self-propelled guns. Target plates were distributed which highlighted the vulnerable areas of the German tanks, and the crews of Soviet anti-tank guns and anti-tank riflemen were urged to target the vision slits of the tanks or the commander's cupola. The latter were vulnerable to fire and were often torn off when badly hit, while the tank commanders were likely to be killed or seriously wounded. An after-action report from the 503rd Heavy Panzer Battalion, which was equipped with *Tigers*, later commented: 'What was striking was how frequently the commander's cupola was penetrated by direct hits or badly damaged [...]. The Russian instruction on how to combat *Tigers* spread surprisingly quickly and was followed by all enemy arms of service with great stubbornness.'[75] It was not until summer 1943 that new commander's cupolas were introduced for the *Tiger* and the *Panther*, which had a projectile-resistant shape and would not be torn off the turret when receiving a direct hit.

What proved particularly effective against German panzer attacks was the method of digging in tanks, that is, digging positions into which the Soviet tanks could be moved for the defence against attacks. These dugouts were so deep that the turret was the only part of the tank's body that remained visible. The digging-in of tanks was effective in two ways. First of all, the turret offered only a small target and was difficult to hit. Secondly, a dug-in tank impeded target designation for the German tank commander and gunner, as it was almost impossible to distinguish a camouflaged tank turret from an anti-tank gun at a greater distance.

75 BA-MA, RH 10/56, Schwere Panzer-Abteilung 503, Abteilung Ia, Erfahrungen, 10.10.1943, fol. 71-3, quote, fol. 73.

Another key element in the defence against German panzer attacks were the countless mines laid by Soviet engineers, who often dug out German anti-tank mines and used these to construct new minefields. This might in fact be one of the reasons why German reports time and again noted that the troops had driven into their own minefields because these had been unmarked and uncharted.

However, the backbone of the Soviet defence were not the trenches, minefields or tanks but the artillery. This arm of service was the pride of the Red Army; and, the Soviet forces had technically excellent guns – and many of them, too. The Voronezh Front had a concentration of 40 guns per kilometre of frontage in the area where the main German thrust was expected, whilst the Central Front even had as many as 70 guns per front kilometre. In terms of training in the preparation phase of the Battle of Kursk, the Soviet artillery also focused on repelling German panzer attacks.

What also requires mentioning here are the Soviet partisans, who were most notably active in the rear area of Army Group Centre. In early July, the German Armed Forces Operations Staff compiled a report on the partisan or 'bandit' movement in the period from April to June 1943. The report concluded that partisan activity had increased further in the whole 'Eastern space', one reasons for which was thought to be the dire food situation of Soviet population under German occupation, as the shortage of food was above all caused by the imposed deliveries by the Germans. Another reason was that the general mood of the Soviet population deteriorated sharply because of the requisitioning of slave labour by the Germans for work in their economy. More and more Soviet civilians were therefore willing to join the partisans. In the spring of 1943, partisans attempted to hamper the German build-up for Operation Citadel by numerous attacks against the railway lines and German trains. In June alone, 1,092 attacks on trains, railway lines and bridges were registered, in which 409 locomotives and 54 railway bridges were damaged according to the report of the Armed Forces Operations Staff. In fact, the Soviet planning for the Battle of Kursk relied on the partisans' contribution to the battle itself as well as on their interference with troop transfers and cutting off supplies.

Following the assumed successful repulse of the German attack on Kursk and the decimation of the enemy forces, the Red Army planned to launch large-scale counteroffensives. In the north of Kursk, the Soviet Western, Bryansk and Central Front were to mount an attack against the Orël salient. This counteroffensive was code-named *Kutuzov*, after a famous Russian field-marshal of the Napoleonic Wars. Operation *Kutuzov* aimed at eliminating the German salient at Orël, followed by a push towards the west.

South of Kursk the formations of the Voronezh Front, the Steppe Military District and the Southwestern Front were given the order to launch Operation *Polkovodets Rumyantsev* (Commander Rumyantsev) as soon as the defensive phase had come to a close. The first goal of this counteroffensive, named after an 18th century Russian field-marshal, was to recapture Khar'kov, after which Soviet troops were to attack towards the southwest and advance as far as the river Dnepr. The Soviet leaders hoped that by autumn 1943, the Red Army could liberate most of the areas that had been part of the Soviet Union prior to the Molotov–Ribbentrop Pact of 1939.

First of all, however, the expected German attack at Kursk had to be withstood, inflicting as severe losses on the enemy forces during the defensive phase as possible. Yet the Germans kept postponing their attack – a fact which made the Soviet leadership increasingly nervous. By mid-May, the Voronezh Front had amassed a considerable combat strength, already having three fourths of the tanks and self-propelled guns and nine tenths of men available compared to the beginning of July. General Vatutin, commander of the Voronezh Front, therefore once again recommended launching a pre-emptive attack rather than waiting for the Germans to mount their offensive. It is possible that his suggestion had something to do with the fact that at the end of April, the commanders-in-chief of the Central and the Voronezh Front had notified the *Stavka* that the preparations for the defensive phase were practically finished. In truth, however, only the first defensive belt was completed by mid May, whereas the other lines of defence were not yet fully fortified. Even by the beginning of June, only half of the assembled mines had been planted. To Vatutin, an offensive attack therefore seemed less risky than a defensive battle in a half-finished defence system. As far as Stalin was concerned, Vatutin was kicking at open doors, since Stalin himself was in favour of beginning their own offensive as soon as possible. Yet, just as in April, Marshal Zhukov again managed to convince Stalin that it would be better to fend off the German attack first, decimate the German forces and then launch a counteroffensive against a severely weakened enemy. Zhukov was supported by Colonel-General Aleksey Innokent'evich Antonov, the Chief of the Operations Directorate of the General Staff, and by General Rokossovskiy, the commander of the Central Front. It is likely that Rokossovskiy's reservations about a pre-emptive strike were heightened by the fact that in the middle of May, his front only had about half the tanks that it had at its disposal by the beginning of July. On the other hand, it was already equipped with more than three fourths of its guns and mortars, which formed the backbone of the defence.

In the ensuing seven weeks, the Soviet fronts had time to reinforce their formations as well as their defensive positions. The Soviet commanders were also constantly informed about the German troop build-up, so they could estimate fairly accurately when the Germans would launch their offensive. On 2 July 1943, Stalin warned the commanders of the Central Front and the Voronezh Front that the German offensive had to be expected between 3 and 6 July. Three days later, on 5 July 1943, the Battle of Kursk began.

Intelligence and Espionage Prior to Operation Citadel

Since the 1960s, how the Soviet leadership knew about the German intentions to attack the Kursk salient so early on has been the cause for much speculation in literature on the Battle of Kursk. Paul Karl Schmidt, the former chief press spokesman for Foreign Minister Joachim von Ribbentrop, sparked a heated discussion when he

– under the *nom de plume* Paul Carell – published his bestseller *Scorched Earth*.[76] In it, he claimed that the German spy Rudolf Rößler supplied the Soviet leadership with first-rate information about the preparations for Operation Citadel from Switzerland. According to Schmidt, Rößler's source was a high-ranking officer known as 'Werther', who was part of Hitler's entourage. As the author did not want to reveal the name of this alleged master spy, the question of who 'Werther' might have been was fiercely debated. Reinhard Gehlen, chief of the Foreign Armies East (*Fremde Heere Ost*) of the Army General Staff, wrote in his memoirs in 1971 that 'the *Führer*'s secretary' Martin Bormann had been the 'most prominent informant and consultant of the Soviets' and that after the war he lived – perfectly shielded – in the Soviet Union.[77] In actual fact, Bormann did not survive the demise of the Third Reich. He was either killed or committed suicide on 2 May 1945 when attempting to flee the embattled city of Berlin. His remains were found in 1972 during construction works.

Serious doubts about the story of the master spy, who had effectively contributed to the failure of Operation Citadel, however, had been raised before. In his book *Verrat im Zweiten Weltkrieg* (Treason During the Second World War), the journalist and military historian Wilhelm von Schramm pointed out as early as 1967 that the intelligence supplied by 'Werther' could not have been nearly as vital for the Soviet leadership as was often assumed.[78] In the same year, Schramm received support from fellow historian and intelligence expert Gert Buchheit, who remarked correctly that the Kursk salient offered such an obvious base for an operation that no betrayal was needed for the Soviets to recognize the German operational intentions. Moreover, Buchheit referred to a report from the *Amt Ausland/Abwehr*, the Office of the Military Foreign Intelligence, dating from 26 March 1943. It stated that the Japanese military attaché in Helsinki had learned from an agent from Moscow that by then the Red Army was assembling its available reserves 'behind the Russian front sector behind Kursk and Donets, which is threatened by our [i.e. by the German] offensive.'[79] This report highlights the fact that the Red Army had been preparing for continued fighting in the area of Kursk since the end of March.

On 29 March 1943, the British War Office received a summary of decoded German wireless messages from the period of 18–26 March 1943, which showed that the Germans were amassing ground-attack aircraft around Khar'kov. The British Intelligence Service concluded that either the German Army was planning to mount an offensive at Khar'kov as soon as the *rasputitsa* was over – which was approximately in the last week of April – or the Germans were apprehensive of a Soviet attack there. In his book *Operation Citadel*, published in 1983, the Polish non-fiction

76 Paul Carell, *Verbrannte Erde: Schlacht zwischen Wolga und Weichsel* (Berlin, 1966).

77 Reinhard Gehlen, *Der Dienst: Erinnerungen 1942–1971* (Mainz, 1971), p. 48.

78 Wilhelm von Schramm, *Verrat im Zweiten Weltkrieg: Vom Kampf der Geheimdienste in Europa* (Düsseldorf, 1967), pp. 143-74, 350-64.

79 Gert Buchheit, 'Verrat der "Kursker Offensive"? Eine Abwehrmeldung gibt Aufschluss', *Die Nachhut*, 1 (1967), pp. 1-3, here, 3.

writer Janusz Piekałkiewicz made a sensation out of this and of another intelligence report, arguing that on 22 March 1943, the War Office had obtained 'irrefutable proof of the German preparations for the summer offensive in the Kursk salient.' By decoding the Luftwaffe's radio traffic, they not only knew everything about the displacement of German panzer divisions to the middle sector of the Eastern Front and of the German *Luftflotte* 4, but also 'that the German offensive was scheduled to begin in late April.' 'This important message was', according to Piekałkiewicz, 'relayed to Moscow at once.'[80]

But did these decoded messages really contain invaluable information? No, they did not. In fact, the second report quoted by Piekałkiewicz only says: 'From two [German] tank returns for 16 [March] it appears probable that five of six panzer divisions of Army Group Centre have been grouped in 2 Panzer Army, in the Orël sector, leaving only two panzer divisions available for the remainder of Army Group Centre's front. This appears to indicate that a strong offensive by the Germans in this sector has been or is to be launched, possibly with a view to cutting off the Russian salient between Orël and Kharkov. There is also some indication that these Panzer divisions have only 15 percent of their establishment in tanks, but this is by no means certain.'[81] Therefore, the documents mainly contain information the Red Army could itself obtain by radio intelligence and by air and ground reconnaissance. So if the British did indeed pass on these pieces of information to the Soviets, they were hardly of vital importance for the latter.

In effect, the Kursk salient lent itself so well to military operations for both sides that an operational surprise was an impossibility – and the German commanders were fully aware of this. As early as the end of March 1943, the Department of Foreign Armies East had recognized that the Soviets were concentrating forces in the area of Kursk–Kupyansk. On 25 April, Army Group South pointed out in an assessment to the Army High Command that the enemy was likely to be fully prepared and that strong counterattacks had to be expected. In the sector of Army Group Centre, the Germans noted that the Soviet 13th Army north of Kursk was being supplied with artillery, rocket launchers and replacement personnel. The Ninth Army Headquarters thus felt vindicated in their assumption 'that the enemy is expecting a German attack here and is reinforcing his troops accordingly.'[82]

Ultimately, it cannot be ruled out that the fairly accurate Soviet intelligence on the German build-up at Kursk was reinforced with decoded German radio messages

80 Janusz Piekalkiewicz, *Unternehmen Zitadelle. Kursk und Orel: Die größte Panzerschlacht des 2. Weltkrieges* (Herrsching, 1989), p. 67.

81 The National Archives of the United Kingdom, Kew (hereafter, TNA), WO 208/3573, War Office, British Military Intelligence, Section 14 (MI14), Weekly summaries for the Chief of the Imperial General Staff (CIGS), 1941-1944, Summary of M.I. 14 indications files for week ending 22 March 43, fol. 265.

82 NARA, T312/317/7886062, Kriegstagebuch Nr. 8, Armee-Oberkommando 9, Führungsabteilung, 26.3.-18.8.1943.

from Britain, or with reports from agents in Switzerland. The British could break the Germans' coded radio and teletype messages and they passed on intelligence to Stalin. But there was actually an easier way for the Soviets to obtain the decoded German messages. John Cairncross, one of the British codebreakers at the top-secret Bletchley Park decryption facility and a Soviet spy, relayed decoded messages directly to Moscow. It is nevertheless difficult to estimate the true importance of these reports for the Soviets. Nor is it possible to judge the impact of the intelligence supplied by the spy ring in Switzerland. At the very least the spies operated so effectively that they commanded the Germans' respect, as an entry for 7 April 1943 in Goebbel's diary illustrates: 'English espionage does outstanding work from Switzerland; we should take this as an example. Compared with the English espionage centres, our Admiral Canaris seems like a dilettante.'[83]

Much more important than agents abroad was Soviet radio monitoring, through which the Red Army was able to gather detailed information about the German build-up. Another crucial source of intelligence were the Soviet agents operating behind German lines. Their presence did not escape the Germans, who repeatedly cautioned their troops. The Ic section (Intelligence) of the SS Panzergrenadier Division *Das Reich*, for instance, announced on 31 May 1943 that during the previous weeks 76 auxiliary volunteers (*Hilfswillige*) of the division had fled. 'In this context', the order further stated, 'it must be pointed out that enemy agents often try to get recruited as auxiliary volunteers.'[84] Despite such problems, the German *Ostheer* could and would not dispense with the Soviet *Hiwis*, as many of them provided reliable and valuable help to the Germans.

Only a week later, the Ic section of the Division *Das Reich* was once more compelled to issue a warning to the troops: 'Various recent incidents suggest that there are dubious Russian elements in the billet area of the division, who are in contact with the Soviets and use every opportunity to spy and to commit sabotage.'[85] The fear of sabotage and the suspicions harboured against Soviet civilians were by no means groundless, as the instance of an interrogation of a captured soldier of the Soviet 72nd Guards Rifle Division on 6 July 1943 illustrates. The prisoner declared that the Soviet side had detailed knowledge of the German 320th and 106th Infantry Divisions' positions opposite his own division down even to regimental level. The claim that 'civilians served as source of information'[86] can be verified by Soviet sources.[87] The Germans'

83 Goebbels, *Tagebücher*, pt. II, vol. 8, p. 67.
84 BA-MA, M 1053, Akte 8, Divisions-Sonderbefehl Ic Nr. 13, SS-Panzergrenadier-Division 'Das Reich', 31.5.1943, no pagination.
85 BA-MA, M 1053, Akte 7, Divisions-Sonderbefehl Ic Nr. 14, SS-Panzergrenadier-Division 'Das Reich', vom 7.6.1943, no pagination.
86 BA-MA, RH 20-8/99, Anlagen zum Kriegstagebuch des Armee-Oberkommandos 8, Ic-Tagesmeldung vom 6.7.1943, no pagination.
87 Leonid D. Grenkevich, *The Soviet Partisan Movement 1941–1944: A Critical Historiographical Analysis* (London, 1999), pp. 121-5, 130-1; Dennis E. Showalter, *Armor*

carelessness actually played into the hands of Soviet informants time and again, as the following example shows. A Soviet 'agent' who was taken prisoner said during his interrogation on 1 August 1943 that the checks carried out by the Germans were so superficial and careless that spies often managed to destroy evidence or hide weapons even when German soldiers were present.

Some German soldiers were negligent not only when it came to spies but also with regards to camouflage and secrecy. The war diary of the Fourth Panzer Army Headquarters noted on 2 May 1943: 'Even though prohibited, there is increased column traffic during daytime on the roads north of Khar'kov.'[88] In a local engagement in the sector of the 258th Infantry Division on 4 June 1943, Soviet soldiers succeeded in obtaining 'a list of codenames with the uncoded and the coded names of all elements of the division.' According to the Ninth Army Headquarter's war diary, a 'court-martial will be initiated against the guilty party.'[89] Ten days later the Headquarters of the Fourth Panzer Army felt compelled to send an admonitory message to the SS Panzer Corps, which stated: 'There is a growing number of cases where officers of panzer formations wearing black uniforms carry out reconnaissance in the area designated for Citadel and do not maintain the necessary secrecy towards the troops. One is reminded again that all reconnaissance has to be carried out using the best possible concealment.'[90] Soviet sources confirm that such careless reconnaissance by officers of the SS Panzer Corps did not escape the vigilant observers of the Red Army.

The War Diary officer of the 292nd Infantry Division noted on 2 July 1943: 'Radio intelligence proves that the enemy observes our movements – where he is able to – as closely as possible, therefore we have to be *even more* careful than at present. Individual mistakes nevertheless happen, such as the limbers of the II battalion of the 292nd Artillery Regiment, who contrary to orders move during daytime, receive observed enemy artillery fire and suffer casualties.'[91] The Red Army were able to detect such blatant German troop movements both by ground and air reconnaissance. In early July 1943, the Ic section of Army Detachment Kempf intercepted enemy radio transmissions, which made clear that Soviet reconnaissance aircraft had observed busy motor traffic on the road to Belgorod and that the Soviets expected a German attack on Belgorod. And they were right.

and Blood: The Battle of Kursk (New York, 2013), p. 66.

88 BA-MA, RH 21-4/104, Kriegstagebuch des Oberkommandos der 4. Panzerarmee, Ia, 25.3.-31.7.1943, fol. 23.

89 NARA, T312/317/7886114, Kriegstagebuch Nr. 8, Armee-Oberkommando 9, Führungsabteilung, 26.3.-18.8.1943.

90 BA-MA, RH 21-4/122, Anlagen zum Kriegstagebuch des Oberkommandos der 4. Panzerarmee, Ia, Operation 'Zitadelle', 15.5.-9.7.1943, fol. 88.

91 BA-MA, RH 26-292/43, Kriegstagebuch Nr. 6 der 292. Infanterie-Division, Ia, für die Zeit vom 11.6.-30.9.1943, no pagination [emphasis in original, RT].

On 3 July 1943, *General der Infanterie* Hans Zorn, the Commanding General of the XXXXVI Panzer Corps, noticed on a drive to his subordinate divisions that 'the troops in the final assembly areas comport themselves as if they were actually at peace. He immediately orders that the divisions be informed by teletype to ensure complete camouflage.'[92] The visit of Field-Marshal Hans Günther von Kluge, the Commander-in-Chief of Army Group Centre, to the 18th Panzer Division and the 292nd Infantry Division one day before the start of Operation Citadel was hardly beneficial for secrecy either, especially as the Red Army had enough informants among the civilian population to immediately report such incidents.[93]

Another source of information for the Soviet leadership were countless partisans, who for instance carried out surveillance of German rail traffic, providing valuable intelligence as to German offensive plans. There were also various groups of agents who cooperated with partisans and airdropped behind enemy lines, tasked with special missions. The Germans were often impressed by how well organized and equipped partisans and agents were. On 1 July 1943, the 4th Panzer Division deployed part of its reconnaissance battalion to combat a group of partisans or agents, which had been reported by a medical company of the 31st Infantry Division. The war diary of the 4th Panzer Division reported this incident: 'After surrounding the woods northeast of Leninskiy, 4 bandits equipped with 4 submachine guns and silenced rifle, among them one woman, were shot down after fierce resistance. One prisoner was taken. As the result of finding a parachute and supported by the statements of the prisoner, it was determined that the group had been dropped by aeroplane.'[94]

The Red Army also collected vital information through scouting raids and minor attacks. On 30 April 1943, a Soviet battalion with tank support attacked a height which was occupied by parts of the 78th Assault Division. The Soviet soldiers not only succeeded in taking the tactically important height but they also captured several German soldiers. The Soviet side now 'had proof that the German front has been reinforced by a fresh and especially powerful division', as the war diary of the Ninth Army Headquarters put it.[95] Five days later a Soviet reconnaissance patrol managed to knock out a German machine gun nest of the 332nd Infantry Division and capture two soldiers.

On 25 May, the Ninth Army Headquarters issued the order that at night soldiers should never perform sentry or patrol duty alone, and must always be well armed. But during the weeks that followed, the Red Army still managed to take prisoners,

92 BA-MA, RH 24-46/91, Generalkommando XXXXVI. Panzerkorps, Ia, Kriegstagebuch Nr. 7 vom 1.6.-15.8.1943, fol. 56.

93 David M. Glantz, *Soviet Military Intelligence in War* (London, 1990), pp. 238-9.

94 BA-MA, RH 27-4/76, Kriegstagebuch der 4. Panzer-Division, Führungsabteilung, vom 1.7.-30.9.1943, fol. 4.

95 NARA, T312/317/7886066, Kriegstagebuch Nr. 8, Armee-Oberkommando 9, Führungsabteilung, 26.3.-18.8.1943.

who imparted valuable information. An experience report from the 17th Grenadier Regiment of the 31st Infantry Division about Operation Citadel states that the offensive did not come as a surprise to the Red Army – neither in time nor in location – and that the enemy was in fact expecting the German attack. It was clear where the attack area would be mounted because in the weeks before the beginning of Operation Citadel, the division had been assembling in the same spot on several occasions, whilst the exact date for the attack had been divulged by a captured non-commissioned officer of 62nd Grenadier Regiment of the 7th Infantry Division. The attack of the 17th Grenadier Regiment launched at the beginning of Operation Citadel, therefore, had been met by 'a well-prepared opponent and a massive barrage of artillery and multiple rocket launchers.'[96]

In fact, the Soviets often did not even have to make much of an effort to obtain information about the imminent German offensive, as they were again and again provided with good intelligence from deserters. Apart from numerous Ukrainian and Russian 'volunteers' who changed sides in spring and summer 1943, the *Volksdeutsche* also posed increasing problems for the Wehrmacht. Fewer and fewer of these ethnic Germans were willing to risk their lives for Hitler and the Third Reich. The War Diary officer of the Ninth Army Headquarters noted on 17 June 1943: 'A regrettable and by no means trivial incident occurred with the 78th Assault Division. In the past few days, 6 German soldiers, 4 of whom are *Volksdeutsche*, went over to the enemy. … As an immediate measure, it was deemed necessary to pull out 150 *Volksdeutsche* out of the frontline.'[97] In the morning of 4 July 1943, one day before the beginning of Operation Citadel, two Slovene soldiers of the 18th Grenadier Regiment of the 6th Infantry Division deserted. That same evening, the war diary of the 6th Infantry Division commented on this as follows: 'In the late evening hours, loudspeaker propaganda by the Russian[s] in front of our own sector. He discloses [the] number of the regiment and of the division and refers to the imminent attack. The 2 soldiers who deserted in the morning (who had arrived just recently as reinforcements) are to blame for this. Every soldier who is aware of the situation feels a deep loathing from this despicable deed.'[98]

Soldiers from Alsace and Lorraine, too, were increasingly considered to be unreliable. The Operations Officer of the 7th Infantry Division reported on 10 July 1943 that 'highly unpleasant news has already spread' about the replacement personnel from

96 Grenadier-Regiment 17, Kommandeur, Erfahrungen über die Angriffs- und Abwehrkämpfe südlich Orel vom 5. bis 28. Juli 1943, 28.7.1943, reproduced in Ernst Mund (ed.), *Grenadiere, Jäger: Quellen und Darstellungen zu einer Geschichte des Infanterieregiments 17* (Osterode, 1959), p. 183-8, quote, 184.

97 NARA, T312/317/7886128, Kriegstagebuch Nr. 8, Armee-Oberkommando 9, Führungsabteilung, 26.3.-18.8.1943.

98 BA-MA, RH 26-6/47, Kriegstagebuch Nr. 7 der 6. Infanterie-Division vom 1.1.-30.9.1943, Ia, no pagination. For the Soviet view of this incident, see Valeriy N. Zamulin, *The Battle of Kursk: Controversial and Neglected Aspects* (Solihull, 2017), pp. 178-91.

Alsace-Lorraine.[99] *General der Infanterie* Johannes Frießner, Commanding General of the XXIII Army Corps even advised the commander of the 216th Infantry Division on 11 July 1943 to threaten the Alsatian replacements with execution should they attempt to cross the main front line, 'explaining [to them] that all movement must be concealed from enemy observation.'[100]

That deserters divulged information about the planned German summer offensive in the first place was not least due to the fact that by spring 1943, Operation Citadel had become more or less an open secret. Numerous accounts by German soldiers reflect that countless rumours were circulating not only at the front but also in the rear, and even in the homeland. Eventually, even the date of the attack was not a secret anymore, particularly as on 4 July parts of the Fourth Panzer Army already began probing attacks in order to reach a better assault position for Operation Citadel, which was launched the following day. On the same day, Sergeant Günther Josten, a pilot of the 51st *Jagdgeschwader*, aired his frustrations in his diary: 'Tomorrow the ruckus begins in the south, and we have to sit in Bryansk.'[101]

The Correlation of Forces on the Eve of the Battle

In literature on the Battle of Kursk it has often been pointed out that Operation Citadel was bound to fail, not least because in terms of relative strength the German attackers were no match for the Soviets – as German military historian Karl-Heinz Frieser put it, it was an 'assault against an avalanche.'[102] In terms of numbers alone, however, it would not have been the first time that the Wehrmacht achieved remarkable successes on the Eastern Front in the face of a numerically stronger opponent – for example at the beginning of the conflict against the Soviet Union: On 22 June 1941, the Red Army had at least twice as many combat aircraft and at least three times as many tanks at its disposal than the Wehrmacht.

What needs to be considered, though, is that by 1943 the situation was very different in various respects: Compared to 1941, the Red Army was much better organised in the third year of the 'Great Patriotic War' and had gained considerable combat experience against the German Army. The deciding factor, however, was that both sides were well aware of where the main area of concentration for the battles in summer 1943 was going to be. The Germans were no longer going to attempt to push deep into

99 BA-MA, RH 24-46/91, Generalkommando XXXXVI. Panzerkorps, Ia, Kriegstagebuch Nr. 7 vom 1.6.-15.81943, fol. 88.

100 BA-MA, RH 24-23/132, Anlagen zum Kriegstagebuch Nr. 15, XXIII. Armeekorps, Abteilung Ia, Zeit: 22.3.-20.8.1943, Gefechts- und Erfahrungsberichte, Anlage 47, no pagination.

101 Günther Josten, *Gefechtsbericht: Kriegstagebücher 1939–1945*, ed. Kurt Braatz and Wilhelm Göbel (Moosburg, 2011), p. 179.

102 Frieser, 'Schlacht', p. 86.

enemy territory with skilful operational manoeuvres, make large gains in territory and reach ambitious objectives such as the Soviet industrial centres or the oil areas. Now it was only a matter of encircling as many troops as possible in a limited operation. The enemy did not need to be deceived by a large-scale feint, nor should he have the option for evasive manoeuvres; instead, it was hoped he would concentrate his troops where they could most easily be destroyed by the Germans. On 12 June 1943, First Lieutenant Hellmut Wendtlandt, who was responsible for keeping the Ninth Army Headquarters' war diary, wrote that in view of the 'still undeniable superiority of German leadership, ground troops and air force' there is yet 'an intact chance of striking fatal blows to the enemy', which was the one thing which still mattered at this stage of the war. The enemy's '*vital force* had to be decisively weakened', whereas gains in territory were 'of secondary importance.'[103] If Wendtlandt and the staff of the Ninth Army had had any idea how strong a fortress the Soviet defenders had made of the Kursk salient, and what forces and reserves were available to the Red Army, their optimism would have been dampened considerably.

Only in terms of tanks and self-propelled guns did the situation not look as dire for the Germans, even though it is nearly impossible to reconstruct the numbers exactly. Despite wartime losses there is still a sufficient body of contemporary statistics available for the German side. However, most of these are incomplete because the troops did not usually list *all* tanks in their reports to the higher headquarters. This can be illustrated by the example of the SS Panzergrenadier Division *Leibstandarte SS Adolf Hitler*: on 1 July 1943, the Motor Transport Branch of the *Leibstandarte* compiled a list of all armoured vehicles of the division, which shows that the *Leibstandarte* still had three of the completely obsolete light Panzer I at its disposal. These tanks were used as support vehicles by the Tank Destroyer Battalion. Yet by summer 1943, almost no statistic produced by the Fourth Panzer Army, let alone of the Army High Command, still includes Panzer I machines. The same is the case with captured tanks. According to Wilhelm Roes, a member of the staff of the II Panzer Battalion of the *Leibstandarte*, the division was equipped with several captured T-34 in summer 1943. Only one contemporary document, namely a report about repaired vehicles dating from 30 June 1943 from the Quartermaster Department of the *Leibstandarte* lists three captured tanks. Furthermore, the commander of the Panzer Regiment of the *Leibstandarte* used a Panzer IV as command tank in the summer of 1943. At that time, however, the *Panzerbefehlswagen* IV command tank officially did not even exist; they were only produced from March 1944 on. The regimental commander's tank was, in fact, a normal series-production Panzer IV, which had been converted to an armoured command vehicle on the troops' own initiative.

Another difficulty when comparing strengths is that nearly every list of tanks that has been published in the available literature has hitherto been incorrect. On the

103 NARA, T312/317/7886123, Kriegstagebuch Nr. 8, Armee-Oberkommando 9, Führungsabteilung, 26.3.-18.8.1943 [emphasis in original, RT].

one hand, many historians treat available sources – which are often not quite reliable in the first place – too uncritically, on the other hand, the correlation of forces has been skewed even further by misinterpretations. In strength comparisons, armoured command vehicles, that is the staff tanks of the regimental or battalion commanders, are often not taken into consideration. It is true that in the early years of the war, these vehicles were only equipped with machineguns, sometimes with dummy gun barrels, and therefore unsuitable for tank combat. But these thoroughly outdated vehicles were being substituted with properly armed command tanks from summer 1942 onwards. This was necessary because many commanders led their troops from the front and therefore often faced attacking Soviet tanks, against which they had to defend themselves. There are several incidents known from Operation Citadel when command tanks knocked out Soviet tanks which had broken through. In fact, most command tanks used at the front in summer 1943 were armed with tank guns, whereas only very few vehicles with dummy guns were still in use. Armoured command vehicles, therefore, cannot simply be ignored in strength comparisons.

What is just as absurd is categorizing assault tanks as 'armoured artillery' and excluding them from the statistics, as some authors have done.[104] In fact, soldiers of the *Sturmpanzer* battalions did not belong to the artillery branch but to the armoured forces. In summer 1943, the assault tanks were not used as artillery but rather to combat tenacious pockets of resistance with direct fire, just like assault guns. Besides, the statistics of the Army High Command also listed them as tanks rather than self-propelled artillery.

The German light tanks are often ignored in strength comparisons, too. Units taking part in Operation Citadel were equipped with 76 light Panzer II and 38(t) tanks. The argument often advanced that Panzer IIs were unsuitable for tank warfare because of their weak armament and, thus, should not be taken into account, is misleading. Certainly, the Panzer II was equipped with only a 2cm gun and was solely used in reconnaissance units or as staff vehicles in 1943. But they were still employed at the front line and suffered corresponding losses. The 7th Panzer Division, for instance, had to write off three Panzer IIs as total losses during Operation Citadel – two of which were destroyed by armour-piercing rounds, one destroyed by a mine. Aside from that, the Panzer II's Soviet equivalent, the light T-60 tank, is always considered in strength comparisons in historical studies. The T-60, too, was only armed with a 2cm gun and used in reconnaissance units. In early July 1943, the formations of the Voronezh Front had as many as 60 of these vehicles available; the Central Front had even more. Therefore, if one takes all light tanks into consideration for the Soviet side, one cannot simply ignore them when it comes to the German tank tally.

The same holds true for the light, self-propelled, tank destroyer, the *Marder*. At the beginning of July 1943, the Germans had 350 of these vehicles at their disposal in the Kursk salient; 80 more were with the maintenance teams, or on their way to the front

104 See, for example, Frieser, 'Schlacht', pp. 87, 111, 151.

from the German Reich. The *Marder*'s Soviet counterpart was the light SU-76 self-propelled gun. They were technically and tactically comparable to the German *Marder* – and considered as such by the Germans at that time. Contemporary German regulations designate the SU-76 as '7.62cm anti-tank self-propelled gun on a T-70 chassis.'[105] The Germans rated its combat effectiveness very highly, and captured SU-76 tank destroyers were regularly used by frontline units of the Wehrmacht. As late as March 1944, the 752nd Army Tank Destroyer Battalion incorporated six captured SU-76 into its self-propelled gun company. Yet, while the SU-76 self-propelled guns appear in every comparison of strengths, one will search in vain for the *Marder* in most statistics. This is even more striking as the latter took on a crucial importance, not only because the attacking forces of the Wehrmacht were equipped with a large number of these vehicles, but also because they played an important role during the battle. Parts of the Soviet 25th Tank Brigade, for example, were annihilated by the *Marders* of the *Leibstandarte*'s Tank Destroyer Battalion on 12 July 1943 at Prokhorovka. In any strength comparison, the *Marder* tank destroyers must therefore not be forgotten, especially when their Soviet equivalents, the SU-76, are included in the tally of forces.

The best basis for reconstructing the number of German tanks and self-propelled guns on the Eastern Front in summer 1943 are the lists of tanks, assault guns and anti-tank guns, which were compiled by the Quartermaster General of the Army High Command every ten days, based on reports from the troops.[106] The tables contain detailed information on how many tanks and self-propelled guns of each type were available. It is also noted how many of these vehicles were operational, under repair or in transit to the troops, even though these lists are not completely reliable either: on the one hand, only a few units reported the number of captured tanks they used, so these do not appear in the records; on the other, the Quartermaster General's statistics usually contain minor inaccuracies because of human error at troop or headquarters level. According to the summary of the situation regarding self-propelled guns from 13 July 1943, for instance, the 653rd and 654th Heavy Tank Destroyer Battalion had a total of 89 *Ferdinands* – 45 the first, 44 the latter unit. One more *Ferdinand* was listed as being in transit to the 654th Battalion. But these numbers are inaccurate in two ways. First, it was the 654th Battalion which actually had 45 *Ferdinands* at its disposal, whereas the 653rd had 44 only. Second, that last *Ferdinand*, which was supposed to be in transit, was never delivered to the front. The same document from the Quartermaster General also suggested that the 4th Panzer Division had 26 *Marder* tank destroyers in total at the beginning of Operation Citadel. However, the reports from the division state that only 25 *Marders* were available. Another example can be taken from the 18th Panzer Division. According to the tank status report dated 11 July 1943, the division had 10 short-barrelled Panzer IIIs but no long-barrelled ones at

105 Richard Kindel (ed.), *Die 8. Panzer-Division der Deutschen Wehrmacht 1939–1945: Bilder, Texte, Dokumente*, 2 vols. (Wuppertal, 2nd edn, 2007), vol. 2, p. 499.
106 BA-MA, RH 10/60-63.

its disposal. The divisional records, however, state the exact opposite: all Panzer IIIs of the 18th Panzer Division were equipped with long-barrelled guns from the beginning of Operation Citadel.

It will never be possible to provide a complete statistical survey which is accurate to the last tank, as even the most detailed records are incomplete and contain errors. But what the records from the Quartermaster General clearly do show is that so far the total numbers of German tanks and self-propelled guns have been repeatedly underestimated in the literature on the Battle of Kursk. Based on the Quartermaster General's records, the four German armies at the Kursk salient had in total about 1,980 tanks, 570 assault guns, howitzers and assault tanks, 570 tank destroyers and 260 self-propelled artillery pieces at their disposal in July 1943. This is a total of nearly 3,400 tanks and self-propelled guns, roughly 3,150 of which belonged to the units that were to take part in Operation Citadel. At the beginning of July a fair number of these vehicles were under repair or in transit from the German Reich. The number of operational vehicles available to all four armies (including the 2nd Army) totalled approximately 1,700 tanks, 510 assault guns, howitzers and tanks, 470 self-propelled tank destroyers and 160 self-propelled artillery pieces, that is, roughly 2,840 vehicles. About 2,650 of these belonged to the attacking formations.[107]

As difficult as it is to assess the numbers on the German side, it is all but impossible to reconstruct the exact number of tanks and self-propelled guns available to the Red Army in early July 1943. There are numerous Soviet records still available, but with regards to numbers they are so unreliable that one hardly ever finds two documents which agree with each other. The most credible numbers are found in a report by Colonel Dmitriy Ivanovich Zaev, the deputy Chief of Staff of the Armoured and Mechanized Forces of the Red Army, drawn up on 19 July 1943. According to Zaev, the formations of the Central Front had a total of 1,666 tanks at their disposal in early July, whereas the Voronezh Front had 1,826 tanks. By mid-July, both fronts had received 328 tanks in total as 'reinforcements from the headquarters.'[108] However, the report contains no information on available self-propelled guns, or on the tanks, that were at the disposal of the Steppe Front and which took part in the Battle of Kursk. The lists reproduced in the historiography

107 For detailed information, see Roman Töppel, 'Die Offensive gegen Kursk 1943: Legenden, Mythen und Propaganda', MA thesis, Dresden University of Technology (2001), Appendix 4, online at: https://independent.academia.edu/RomanToeppel. The total numbers have been increased slightly here since an additional unknown number of captured vehicles has to be taken into account, too.

108 Spravka o poteryakh tankovykh voysk frontov, poteryakh, nanesënnykh imi protivniku, i vyvody o deystviyakh tankovykh voysk protivnika v operatsiyakh s 5-go po 15-e iyulya 1943 goda [Information about tank losses of the tank formations of the fronts, their losses suffered by the enemy and conclusions about the actions of the enemy tank formations in the operations from 5 to 15 July 1943], copy from the document collection ('Materialsammlung') of the ZMSBw.

suggest that the Steppe Front had 1,513 tanks at the beginning of July 1943, whilst the three fronts altogether had 259 self-propelled guns.[109] In total, the three Soviet fronts thus were equipped with about 5,600 tanks and self-propelled guns including reinforcements, facing roughly 3,400 German tanks and self-propelled guns in the Kursk salient in July 1943.

However, in the first phase of the Battle of Kursk, neither side deployed all their available tanks. The German Second Army remained passive, and both the XX Army Corps of the Ninth Army and the XXXXII Army Corps of Army Detachment Kempf did not join Operation Citadel, whereas the Soviet side withheld some formations of the Steppe Front as well as the armies stationed in the western part of the Kursk salient. An indication of how many Red Army tanks were actually employed in the great tank battle at Kursk in July 1943 is again given by Colonel Zaev. According to a list dating from 23 July 1943, 4,400 Soviet tanks took part in the fighting for the Kursk salient until mid-July 1943; another 328 tanks have to be added to this number, which were sent to the Central and the Voronezh Front as reinforcements. What is also missing in Zaev's report is the number of self-propelled guns and of captured German tanks used by the Red Army against their former owners. Adding these gives a total number of roughly 5,000 tanks and self-propelled guns deployed by the Red Army in the first phase of the Battle of Kursk.

As for the German side, a number of vehicles have to be added to the total of 2,650 operational tanks and self-propelled guns available in early July, namely, those that were delivered to the frontline troops from the maintenance units or from the German Reich during the battle. At a rough estimate, about 2,900 German tanks and self-propelled guns were used in Operation Citadel altogether.

In terms of troops, aircraft and guns, the correlation of forces was even less favourable for the Germans. According to various figures given in the literature about the Battle of Kursk, the roughly 780,000 German soldiers assembled at the Kursk salient were facing more than 1.9 million Red Army soldiers, whilst about 1,800 aircraft of the Luftwaffe had to fight against more than 3,600 Soviet aeroplanes in the first phase of the operation alone. Even more dire for the Germans was the overwhelming Soviet artillery superiority. While the Germans had 7,400 guns and mortars at their disposal, the Red Army had 31,400, that is, more than four times as many. What must be taken into consideration when comparing these numbers, though, is that the body of source material is even more problematic than it is for assessing the numbers of tanks. The numerical data provided here must, therefore, be treated with some degree of caution.

109 Grigori A. Koltunov, 'Kurskaya bitva v tsifrakh', *Voenno-istoricheskii Zhurnal*, 6 (1968), pp. 61-3.

Correlation of Forces at the Kursk Salient, Beginning of July 1943

	Wehrmacht	Red Army	Strength Ratio
Men	780,000	1,910,000	1:2.4
Tanks and SP Guns[1]	3,400	5,600	1:1.6
Aircraft	1,800	3,600	1:2
Guns and Mortars	7,400	31,400	1:4.2

Note
1 These figures include vehicles under repair and reinforcements on the way to the front.

In the end, the Wehrmacht and Waffen-SS formations in the Kursk salient had a substantial number of tanks and self-propelled guns available. Yet the price for this massing was high, as the other sectors of the Eastern Front had as a consequence to make do with a very limited number of tanks and self-propelled guns. This became a severe problem, particularly during the second phase of the battle when the Soviet Bryansk Front and the Western Front mounted their counteroffensive at Orël. Both these fronts had a total of 3,260 tanks and self-propelled guns, whereas the opposing German Second Panzer Army, tasked with defending the Orël salient, only had about 550 tanks and self-propelled guns, including those still on the way to the front. In the Donets Basin, where the Red Army began its attack on 17 July 1943, the situation was slightly less critical for the Germans. Defending the Donets Basin against the Soviet Southwestern and Southern Front, which had almost 2,000 tanks and self-propelled guns at their disposal, were the German 1st Panzer Army and the 6th Army with 560 tanks and self-propelled guns including reserves. If the 23rd Panzer Division and the SS Panzergrenadier Division *Wiking* had indeed been committed to Operation Citadel, as Manstein had requested, only 410 tanks and self-propelled guns would have remained for the defence of the Donets Basin. This was not a risk Hitler was willing to take. On 3 July 1943, the Intelligence Department 'Foreign Armies East' predicted that the Red Army would mount a large-scale attack against the German 6th Army and 1st Panzer Army to retake the Donets Basin soon after the beginning of Operation Citadel. The Germans' only chance of weathering the expected crises on the weak sectors of the Eastern Front was a swift victory at Kursk. The forces freed up after the conclusion of Operation Citadel would then be available for counterattacks in other front sectors. As Manstein believed, they simply had to keep their nerve and accept temporary setbacks. Kursk, as he pointed out to Zeitzler even on 16 July 1943, was the decisive battle.

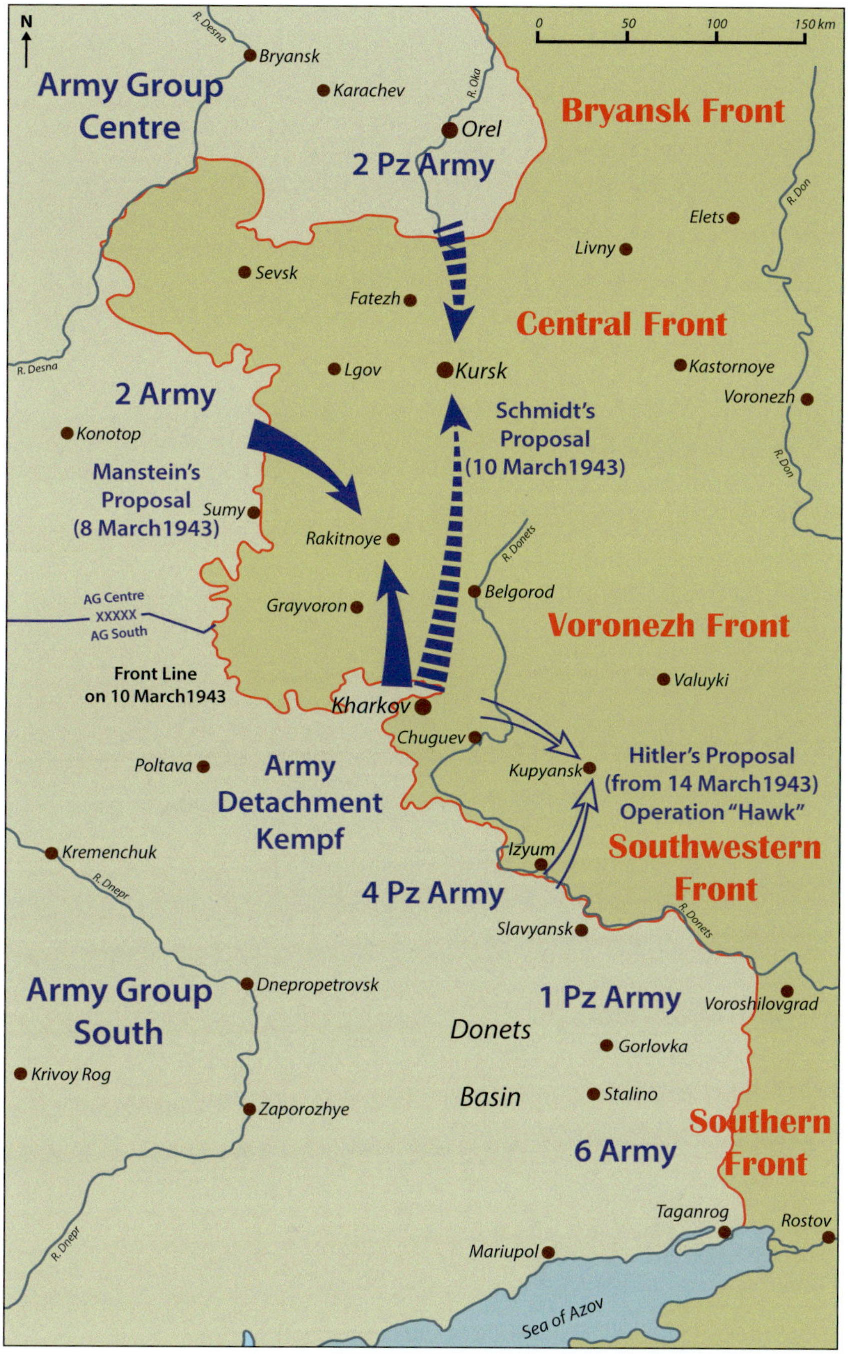

Map 1: German proposals for offensive operations, March 1943

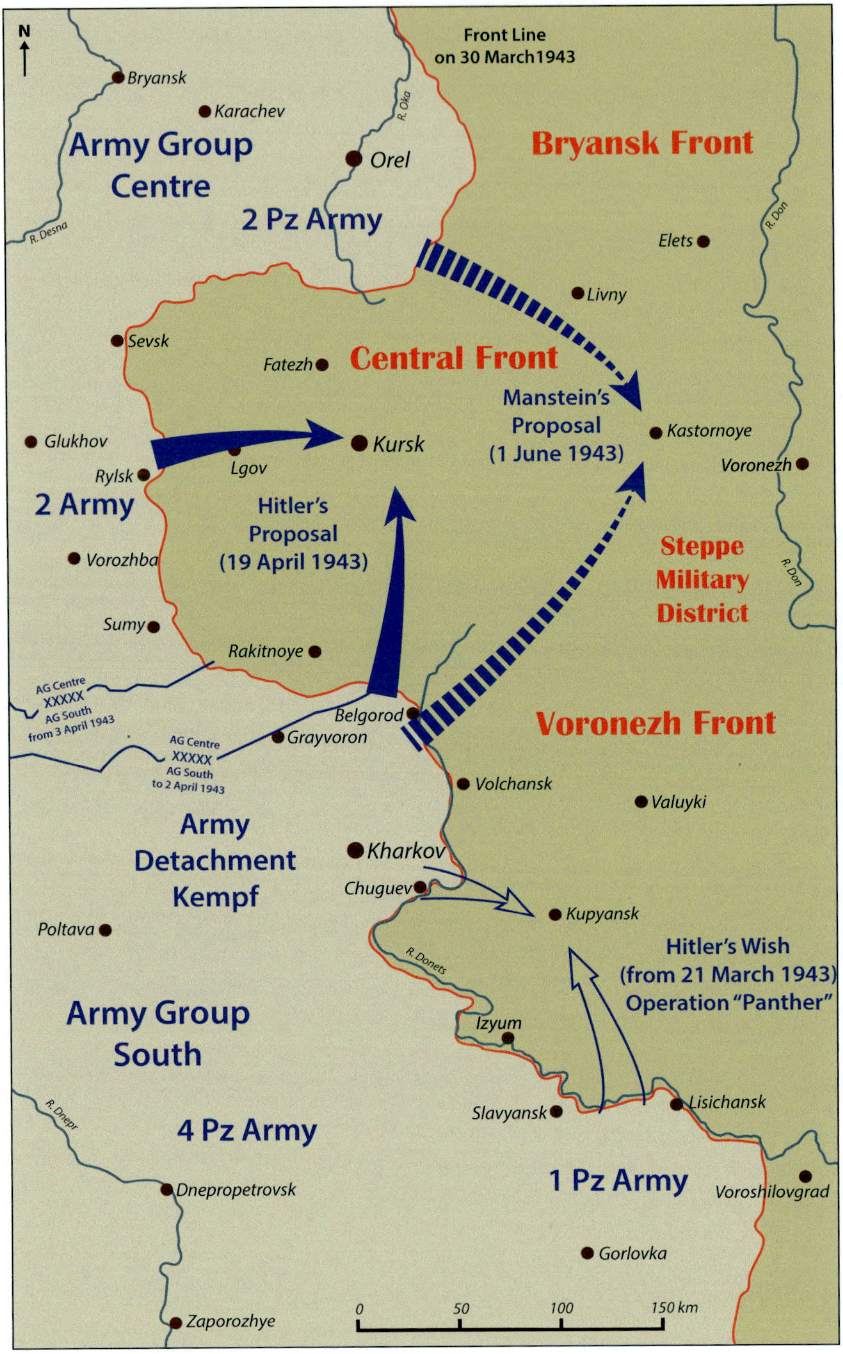

Map 2: Alternative proposals to Operation Citadel

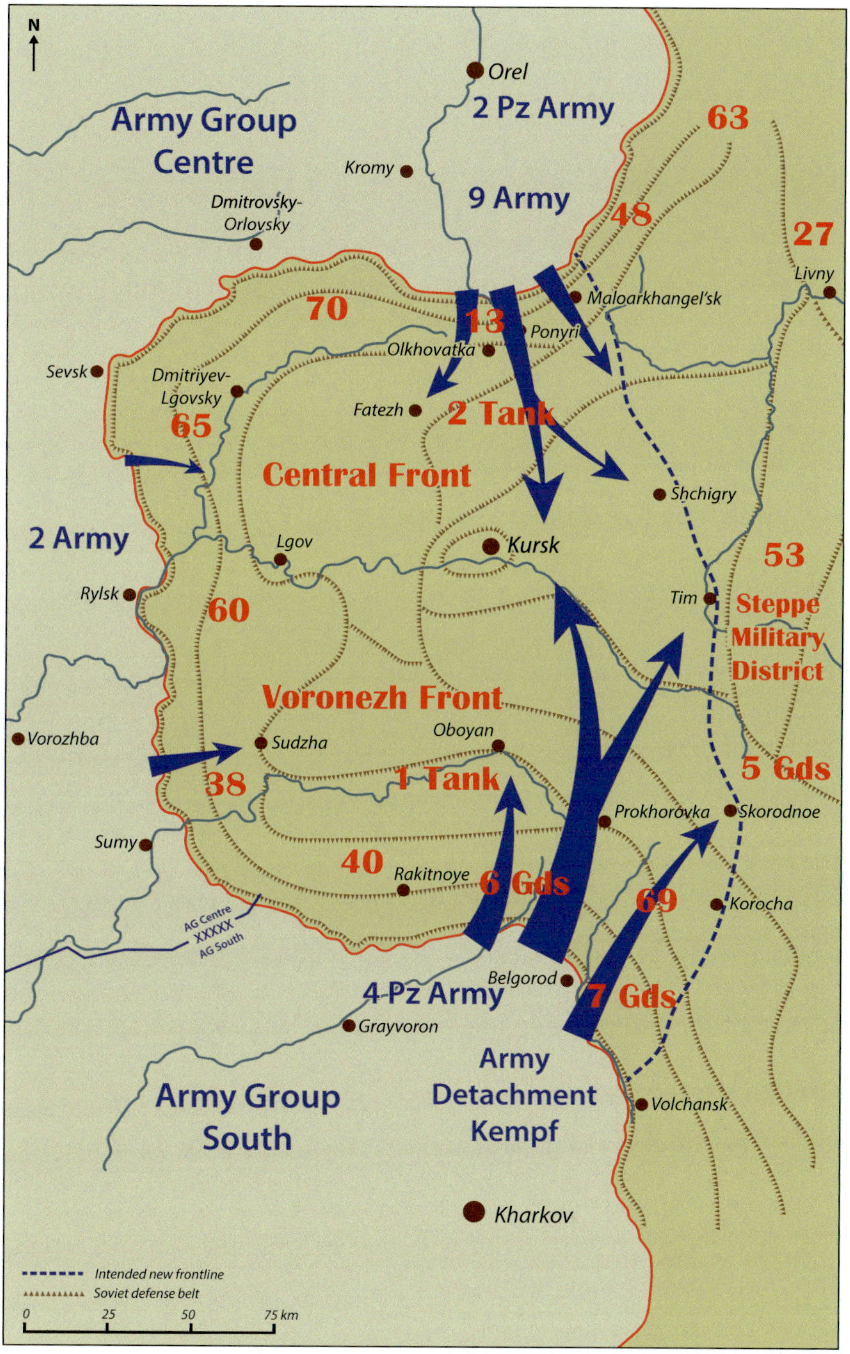

Map 3: Kursk Salient and plan for Operation Citadel

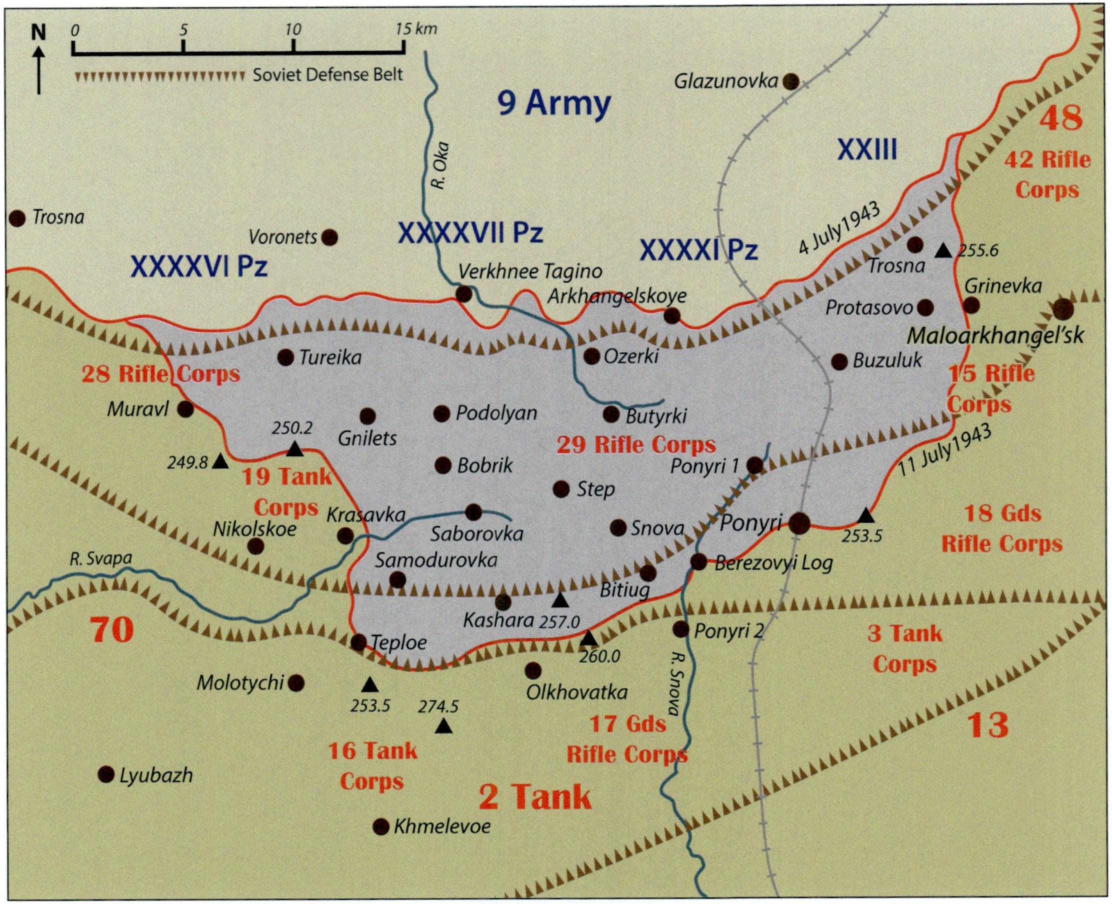

Map 4: Territorial gains of the German Ninth Army, 5-11 July 1943

Map 5: Territorial gains of the Fourth Panzer Army and Army Detachment Kempf

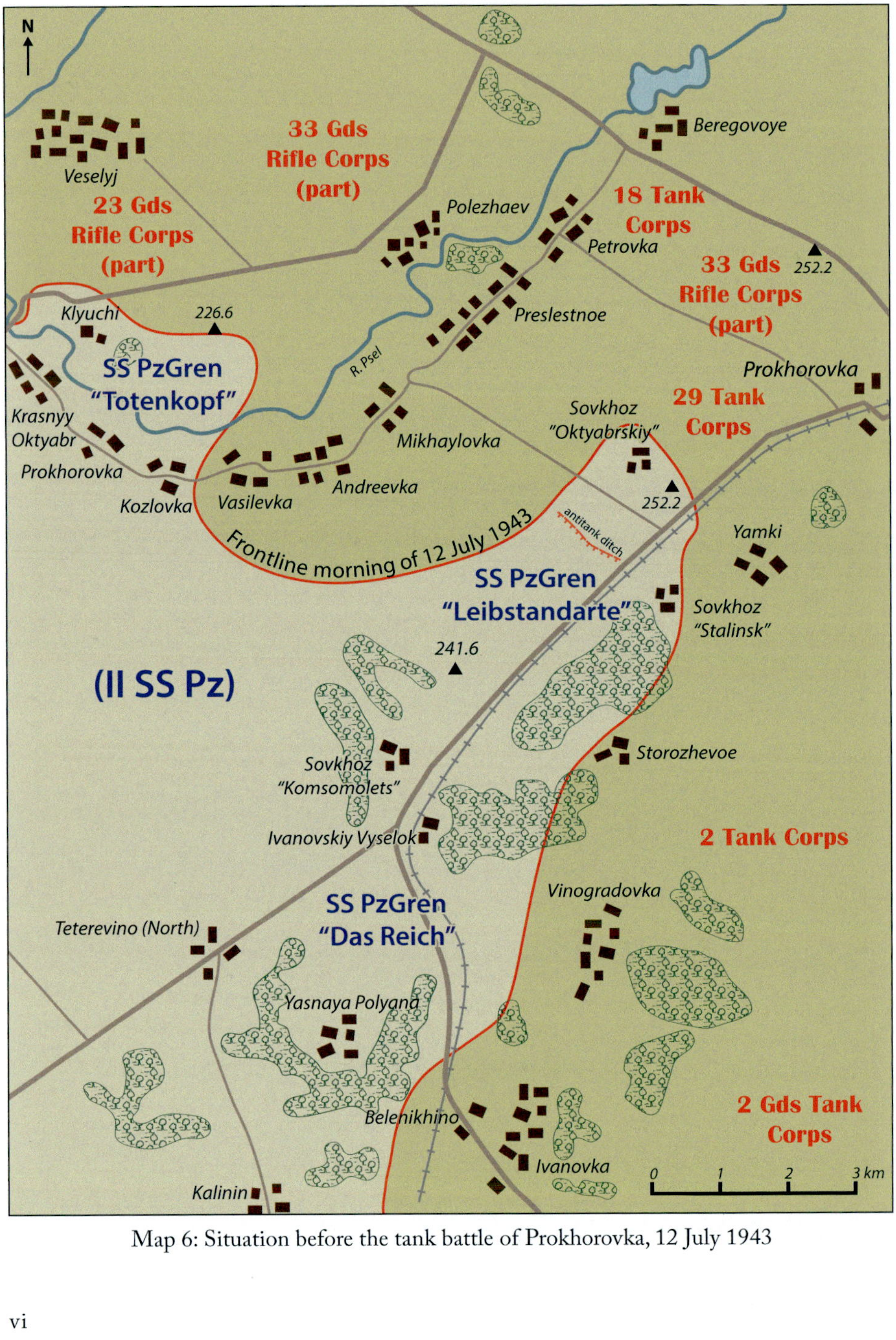

Map 6: Situation before the tank battle of Prokhorovka, 12 July 1943

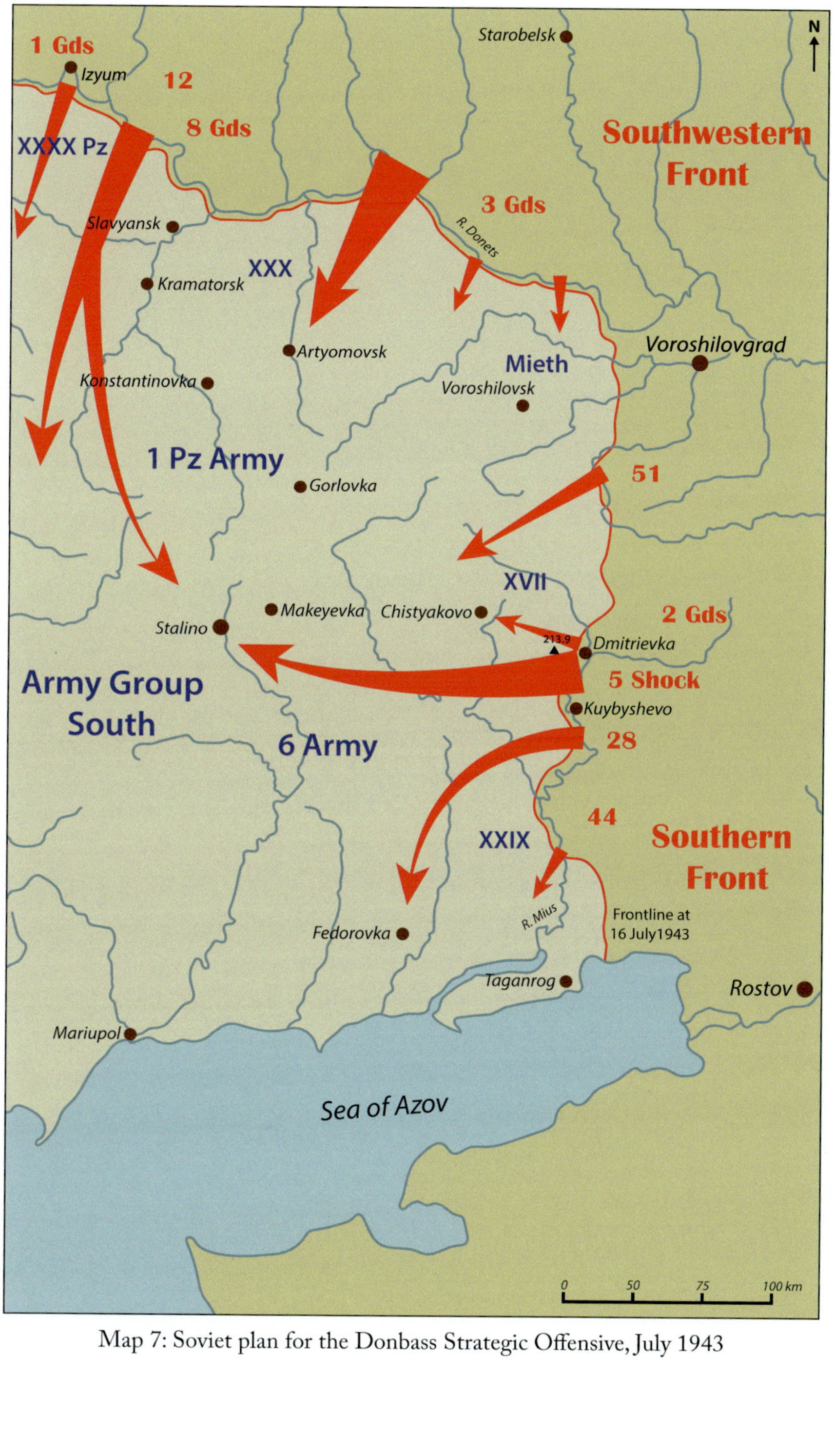

Map 7: Soviet plan for the Donbass Strategic Offensive, July 1943

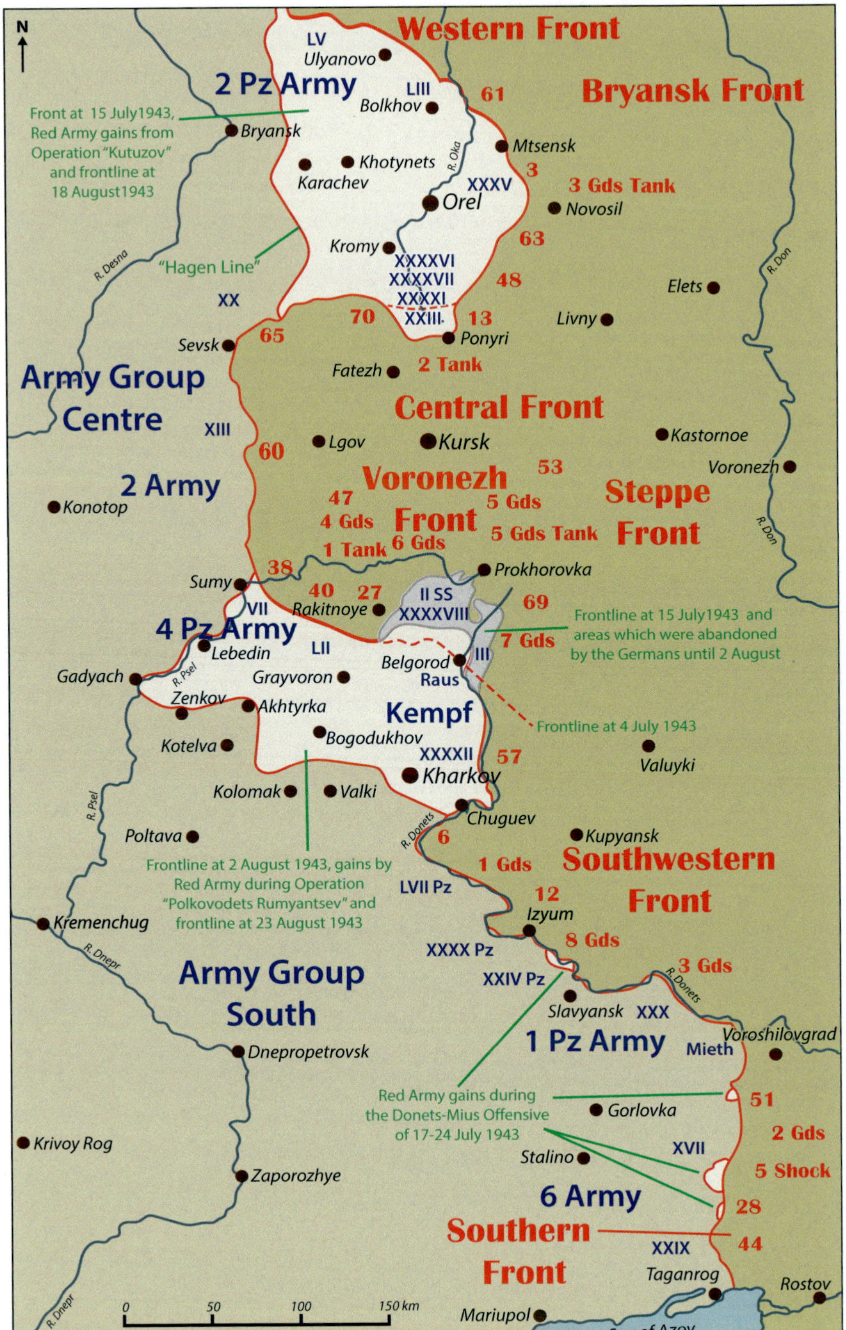

Map 8: Soviet counteroffensives, July-August 1943

2

The Bulge of Fire: The Battles of Kursk, Orël and Khar′kov in Summer 1943

The Probing Attack by XXXXVIII Panzer Corps, 4 July 1943

A day before the official opening of Operation Citadel, the XXXXVIII Panzer Corps with its five subordinate divisions launched the Battle of Kursk. This early attack was a prerequisite for the entire operation because the no man's land between the German forward lines and the first Soviet defensive belt in the corps' sector stretched several kilometres. This ground was dominated by a set of hills, which blocked the Germans' line of sight of the Russian positions. Furthermore, there were Soviet combat outposts dug in on top of the hills. Before Citadel could be launched, these outposts had to be neutralized and the hills had to be captured in order to get a better view of the Soviet defensive system and also to observe the effects of the artillery fire on the day of the attack.

This preliminary attack was planned as an infantry thrust with support from engineers, assault guns and tank destroyers, but without any tanks. At 1455 German Ju 87 *Stukas* (*Sturzkampfflugzeuge* or dive bombers) appeared over the target area, commencing the attack. It was 1555 Moscow time – there was a one hour difference because, unlike the Soviet Union, the German Reich had reintroduced daylight saving time in 1940. At 1500 German time, the XXXXVIII Panzer Corps began its advance. On the far left, the 332nd Infantry Division joined the attack; this division was actually subordinate to the LII Army Corps but at the beginning of Operation Citadel it was temporarily attached to the XXXXVIII Panzer Corps. It came up against units of the 71st Guards Rifle Division, which at first did not offer too much resistance. Fifty-seven Red Army soldiers were taken prisoner, nine more crossed over to the German lines. Only when the German infantry reached the railway line west of Gertsovka, did Soviet resistance begin to stiffen (Map 5).

Advancing to the right of the 332nd Infantry Division was the 3rd Panzer Division (attacking without its tanks). Its commander, Lieutenant-General Franz Westhoven, took part in the attack with one of the panzergrenadier regiments, exemplifying a tactical concept which had made many of the Wehrmacht's successes possible – leading from the front (*Führen von vorn*). The objective of the 3rd Panzer Division was Gertsovka, which was defended by elements of the Red Army 71st Guards Rifle Division. The Soviet soldiers here offered far more determined resistance than the 332nd Infantry Division had encountered. In spite of effective *Stuka* support, it was only in the late evening that the 3rd Panzer Division managed to secure Gertsovka. This success cost the division 130 casualties: 24 soldiers were killed in action, 102 were wounded and four were missing. Until the early morning the infantrymen were busy clearing Gertsovka of the enemy, mopping up sporadic resistance and capturing enemy stragglers.

East of the 3rd Panzer Division, the Panzergrenadier Division *Großdeutschland* attacked the ridge between the villages of Gertsovka and Butovo. Their attack hit the boundary between the Soviet 71st and the 67th Guards Rifle Division. At first the advance was met with little resistance and proceeded well. But soon the Germans started to receive Soviet enfilade artillery fire. They were also caught up in a minefield and a number of soldiers, among them several officers, were badly wounded. Eventually the soldiers of the Division *Großdeutschland* reached their objectives of the day but the loss in officers was very serious: the III Battalion of the Panzer Fusilier Regiment *Großdeutschland* lost its commanding officer, the Panzer Artillery Regiment *Großdeutschland* one of its battery commanders.

The village of Butovo was attacked by the 11th Panzer Division. Initially, the division advanced fairly quickly south of Butovo, but the village itself was fiercely defended by units of the Soviet 67th Guards Rifle Division. Butovo could not be fully captured that evening and it would not be before the morning of 5 July, after the beginning of the actual Operation Citadel, that the final Russian resistance in the village was broken.

Of all the five German divisions involved in the attack, it was the 167th Infantry Division which made the most progress. At Streletskoe it pushed northwards, led from the front by its commander, Lieutenant-General Wolf Trierenberg. Facing the division and defending the front sector between Streletskoe and Yakhontov were elements of the 52nd Guards Rifle Division. The daily report from the 167th Infantry Division states: 'After attacking according to plan and against slight enemy resistance, the day's objective was reached around 1700. During the attack [there was] only weak artillery and mortar fire, particularly against [the] left flank.'[1]

At the end of 4 July, the XXXXVIII Panzer Corps had reached most of its objectives of the day and fought its way to the Soviet main line of defence. The Soviet combat outposts had been destroyed, the Soviet positions lay in sight. Yet the day also gave a bitter foretaste of the battles that were to follow: the Russian troops had defended themselves 'surprisingly well.'[2] The German divisions had suffered their first

1 BA-MA, RH 24-48/121, Anlagen zum Kriegstagebuch des Generalkommandos XXXXVIII. Panzerkorps, Abteilung Ia, Juli 1943, no pagination.

2 BA-MA, RH 24-48/115, Kriegstagebuch des Generalkommandos XXXXVIII. Panzerkorps, Ia, 1.7.-31.7.1943, fol. 12.

severe losses, some of which were caused by their own air force when the Luftwaffe twice accidentally bombed the 11th Panzer Division at Butovo. The Soviet minefields also proved to be of unexpected depth. Lastly, an accident happened in the rear of the German front which could have been taken as a bad omen for the forthcoming first commitment of the new *Panther* tank. A *Panther* of the 51st Panzer Battalion crashed through a bridge at Borisovka, fell into the Vorskla River and caught fire, managing to set the bridge alight as well. As the risk of explosion thwarted any attempts of putting out the fire, the *Panther* burned out and the bridge, too, was destroyed.

The Germans concluded that the Soviet troops had been completely taken by surprise by the preliminary attack of the XXXXVIII Panzer Corps. Now, however, even the most junior Red Army soldier was aware that the German main attack was imminent. The Russians, however, expected the main thrust of the German summer offensive to originate from the Ninth Army, north of Kursk, which is why the Soviet artillery laid the main focus of its defensive preparations there.

The Soviet Counter-Preparations during the Night of 4-5 July 1943

Several months before the battle for Kursk began, the Soviet commanders planned time-on-target artillery fire on the German assembly area to pre-empt the German attack. Its goal was not only to demoralize the enemy troops but also inflict heavy losses and debilitate the attack forces. The crucial element was to open fire at the right moment – when the German formations had moved into their pre-assault positions. The Soviet leaders had been aware for months of where the German offensive would be mounted, and the probing attacks on 4 July suggested that the German main attack would quite probably be launched on 5 July. However, what the Red Army did not know was the exact time of the attack.

During the night of 4-5 July, an engineer of the German 6th Infantry Division was taken prisoner near Verkhnee Tagino by soldiers of the 15th Rifle Division. During interrogation the German soldier revealed that Operation Citadel was to begin between 0100 and 0200 German summertime (0300 Moscow time).[3] Based on this information, General Rokossovskiy, the commander of the Central Front, ordered that artillery counter-preparations should begin at 0220 Moscow time. According to Rokossovskiy's memoirs, more than 500 guns, 460 mortars and 100 rocket launchers opened up in the sectors of the Thirteenth and the Forty-Eighth Army, hitting the enemy troops, who were just getting ready for the attack, with devastating fire. Allegedly the Germans suffered heavy losses and it took them two hours to recover from the blow and finally launch their own attack.[4] Even though this depiction is

3 Zamulin, *The Battle of Kursk: Controversial and Neglected Aspects*, pp. 178-91.
4 Konstantin K. Rokossowski, *Soldatenpflicht: Erinnerungen eines Frontoberbefehlshabers* (East Berlin, 1970), p. 262.

far from accurate, it has had a considerable influence on the historiography of the Battle of Kursk. Olaf Groehler, a historian from the German Democratic Republic, for instance, embellished Rokossovskiy's account and claimed that Soviet artillery fire annihilated whole German batteries, companies and regiments.[5] Western historians, too, have adopted such narratives without question. The American author Martin Caidin, for example, claimed that the Soviet counter-preparations had a decisive impact on the course of the Battle of Kursk.[6]

While the effect of the pre-emptive Soviet artillery fire is rarely described as drastically as in the writings of Groehler and Caidin, many studies on Kursk, even recent ones, claim that the Soviet artillery fire inflicted heavy losses on the German formations readying themselves for battle and that, because of it, the attack had to be postponed by two hours. The daily reports and the war diaries of the divisions launching Operation Citadel in the early hours of 5 July 1943, however, demonstrate that in fact this was not the case. Fortunately most of these crucial records survived the war and are still available today, yielding valuable information on how effective the Soviet artillery counter-preparations really were. The XXXXVI Panzer Corps with the 258th, the 7th and the 31st Infantry Divisions was assembled in the far western sector of Model's Ninth Army. Soviet sources state that this sector, defended by the 70th Army, was not shelled, which is corroborated by the German reports.

The eastern neighbour of the XXXXVI Panzer Corps, the XXXXVII Panzer Corps, joined the offensive with only two divisions at first, namely the 6th Infantry Division and the 20th Panzer Division. The war diary of the latter division reports: '[0115:] Beginning of massive enemy time-on-target fire from all heavy weapons. Russian expects our attack at 0200, confirmed by the statements of two deserters of the 6th Infantry Division.'[7] Except for this remark, there is no mention of the counter-preparations in the war diary – had they really inflicted such a heavy toll, it undoubtedly would have been noted. In the war diaries of the 6th Infantry Division and the panzer battalion of the 20th Panzer Division, the counter-preparations are not brought up at all.

According to Soviet sources, the focus of the Soviet artillery time-on-target fire was on the area north of Ponyri, where Rokossovskiy expected the German main attack. This is where in the early morning hours the men of the 292nd and the 86th Infantry Division (XXXXI Panzer Corps) and – further to the east – the regiments of the 78th Assault Division and the 216th Infantry Division (XXIII Army Corps) were preparing for the attack, which was to begin at 0330 German time (0430 Moscow time). The war diary of the 292nd Infantry Division states: 'The assembly is carried out

5 Olaf Groehler, *Kampf um die Luftherrschaft: Beiträge zur Luftkriegsgeschichte des zweiten Weltkrieges* (East Berlin, 2nd edn, 1989), p. 128.

6 Martin Caidin, *The Tigers are Burning* (New York, 1974), p. 172.

7 BA-MA, RH 27-20/163, Kriegstagebuch der 20. Panzerdivision, Ia, pt. 7, 1.7.-8.10.1943, fol. 9.

as scheduled and concluded by 0200. The Russian seems to have become suspicious though, because from 0100 until 0145 he delivers heavy harassing fire on the main line of resistance and on [the] rear; there is not much damage.'[8]

The war diaries of the 86th Infantry Division for the period of Operation Citadel unfortunately no longer exist, and the war diary of the XXXXI Panzer Corps has also been lost. What is still available though are the corps' daily reports. The morning report of 5 July notes: 'After a quiet late evening, [the] enemy directed heavy harassing fire on the main line of defence in the whole sector of the corps from 0100-0300. Other than that [there were] no specific incidents until the beginning of our own attack.'[9] In the reports from the corps there are no remarks about casualties, which suggests that in the area of the 86th Infantry Division 'there cannot have been much going on [i.e. causing damage]' either, as a soldier of the 653rd Heavy Tank Destroyer Battalion later recalled.[10] This battalion began its attack on 5 July together with the 86th Infantry Division. One of the rare available records on the employment of this division in Operation Citadel, a divisional history written after the war, gives the following account of the Soviet counter-preparations: 'Before our own artillery preparations began, [the enemy] suddenly began opening up with all guns blazing on what he thought to be our assembly areas, but he did not interfere with the beginning of our attack.'[11]

One of the most revealing documents on the counter-preparations is the daily report of the XXXXI Panzer Corps Artillery Commander: 'At 0110, the enemy all of a sudden began shelling the main line of defence, the woods behind it and the rearward area with about 15-18 batteries and mortars, using large amounts of ammunition. The fire abated around 0200. Until the beginning of [our] attack the enemy remained quiet. Due to poor fire control, the effect of the artillery strike was minimal considering the amount of ammunition expended.'[12]

Soviet accounts claim that apart from the 86th Infantry Division, the 78th Assault Division suffered particularly bloody losses through the counter-preparatory fire. The division's war diary for the period in question no longer exists, but that of the XXIII Army Corps, to which the 78th Assault Division was subordinate, is available. It includes a report from the division according to which it received 'unusually lively harassing fire' at 0130, which destroyed a few telephone lines. At 0320 another

8 BA-MA, RH 26-292/43, Kriegstagebuch Nr. 6 der 292. Infanterie-Division, Ia, für die Zeit vom 11.6.-30.9.1943, no pagination.
9 BA-MA, RH 24-41/84, Unterlagen zum Tätigkeitsbericht des Generalkommandos XXXXI. Panzerkorps Ic für die Zeit vom 24.3.-18.7.1943, no pagination.
10 Letter from Karl Neunert to the author, 11 November 2003.
11 ZMSBw Library, Der Ostfeldzug der 86. rhein.-westf. Inf.-Division, dargestellt aufgrund von Tagebuchnotizen, Karten, Fotos, Briefen und unvergessenen und unvergesslichen Eindrücken und Erlebnissen, copy of manuscript, s.l., 1962, ref. F.500.2373.
12 BA-MA, RH 24-41/84, Unterlagen zum Tätigkeitsbericht des Generalkommandos XXXXI. Panzerkorps Ic für die Zeit vom 24.3.-18.7.1943, no pagination.

message from the 78th Assault Division was noted down in the war diary: 'Some casualties due to enemy artillery, otherwise everything is all right.'[13] Its neighbour to the east, the 216th Infantry Division, on the other hand, did not report anything about the counter-preparations to the XXIII Army Corps.

The Ninth Army Headquarters did not even find the counter-preparations worth mentioning in their war diary, in fact all divisions began the attack as scheduled. The Soviet statement that the Germans had to postpone their attack by two hours is based on misinformation. The captured German soldier of the 6th Infantry Division, who told his interrogators that Operation Citadel would begin at 0200 German summertime or 0300 Moscow time respectively, unknowingly or deliberately gave an incorrect time. In fact, as early as mid-April 1943 the time of the attack had been fixed on 0330 German summertime for the XXXXI Panzer Corps and the XXIII Army Corps, and on 0630 for the XXXXVI and the XXXXVII Panzer Corps.

Yet, the Red Army did not only make counter-preparations in the German Ninth Army's sector north of Kursk but also in the southern sector, in the area of the Fourth Panzer Army and Army Detachment Kempf. The war diaries covering the period of the Battle of Kursk of nearly all the divisions attached to these two armies have been lost – but those of all the corps of the two armies still exist, so it is possible to draw a comparison with the southern sector as well. According to Soviet sources, the artillery of both the 6th and the 7th Guards Army fired two time-on-target concentrations against the German assembly areas in the course of Soviet counter-preparations. An artillery report from the 6th Guards Army indicates that the first strike began at 2230 Moscow time (2130 German summertime) and lasted only five minutes. At 0330 Moscow time (0230 German summertime), Soviet artillery again opened fire, shelling the German initial positions for 40 minutes. Allegedly, the counter-preparations also inflicted heavy casualties in the ranks of the German formations south of Kursk and delayed the beginning of the German offensive by several hours.

Comparing this account with available German records gives the following picture. The war diary of the LII Army Corps, which had to cover the western flank of the Fourth Panzer Army, reports that 'the enemy in front of the corps' whole front remained quiet.'[14] At 0230, the 332nd Infantry Division, which had advanced as far as the area of Bubny on 4 July, reported Soviet counterattacks and 'strong enemy resistance with concentrated [fire] from artillery, mortars and rocket launchers.'[15] Before the division could start Operation Citadel, it first had to fend off Soviet counterattacks and clear up the situation; therefore it had to postpone the time of attack scheduled

13 BA-MA, RH 24-23/123, Kriegstagebuch Nr. 15, XXIII. Armeekorps, Abteilung Ia, 22.3.-22.7.1943, fol. 159.

14 BA-MA, RH 24-52/136, Kriegstagebuch Nr. 5 des LII. Armeekorps, Abteilung Ia, vom 4.3.-5.7.1943, fol. 181.

15 NARA, T315/2076/559, Kriegstagebuch Nr. 4 des Stabes der 332. Infanterie-Division, Führungsabteilung, vom 27.6.-11.8.1943.

for 0500 until 0930 – which was a result of the combat actions rather than the Soviet counter-preparations.

The four other divisions of the XXXXVIII Panzer Corps (the 3rd Panzer Division, the Panzergrenadier Division *Großdeutschland*, the 11th Panzer Division and the 167th Infantry Division) all registered heavy Soviet artillery, mortar and rocket fire in their sectors during the night, but none of them reported any casualties. Consequently, the war diary of the XXXXVIII Panzer Corps remarked succinctly: 'The night passes more or less quietly. There is heavy enemy fire from artillery, rocket launchers and mortars on the whole corps sector.'[16] What is not mentioned, though, is any postponement of the attack due to the Soviet shelling. The same holds true for the II SS Panzer Corps. Even though the SS divisions reported the Soviet counter-preparations and various other time-on-target strikes, there is no mention of casualties. Only the divisional histories published after the war note that a few soldiers were wounded by the Soviet artillery fire.[17] However, all in all, the number of casualties was so low that it was not listed in the reports from the divisions to the corps, nor was it registered in the war diary of the Fourth Panzer Army or the personal files of the commander of Army Group South, Field-Marshal Erich von Manstein. In the sector of Army Detachment Kempf, the Corps Raus (106th and 320th Infantry Division) hardly even noticed the Soviet counter-preparations and did not mention it in the war diary or in its morning and daily reports. Here, the attack was launched as scheduled at 0225 German summertime.

In the case of the III Panzer Corps, the Soviet counter-preparations undoubtedly had detrimental effects. According to Soviet records, the focus of the second counter-preparation lay on the Mikhaylovka bridgehead east of Belgorod in the sector of the 7th Guards Army. This is confirmed by German records, though the times mentioned differ. The Soviet account states that the second counter-preparation began at the same time as the attack of the III Panzer Corps, that is at 0330 Moscow time (0230 German summertime). The divisions of the III Panzer Corps did indeed launch their attack on schedule at 0225 German summertime. However, according to the morning report from the 19th Panzer Division, Soviet artillery had already been shelling the Mikhaylovka bridgehead for half an hour by that time. This interfered seriously with the construction of the bridges over the Donets, which had to be completed by the time the attack was to begin. Yet, by 0225, only footbridges for the infantry crossings were finished. The *Tigers* of the 503rd Heavy Panzer Battalion, tasked with leading the III Panzer Corps' attack, needed bridges with a load capacity of 60 tonnes. Two such bridges were being built in the sector of the 6th and of the 19th Panzer Division when the Soviet shelling began. The 60-tonne bridge in the sector of the 6th

16 BA-MA, RH 24-48/115, Kriegstagebuch des Generalkommandos XXXXVIII. Panzerkorps, Ia, 1.7.-31.7.1943, fol. 13.

17 Wolfgang Vopersal, *Soldaten, Kämpfer, Kameraden: Marsch und Kämpfe der SS-Totenkopfdivision* (Bielefeld, 1987), vol. 3, pp. 326, 328.

Panzer Division, which was all but completed, was destroyed by a direct hit, whilst the construction site of the second 60-tonne bridge in the sector of the 19th Panzer Division was taken under such accurate enemy artillery fire that the German engineers could not continue their work. When the attack was launched, no *Tiger* could therefore cross the Donets River, and without these 'crowbars' the attacking formations of the III Panzer Corps were initially pinned down by enemy defensive fire.

Summarizing the findings from German records, it can be concluded that the Soviet counter-preparations in the sector of both the Ninth Army and the Fourth Panzer Army were fairly ineffective. As far as Army Detachment Kempf was concerned, the counter-preparations inflicted only light casualties but, much more importantly, it prevented the *Tigers* of the 503rd Heavy Panzer Battalion crossing the Donets in time. However, whether the first attack might have been more successful if the *Tigers* had been able to get across the river as planned is questionable because when the tanks finally did cross they ended up stuck in the Soviet minefields which had been laid in depth.

Ultimately, the counter-preparations had an adverse consequence for the Red Army, too. The Soviet leadership had planned to provide a rude surprise for the Germans with time-on-target artillery fire and air strikes before the Germans could mount Operation Citadel. Strong formations of the Soviet 2nd and 17th Air Armies had orders to destroy as many German aircraft as possible in the early morning of 5 July. This way, both the Fourth Panzer Army and Army Detachment Kempf would have lost their air support, while at the same time the Red Army Air Forces could have achieved air superiority without suffering too heavy losses in aerial combat. But things did not go as planned. In the Kursk area in early July 1943, dawn broke around 0230 German summertime, and the sun began rising at 0320. This was the time Soviet aircraft were supposed to have started their surprise attacks on the German advanced airstrips at Khar'kov. In his memoirs, Walter Lehweß-Litzmann, who at that time was a Lieutenant-Colonel and wing commander of *Kampfgeschwader* 3, listed one of the reasons why the Soviet plan failed: 'In the morning of 5 July, the troops assembling for battle were in for an unpleasant surprise: the Soviet forces initiated the attack with an unexpected time-on-target strike on the troops that were just forming for the attack. They called me excitedly – I had just gathered the commanders for a last briefing in my headquarters – and changed the orders. We had to take off at once in order to suppress Soviet artillery, even though it was still dark.'[18] Many German aircraft were therefore already airborne when the Soviet aeroplanes took off to attack the German airfields. Moreover, the Soviet formations were located by German radar stations and, a little later, by signal intelligence and air observers before they even reached the German lines. As a result, numerous German fighters scrambled – sooner than originally planned – to intercept the Soviet aeroplanes. The Soviet surprise attack

18 Walter Lehweß-Litzmann, *Absturz ins Leben*, ed. Jörn Lehweß-Litzmann (Querfurt, 1994), p. 204.

thus turned into a nasty surprise for the Soviet pilots and, in the morning sky over Khar'kov, a fierce aerial battle began.

The Air Battle over the Kursk Salient, 5 July 1943

On the morning of 5 July 1943 at 0310, a few German fighters of the II Group of *Jagdgeschwader* (Fighter Wing) 3 took off from their airfield Khar'kov-Rogan in the southeast of Khar'kov for a *freie Jagd* ('free hunt', or fighter sweep) in the area of Belgorod. The II Group of *Jagdgeschwader* 3 was one of four fighter groups which were at the disposal of the VIII Air Corps under the command of Major-General Hans Seidemann. Seidemann's corps was ordered to support the attack forces of the Fourth Panzer Army and of Army Detachment Kempf. The fighters had the task of protecting German bombers, dive bombers and ground-attack aircraft from attacking Soviet fighters. Additionally, small groups of German fighters kept flying fighter sweeps over the combat zone in order to combat any unexpected appearances of Soviet aircraft.

In total, Seidemann's four fighter groups had about 150 Messerschmitt Bf 109 G fighters, roughly 120 of which were operational. The fact the Germans only had a handful of aircraft available illustrates the impact of the war on multiple fronts the German Reich was waging in 1943. Most German fighter groups were by now engaged in Western Europe, in the 'defence of the Reich' over German skies and in the Mediterranean against the British and the Americans. In contrast, the Red Army did not have to fight on multiple fronts and was therefore able to use the bulk of their air forces against the Wehrmacht on the Soviet-German front. In early July 1943, the 150 fighters of the German VIII Air Corps were thus faced by roughly 700 fighter aircraft of the Soviet 2nd and 17th Air Armies.

According to Soviet planning, almost 420 aeroplanes were to join the surprise attack on the German advanced airstrips; roughly a third of these were Ilyushin Il-2 ground-attack aircraft and two-thirds were Yakovlev Yak-1 and Yak-7B, in addition to Lavochkin La-5 fighter aircraft. In reality, only about 300 planes – 100 ground-attack and 200 fighter aircraft – actually took to the air. In theory that still would have been an impressive force – had it been deployed *en masse*. But the ground-attack aircraft were at first assigned five German airfields as targets, which had to be hit at the same time rather than one after the other. This is why every airfield was attacked by only about 20 ground-attack and 20-30 fighter escort aircraft, while the remainder of Soviet fighters were patrolling over other airfields to prevent German fighters from taking off.

The fighters of the II Group of *Jagdgeschwader* 3 had flown only 10 kilometres northwards for a 'free hunt', when they were informed that Soviet ground-attack aircraft were approaching. They turned at once to intercept the Soviet formation, while more fighters of the II Group as well as of the other three fighter groups (the III Group of *Jagdgeschwader* 3 and the I and III Group of *Jagdgeschwader* 52) were scrambled. Shortly before 0330 the German fighter planes intercepted the Soviet ground-attack aircraft, broke through their fighter escort and shot down the first Ilyushins. Instead of attacking their assigned targets, the Soviet pilots now had to fight for their very lives. A *Stabsarzt* of the III Group of *Kampfgeschwader* 27 who observed the battle over the airfield Khar'kov-Osnova wrote to his wife on the following day, telling her that the Soviet planes had 'tumbled from the sky like dead flies.' He continued: 'Yesterday in the early morning, the Russians ventured just one attack on our [air] field. I doubt that a single machine made it back home. A squadron of our *Jagdgeschwader* [alone] shot down 25 Russians. No Russian has shown up since then!'[19]

After the morning's air battles over the airfields, the German fighters claimed 50 Soviet fighter and ground-attack aircraft shot down, of which the II Group of *Jagdgeschwader* 3 alone accounted for 30 victories. According to Soviet sources, the 2nd and 17th Air Armies lost about 35 aircraft in the attack, not including the heavily damaged ones that managed to crash land behind their own lines. However, this was only the beginning of a major air battle, which raged over the Kursk salient on 5 July 1943. Both sides supported the ground combat on a large scale, with the VIII Air Corps primarily supporting the II SS Panzer Corps. The Division *Leibstandarte SS Adolf Hitler* reported: 'Outstanding support from our *Stukas*.'[20] About 200 Ju 87 D dive bombers were at the VIII Air Corps' disposal; they were in almost continuous action, with some crews flying six missions a day. The fighter pilots, too, had to make up for their inferiority in numbers by flying four to six sorties daily.

All in all, the VIII Air Corps flew nearly 2,700 missions on 5 July 1943: the *Sturzkampfgeschwader* (Dive-Bomber Wings) 2 and 77 both flew about 1,070 sorties, the four groups of *Jagdgeschwader* 3 and 52 more than 600; bombers, ground-attack and reconnaissance aircraft accounted for the rest. Even though the Soviet 2nd and 17th Air Armies had more than twice as many operational aircraft than the German VIII Air Corps (which had 730 planes at its disposal), the Red Army Air Forces flew only 1,720 sorties in the southern sector of the Kursk salient on 5 July – that is nearly 1,000 less than the Germans. Nevertheless, the Soviet air attacks posed quite a problem for the German ground troops. The XXXXVIII Panzer Corps reported on the morning of 5 July 'extremely heavy air attacks by strong Il-2 and bomber formations' and urgently requested fighter cover.[21] The troops of the II SS Panzer Corps, too, were repeatedly bombed and strafed by Soviet bombers and ground-attack aircraft. The formations suffering most from Soviet air attacks, however, were the divisions of Army Detachment Kempf, since on the first day of the attack, the VIII Air Corps almost solely supported the Fourth Panzer Army, whereas the Soviet 17th Air Army concentrated all its forces against Army Detachment Kempf in the afternoon. The war

19 A *Stabsarzt*, literally 'staff physician', is a medical officer with the rank equal to a Captain. Walter Waiss, *Chronik Kampfgeschwader Nr. 27 Boelcke, pt 4: 01.01.1943–31.12.1943* (Aachen, 2007), p. 159.

20 Stadler, *Offensive*, p. 43.

21 BA-MA, RH 24-48/115, Kriegstagebuch des Generalkommandos XXXXVIII. Panzerkorps, Ia, 1.7.-31.7.1943, fol. 15.

diary of the army detachment accordingly states: 'All along the Donets Front strong enemy air superiority, air attacks especially on crossing sites.'[22]

For the vigorous support of their own ground troops, the Red Army Air Forces paid a high price. While the bulk of the German aircraft were engaged in the sky over the Fourth Panzer Army, the VIII Air Corps nevertheless kept sending fighters to the combat zone of Army Detachment Kempf. They did not achieve air superiority, but still managed to inflict heavy losses on the Soviet air formations. On 5 July 1943, the units of VIII Air Corps claimed 260 Soviet planes shot down – 220 downed in aerial combat and 40 by anti-aircraft fire. Soviet records indicate that the 17th Air Army in total lost 76 aircraft on 5 July 1943. Of these, 55 Il-2 ground-attack aircraft were shot down in the afternoon's attacks on the German crossing sites over the Donets alone. The 2nd Air Army suffered even heavier losses: 91 aircraft were destroyed, 23 were damaged and had to make an emergency landing. Some of these were written off later as total losses because they were not worth repairing anymore. Of the number of planes claimed shot down by the Germans, 190 (including about 170 total losses) are thus confirmed by Soviet sources.

The Soviet fighter pilots of the 2nd and the 17th Air Armies claimed to have shot down a total number of 173 German aircraft in the air battle on 5 July. Soviet ground-attack aircraft furthermore reported the destruction of 60 planes on the ground during the attacks on German airfields. However, German records indicate that the attack on the airfields was really a complete failure and that not one German plane was destroyed on the ground. The 173 Soviet air victories are also far from reality; in truth, only 33 aircraft of the VIII Air Corps were lost in aerial combat, due to anti-aircraft fire or because of technical failures and accidents, either destroyed or so badly damaged that they could not be repaired.[23]

On 5 July 1943, heavy aerial combat also raged to the north of Kursk, where Model's Ninth Army mounted its attack. The German 1st Air Division under the command of Major-General Paul Deichmann faced the Russian 16th Air Army under Lieutenant-General Sergey Ignat'evich Rudenko, who had about 1,030 aircraft available, compared to Deichmann's 640 operational aircraft. In fact, the numerical

22 BA-MA, RH 20-8/83, Kriegstagebuch Nr. 2 (vol. 1) des Armee-Oberkommandos 8, Ia (Armee-Abteilung Kempf) vom 1.7.-31.7.1943, fol. 19.

23 The deployments and losses of the German Luftwaffe were compiled based on the records of the Quartermaster General of the Luftwaffe (BA-MA, RL 2 III/1191-1193), the reports from the Luftwaffe's liaison officer at the Second Army Headquarters (BA-MA, RH 20-2/1337), as well as the histories of various Luftwaffe formations written after the war. For the Soviet side, the compilation is primarily based on Mikhail N. Kozhevnikov, *The Command and Staff of the Soviet Army Air Force in the Great Patriotic War 1941–1945: A Soviet View* (Washington, D.C., 1977); Dmitriy B. Khazanov and Vitaly G. Gorbach, *Aviaciya v bitve nad orlovsko-kurskoy dugoy: Oboronitel'nyy period* (Moscow, 2004); Christer Bergström, *Kursk: The Air Battle, July 1943* (Hersham, 2007); Vitaly G. Gorbach, *Nad Ognennoy Dugoy: Sovyetskaya aviaciya v Kurskoy bitve* (Moscow, 2007); and, Christopher A. Lawrence, *Kursk: The Battle of Prokhorovka* (Sheridan, CO, 2015).

imbalance was even greater, since the Soviet 15th Air Army, attached to the Bryansk Front, also joined in the fighting on 5 July. In total, the two Soviet air armies flew approximately 1,670 sorties – roughly 1,150 by the 16th Air Army and 520 by the 15th Air Army.

Like the formations in the south, the German air forces to the north of Kursk also had to compensate for their numerical inferiority by flying up to six sorties a day. In the early morning hours they had the task of supporting the attack of the XXXXI Panzer Corps and the XXIII Army Corps scheduled for 0330 German summertime. At 0630, the 1st Air Division had to employ all available forces to back up the attack of the XXXXVI and the XXXXVII Panzer Corps. The flight log of First Lieutenant Erhard Jähnert, a pilot of the III Group of *Sturzkampfgeschwader* 3, offers a telling example of the missions flown on 5 July 1943.[24] As early as 0250, Jähnert took off from the Konevka airfield near Orël to fly the first attack, supporting the formations of the Ninth Army which initiated the offensive at 0330. After a flight of 70 minutes, Jähnert returned to the airfield at 0400. At 0540 he took off again for a mission in support of the two corps which launched their attack at 0630. During the course of the day, he added four more flights to his logbook. When he finally landed at 1840, after his last sortie of the day, he had a total flight time of seven hours for the day. The other pilots of the 1st Air Division experienced a similar day; all in all, they flew nearly 2,100 sorties that day.

As Model's Ninth Army launched Operation Citadel in the morning of 5 July, Lieutenant-General Rudenko, the commander of the 16th Air Army, was at first unsure whether this was the German main attack, or whether more offensive thrusts would follow; he withheld, therefore, the majority of his aircraft. This was much to the advantage of the Germans, because the four groups of the 51st and the 54th *Jagdgeschwader* – including one Spanish fighter squadron – only had 145 operational Focke-Wulf Fw 190 A at their disposal. The 16th Air Army, by contrast, had 455 fighter aeroplanes available, and the 15th Air Army another 265. The fact that not all of these joined the attack from the beginning made it easier for the German fighters to protect their own combat aircraft, inflicting heavy losses on the Soviet air formations. Already in the first aerial combats in the area of Maloarkhangel'sk, Captain Vladimir Nikolaevich Zalevskiy was shot down and killed in his Yak-7B. His death was a great loss for the Red Army Air Forces because Zalevskiy was one of the Soviets' most experienced fighter pilots and a recipient of the title 'Hero of the Soviet Union.'

Within a short time, the German fighters managed to achieve air superiority in the northern sector of the Kursk salient on the morning of 5 July. The commander of the 10th Panzergrenadier Division, which was held in reserve south of Orël at that time, later remembered: 'Starting from dawn, strong German bomber squadrons and fighter

24 Erhard Jähnert, *Mal oben – mal unten: Einer, der immer dabei war* (Bad Kissingen, 1992), p. 345.

escorts ceaselessly flew southwards. The Soviet Air Forces seemed to be neutralized.'[25] In the course of the morning, however, the number of Soviet missions increased, and in the afternoon and evening of 5 July, the Red Army Air Forces flew numerous bombing attacks on the formations of the Ninth Army. Around 2000 German summertime, the Ic section (intelligence) of the Ninth Army Headquarters reported that the deployment of the Russian Air Forces on this day had been 'haphazard and fragmented at first' but 'gained in intensity and unity in the meantime … The XXIII Army Corps in particular is being attacked by strong enemy forces flying continuous sorties.'[26]

Since the German fighters repeatedly intercepted the Soviet fighter and ground-attack formations, fierce air battles raged over the battlefield. The Soviet fighters of the 16th Air Army claimed 106 victories – which was a gross exaggeration, as on 5 July, the German 1st Air Division in truth had to write off only 23 planes as total losses or as ready for the scrap heap. Six of these were lost not to enemy fire but because of technical defects or accidents. Of the remaining 17 aircraft at least six were shot down by anti-aircraft fire, one more was lost due to sabotage. This leaves just 10 planes which were either confirmed or likely to have been shot down by Soviet fighters. By contrast, the Germans reported the destruction of 165 Russian planes in total – 163 shot down in aerial combat, two to anti-aircraft fire. According to Soviet records, the 16th Air Army lost exactly 100 planes: 83 fighters, 16 ground-attack aircraft and one bomber. These numbers prove that the Soviet fighter pilots performed well in their escort duties, albeit at a high cost. Unfortunately, the exact number of losses of the 15th Air Army remains unknown, but it can be assumed that it did suffer a number of losses in the numerous missions it flew that day.

When the first day of the battle in the Kursk salient ended, the Soviet 2nd, 16th and 17th Air Armies reported 267 planes lost. Adding to this were some losses of the 15th Air Army and possibly some of the local air defence of Kursk and of the long-range aviation. And if one takes into account the aeroplanes which were so badly damaged that they were later reported as total losses, one can without exaggeration assume a number of 300 total losses suffered by the Red Army Air Forces on 5 July 1943. On the other hand, the German Luftwaffe lost 56 aircraft north and south of Kursk in total; these were either shot down or damaged so badly that they were beyond repair. Only 43 of the 56 were actually shot down by Soviet fighters or anti-aircraft fire, whilst 13 planes were lost because of technical defects, accidents or sabotage.

Why did the Red Army Air Forces suffer such severe losses at Kursk? For one, there was the quality of their fighter aircraft. For decades, Soviet authors have circulated

25 August Schmidt, *Geschichte der 10. Division: 10. Infanterie-Division (mot), 10. Panzer-Grenadier-Division, 1933-1945* (Bad Nauheim, 1963), p. 176.

26 BA-MA, RH 20-9/302, Beilage zum Kriegstagebuch des Armee-Oberkommando 9, Anlage 1b zum Tätigkeitsbericht der Abteilung Ic/A.O., Berichtszeit: 26.3.-17.8.1943, Ic Tagesmeldungen, 1.6.-17.8.1943, no pagination.

the legend of the technical superiority of the Red Army. The 728th Fighter Aviation Regiment, for instance, was equipped with Yak-7B before the Battle of Kursk. In his memoirs, Arseniy Vasil'evich Vorozheykin, the most successful pilot of the regiment, described this plane as follows: 'One simply had to be thrilled about these aircraft: the world's best fighter aeroplanes, their manoeuvrability surpasses that of the German [fighters], and [they are] not inferior in terms of speed either.'[27] In truth, nearly all Soviet fighter aircraft employed at Kursk were inferior to the German Messerschmitt Bf 109 G and Focke-Wulf Fw 190 A – and in contemporary internal Soviet reports this was sometimes admitted. The Yak-7B, praised by Vorozheykin, was fitted with an engine with a take-off output of only 890kW (1,210hp) – like most Yakovlev fighters at that time. The German Bf 109 G, by contrast, had an engine with a take-off power of 1,085kW (1,475hp); at medium altitude it was 30-50km/h faster than the Yak and it also had a better rate of climb. The Fw 190 A had an engine with 1,250kW (1,700hp) take-off power and was even 50-70km/h faster than the Yak in medium altitude. Like the Focke-Wulf 190 A, the Soviet Lavochkin La-5 fighters were equipped with a 1,250kW engine; in terms of speed, however, they were about equal to the Yak-1, Yak-7B and Yak-9. The first versions of the La-5 were no match for both the Messerschmitt and the Focke-Wulf fighters. This changed with the improved version, the La-5FN, which was fitted with an engine with 1,360kW (1,850hp) take-off power and was on a par with – and in some aspects even superior to – the German fighter planes. Like nearly all Soviet fighters it performed best at low altitude and was very nimble. Experienced German pilots thus tried to avoid turning combat with Soviet fighters at low altitude. The La-5FN was delivered to the front in summer 1943 and was first employed in larger numbers at Kursk. Still, there was little it could do to change the fact that the Luftwaffe technically remained clearly superior to the Red Army Air Forces in summer 1943.

Nonetheless, the high rate of losses of the Soviet Air Forces at Kursk cannot only be explained by the superiority of German fighter aircraft. As a matter of fact, the Soviet fighters were by no means so hopelessly inferior to the German aircraft that they stood no chance in aerial combat. With an experienced pilot at the controls, a Yak or a La-5 was a dangerous opponent. The real issue was that the tactics of the Red Army Air Forces were lacking. At the beginning of the battle, Soviet fighters usually flew close escort for the ground-attack aircraft. Since the latter were mainly employed at low altitude, the escort fighters also had to fly at low altitude. Even though this was an advantage for the Soviet fighters insofar as their planes performed best at low altitudes, this tactic also led to heavy losses because German fighters preferred to fly at altitudes of 4,000-6,000 metres. Spotting Soviet aircraft, they would attack in a dive, approaching the enemy at high speed and, once they were at the same level, they would give a short burst of fire and pull right back up to commence another attack or disengage. Of the 200 downed enemy aircraft the fighter pilots of the 3rd and

27 Arseni W. Woroshejkin, *Jagdflieger*, vol. 2 (East Berlin, 3rd edn, 1985), pp. 113-4.

the 52nd *Jagdgeschwader* reported on 5 July 1943, three-quarters had been shot down at altitudes lower than 2,000 metres. It took the Soviet pilots some time until they changed their tactics, but then they began distributing their escort forces at different altitudes, with individual groups of fighters flying high-altitude escort to ward off German fighters attacking from above.

However, there were other crucial reasons for the heavy Soviet losses which could not be remedied so easily. In order to make up for the high numbers of casualties the Soviet Air Forces had suffered since the beginning of the war, many inexperienced and poorly trained pilots were sent into combat. In addition, the Red Army lacked experienced officers at medium command level – partly a result of Stalin's purges in the 1930s. Finally, Soviet commanders were used to receiving detailed instructions, which left little room for improvisation. This 'leading by order' was in contrast to the German 'leading by mission', a concept which offered the commanders at the lower command level much more accountability and opportunity for independent action – in fact, demanded it from them, as this often made the difference between success and failure. The Battle of Kursk provides several impressive examples of this, especially in the sector of Model's Ninth Army.

The Attack of the Ninth Army on Kursk

At 0330 German summertime, the attack of Model's Ninth Army was led by the XXIII Army Corps. The corps was tasked with capturing Maloarkhangel'sk and protecting the eastern flank of the Ninth Army in its attack on Kursk. Maloarkhangel'sk was a particularly heavily fortified element of the defence front of the 13th Army under the command of Lieutenant-General Nikolay Pavlovich Pukhov and a cornerstone of this section of defences. Three divisions of the 15th Rifle Corps were assembled for the defence there; the density of Soviet artillery was exceptionally high in that sector, with 68 guns and mortars per kilometre of front on average. Only at Ponyri had Pukhov concentrated even more artillery – approximately 86 guns and mortars per front kilometre.

Ninth Army Headquarters was fully aware from the start that the enemy would defend Maloarkhangel'sk to the last man, so in addition to the 216th Infantry Division it also chose the powerful 78th Assault Division to carry out the attack. Unlike the infantry divisions the 78th Assault Division contained a tank destroyer battalion with 26 *Marder* self-propelled guns. It also had the 189th Assault Gun Battalion, equipped with 31 assault guns, permanently attached to it. Another assault gun battalion, the 185th, supported the attack of the 216th Infantry Division. But the 216th Infantry Division and the 185th Assault Gun Battalion turned out to be the Achilles' heels of the XXIII Army Corps. While the attack of the 78th Assault Division proceeded well initially, the 216th Infantry Division was caught in a Soviet barrage shortly after the attack was launched. The assault guns of the 185th Battalion, which should have supported the attack, suffered losses from artillery fire and mines. At 0750, the 533rd

Grenadier Regiment reported that six of ten assigned assault guns had already been put out of action and that at the moment only one assault gun was supporting the unit – the rest had gone back to resupply with ammunition. Four hours later, the attack was still stalled. The 216th Infantry Division informed the XXIII Army Corps that for the moment only two assault guns were available, whereas the others were 'not to be found.'[28] Without this support, the commander of the 533rd Grenadier Regiment, Colonel Kurt Gruner, refused to renew the attack. According to the war diary of the XXIII Army Corps, 'the regimental commander seems to be a bundle of nerves.'[29] This was hardly surprising. By noon, Gruner's regiment had already lost more than half of its frontline soldiers.

In the evening, *General der Infanterie* Johannes Frießner, the Commanding General of the XXIII Army Corps, informed Model of his decision to withdraw the 216th Infantry Division to its start position. Model agreed and gave the instruction that the 216th Infantry Division should not be deployed for any attacks the following day, even if a good opportunity arose. As the 383rd Infantry Division's attack against the sector of the Soviet 16th Rifle Division north of Maloarkhangel'sk had failed with heavy casualties, too, the 78th Assault Division was to continue the advance on its own.

There can be no doubt that the XXIII Army Corps failed because of the fierce resistance, the superior Soviet artillery and the deep minefields. However, it should also be mentioned that shortcomings in German leadership played a role as well. On the evening of 5 July, General Frießner learned that the commander of the 216th Infantry Division attributed 'the considerable difficulties of this day of the attack to deficient officers and non-commissioned officers… who were unable to assert themselves.'[30]

Similar criticism can be found in the reports concerning the attack of the XXXXI Panzer Corps, which advanced west of the XXIII Army Corps towards Ponyri. This village consisted of three elements. The main settlement with the train station was located next to the railway line Orël–Kursk. Northwest of it, in the Second Army defence line, was Ponyri 1, a few kilometres south, behind the Third Army defence line, Ponyri 2. The defenders had reinforced the terrain in front of the fortified settlements with numerous trenches, obstacles, anti-tank strongpoints and mines. Instead of the usual anti-tank mines, Soviet engineers had laid mines linked with large-calibre artillery shells and aircraft bombs to inflict heavy damage on the attacking German tanks. Soon after the beginning of the attack, the commander of the 2nd Battery of the 244th Assault Gun Battalion, First Lieutenant Hans-Dietrich Rade, had the bad luck to hit such a booby trap with his assault gun. The war diary of the 244th Assault

28 BA-MA, RH 24-23/123, Kriegstagebuch Nr. 15, XXIII. Armeekorps, Abteilung Ia, 22.3.-22.7.1943, fol. 163.
29 BA-MA, RH 24-23/123, Kriegstagebuch Nr. 15, XXIII. Armeekorps, Abteilung Ia, 22.3.-22.7.1943, fol. 163.
30 BA-MA, RH 24-23/132, Anlagen zum Kriegstagebuch Nr. 15, XXIII. Armeekorps, Abteilung Ia, Zeit: 22.3.-20.8.1943, Gefechts- und Erfahrungsberichte, Anlage 44, no pagination.

Gun Battalion described the incident as follows: 'Gun [of] First Lieutenant Rade [is a] total loss. The hull was ripped open, the turret blown away[31]. First Lieutenant Rade [was] wounded, driver Sergeant [Paul] Rütze [is] dead, the rest of the crew was wounded.'[32] Rade himself recounted: 'I banged my head against the telescope, had a damaged eye and a concussion. I was in hospital until August. They later completely cannibalized the assault gun.'[33]

The 244th Assault Gun Battalion supported the attack of the 292nd Infantry Division. On the westernmost side, the 101st Panzergrenadier Regiment was advancing under the command of Lieutenant-Colonel Paul Fleischauer. It was actually part of the 18th Panzer Division, but had been assigned to the 292nd Infantry Division for the attack. After making good progress at first, the regiment was met with heavy resistance from the Soviet 676th Rifle Regiment at Ozerki. Fleischauer's men were pinned down by Soviet mortar fire and suffered heavy casualties because the commanding officer had failed to disperse his units to minimize losses. The close formation was not Fleischauer's only mistake. *General der Panzertruppe* Josef Harpe, the commander of the XXXXI Panzer Corps, also criticized him for 'a total failure of reconnaissance', and said: 'When a regiment has not done anything for hours to assess the situation on its flanks, as is crucial for operations, or when a strong enemy formation can escape unnoticed from an all but encircled large forest area, then the unit commander in question must be held liable as such negligence has to be paid in blood.'[34] On the morning of 7 July, the order was given that Lieutenant-Colonel Fleischauer should be relieved of his command and transferred to the *Führerreserve* (Leaders Reserve) of the Ninth Army. The 'nearly surrounded enemy formation' Fleischauer's regiment had let escape was the Soviet 676th Rifle Regiment. In the course of 5 July it had indeed been temporarily cut off, but in the evening it managed to break out and reach the new defence line of the 15th Rifle Division.

The failure of the 101st Panzergrenadier Regiment at Ozerki also affected the rest of the attack sector of the 292nd Infantry Division because, in the afternoon, the 508th Grenadier Regiment, which had initially made good progress, had to break off the attack southeastwards. Instead, it had to turn southwest to lend support to the 101st Panzergrenadier Regiment south of Ozerki. This presented a good opportunity to cut off the Soviet 676th Rifle Regiment's route of withdrawal. However,

31 According to the German original, 'der Turm flog weg.' This statement is misleading as assault guns obviously did not have turrets. Photos of the badly damaged vehicle show that the superstructure's roof including the commander's cupola had been blown off. See Christian Bauermeister and Jason Mark (eds.), *Iron Cross Brigade: The Story of Werner Gösel and Sturmgeschütz-Abteilung 244* (Sydney, 2016), p. 233.

32 Garnisongeschichte Jüterbog, Kriegstagebuch Nr. 1 der Sturmgeschütz-Abteilung 244, 27.3.-31.12.1943 [no signature], p. 7.

33 Interview with Hans-Dietrich Rade, 16 November 2011.

34 BA-MA, RH 27-18/140, 18. Panzerdivision, Ia, Anlageband zum Kriegstagebuch 'Zitadelle', Russland, 5.7.-12.7.1943, Anlage 54, no pagination.

again things turned out differently. The attack should have begun at 1500, but was delayed by two hours because the 244th Assault Gun Battalion first had to refuel and replenish ammunition. The Soviet troops used this delay to withdraw to the south. It is quite revealing that the war diary of the 244th Assault Gun Battalion makes no mention of the delay – on the contrary, it claims that heavy losses were inflicted on the Red Army troops withdrawing from the area south of Ozerki. This is an excellent example of the whitewashing often found in contemporary sources when it comes to covering up mistakes and negligence. Even though the German war diaries are generally reliable, it must not be forgotten that their explicit purpose was to serve as an 'indispensable foundation for historiography'[35] – and what commander wanted to go down in history as a failure?

Of all the divisions of the Ninth Army that began the attack as early as 0330, it was the 86th Infantry Division which made the most progress. It advanced southwards along the Orël–Kursk railway line and was supported by the 656th Heavy Tank Destroyer Regiment, which consisted of two battalions of *Ferdinand* tank destroyers and one battalion of assault tanks. In addition, the division was assigned the 177th Assault Gun Battalion. For decades, it has been claimed in literature that the attack of the XXXXI Panzer Corps had been hampered because the *Ferdinands* did not accomplish enough. Above all the *Ferdinand* was criticized because it had no machine gun for close defence and was thus particularly vulnerable to attacks from Soviet infantry. According to Soviet propaganda, which still finds its way into accounts of the Battle of Kursk, many *Ferdinands* were destroyed by Soviet infantrymen using Molotov cocktails. However, records from members of the 656th Heavy Tank Destroyer Regiment paint a very different picture. As an example, the after-action report of Captain Rolf Henning, commander of the 654th Heavy Tank Destroyer Battalion, states: 'The initial apprehension that the *Ferdinand* was very vulnerable to enemy infantry was, in reality, baseless. The bang of the detonation when firing and the *Ferdinand*'s huge impact on morale ensured that during combat no enemy infantryman got close to the *Ferdinand*.'[36] This experience was shared by the members of the 653rd Heavy Tank Destroyer Battalion. Karl Neunert, who at that time was a Sergeant and gunner in a *Ferdinand*, later remembered: 'I never witnessed any enemy soldier coming near our gun. Besides, the following infantry knew they had to protect us from such attacks.'[37] These statements are confirmed by Soviet records. On 15 July 1943, a Red Army commission scrutinized the *Ferdinand* tank destroyers left behind by the Germans on the battlefield at Ponyri. It concluded that some of them had indeed been set afire

35 Oberkommando des Heeres, Kriegswissenschaftliche Abteilung des Generalstabs des Heeres, Bestimmungen über die Führung von Kriegstagebüchern und Tätigkeitsberichten, Berlin, 23 April 1940, with one example at BA-MA, RH 21-4/104, Kriegstagebuch des Oberkommandos der 4. Panzerarmee, Ia, 25.3-31.7.1943, fol. 4.

36 Karlheinz Münch, *Einsatzgeschichte der schweren Panzerjäger-Abteilung 654 1943–1945, ehemalige Panzerjäger-Abteilung 654 1940–1943* (Schwetzingen, 2002), p. 63.

37 Letter from Karl Neunert to the author, 11 November 2003.

with Molotov cocktails – however, not by Soviet soldiers but by their own crews after their vehicle had been put out of action either by mines or enemy fire or because it had bogged down and could not be recovered.[38] In addition, the recollections of various former members of the 656th Heavy Tank Destroyer Regiment as well as contemporary war diaries and after-action reports show that the *Ferdinand* proved itself in battle and was well liked by the troops. On the Soviet side it spread terror, as a report of the XXXXI Panzer Corps relates: '[The] enemy in some places retreats headlong because of their fear of [the] *Ferdinand*.'[39]

The 653rd Heavy Tank Destroyer Battalion attacked east of the Orël–Kursk railway line. For the duration of the attack, it was assigned the 314th Remote Control Panzer Company equipped with Borgward B IV demolition carriers. On the morning of 5 July, the company successfully cleared three lanes in the minefield in front of the Soviet main defence line with their demolition carriers. Since the minefield was so deep, the remote control company had to use up 12 of its 36 carriers to do so. However, due to heavy Soviet artillery fire, their engineers could not mark out the minefield lanes, so the *Ferdinand* crews could not identify the cleared area and several tank destroyers hit mines.

West of the Orël–Kursk railway, the 654th Heavy Tank Destroyer Battalion led the attack. The battalion was supported by the 313th Remote Control Panzer Company, which also used B IV demolition carriers. Yet the company was desperately unfortunate. In the assembly area a B IV was hit by Soviet artillery, its detonation blowing up two more demolition carriers. In addition, when moving up for the attack, a platoon of the company ended up in a minefield, in which four B IV were destroyed and nearly a third of the *Ferdinands* put out of action. Crews who left their vehicles to repair the broken tracks were killed by heavy Soviet artillery fire. Those *Ferdinands* that made it through the minefields unscathed and carried the attack forward drew concentrated enemy artillery fire. This not only prevented the engineers from clearing the next minefields but it also made it impossible for the infantrymen of the 86th Infantry Division to follow the *Ferdinands*. To make things worse for the Germans, the soldiers of the Soviet 81st Rifle Division had by now overcome the fear the first appearance of the *Ferdinand* assault guns had created. In the evening, the XXXXI Panzer Corps reported to the Ninth Army Headquarters: '[The] enemy put up stiff infantry resistance and defended himself until the last.'[40]

38 Michail N. Svirin, *Das Schwere Sturmgeschütz Ferdinand* (Moscow, 2002), pp. 22, 25, 46. Both the Red Army and the Wehrmacht used Molotov cocktails during the Battle of Kursk. According to the minutes of a meeting at Ninth Army Headquarters on 9 June 1943, 20,480 incendiary bottles had by then been delivered to Ninth Army's engineer forces. BA-MA, RH 20-9/138, no pagination.

39 BA-MA, RH 24-41/84, Unterlagen zum Tätigkeitsbericht des Generalkommandos XXXXI. Panzerkorps Ic für die Zeit vom 24.3.-18.7.1943, no pagination.

40 BA-MA, RH 24-41/84, Unterlagen zum Tätigkeitsbericht des Generalkommandos XXXXI. Panzerkorps Ic für die Zeit vom 24.3.-18.7.1943, no pagination.

In reality, it was not the XXXXI Panzer Corps which made the main effort of Model's Ninth Army, as the Soviet leadership believed, but the XXXXVII Panzer Corps, which began its advance at 0630 and first came upon the Soviet 47th Rifle Regiment. This regiment had taken heavy casualties from enemy preparatory artillery fire as well as air strikes in the morning of 5 July. Two thirds of its anti-tank guns were knocked out and the telephone lines to the headquarters of the 15th Rifle Division had been cut. As a result, the men of the 6th Infantry Division encountered only minimal initial resistance. The first penetration of the Soviet positions was made by infantry only. At 0800, the 6th Infantry Division used its crowbar, namely two companies of the 505th Heavy Panzer Battalion with 31 *Tigers*, which in turn were supported by the 312th Remote Control Panzer Company with B IV demolition carriers. Unlike the two remote control panzer companies attached to the 656th Heavy Tank Destroyer Regiment, which were primarily employed to breach lanes into the minefields, the 312th Company also conducted combat reconnaissance in advance of the *Tigers*. This tactic proved to be effective. As soon as a Soviet anti-tank or gun emplacement or a bunker was spotted, a demolition carrier was set to destroy it. In one case, a Soviet tank tried to knock out a B IV by ramming it. The B IV's charge was detonated and the Soviet tank was destroyed by the tremendous explosion. The carriers were also used to horrific effect against Soviet infantry. According to a report: '1 B IV reached a Russian position, was pelted with incendiary bottles and because of this blew up. Its explosion had a devastating effect on the enemy position.'[41] However, in the attack sector of the 505th Heavy Panzer Battalion the minefield lanes had not been sufficiently marked out by the engineers either, so numerous *Tigers* hit mines; and there were not enough spare parts to repair all damaged vehicles. Still, the attack proceeded well, with the *Tigers* being the decisive battering ram of the XXXXVII Panzer Corps on 5 July.

At the same time west of the 505th Heavy Panzer Battalion, the 20th Panzer Division advanced southwards. It hit the boundary between the Soviet 28th Rifle Corps, which was attached to Lieutenant-General Galanin's 70th Army, and the 29th Rifle Corps, subordinate to Lieutenant-General Pukhov's 13th Army. Such boundaries were often inherent trouble spots, because no effective and coherent tactical command and control was possible when the enemy attacked two formations belonging to different armies. Already in the morning, the 20th Panzer Division succeeded in opening up the defensive front of the Soviet 15th Rifle Division. At 1030 German summertime, the division took Podolyan, thus reaching its day's objective. *General der Panzertruppe* Joachim Lemelsen, the Commanding General of the XXXXVII Panzer Corps, had the armoured formations continue their advance. The 20th Panzer Division thrust further southwards, capturing Bobrik by 1500, whilst

41 BA-MA, RH 19 II/167, Kommandeur Panzerabteilung (Funklenk) 301, Denkschrift über die weitere Verwendung der FKL-Waffe unter Auswertung der Erfahrungen des Einsatzes vom 5.-8.7.43 bei Unternehmen 'Zitadelle', fol. 222-9, quote, fol. 223.

the 505th Heavy Panzer Battalion advanced from Podolyan towards the southeast and reached the settlement of Step. By now, however, Model's operational concept came into conflict with his panzer formations pushing forward. Model was anticipating unexpected Soviet artillery time-on-target fire and air strikes, in addition to counterattacks by Soviet armoured formations. This is why he wanted to ensure sufficient flank protection and defensive measures instead of having the panzer units push too far ahead. As a matter of fact, in the night of 4-5 July 1943, only a few hours before the attack, he had issued the following order: '1) lead with tight reins, 2) always set up the heavy guns and artillery protection from all batteries by sector, 3) heavy guns should not follow too closely, 4) exploit [former] enemy positions and field fortifications by own infantry.'[42] Model had not reckoned with such a speedy advance by the 20th Panzer Division and the 505th Heavy Panzer Battalion. After the war, Lieutenant-General Horst Großmann, commander of the 6th Infantry Division, wrote that by the end of the first day of the attack, the divisions of the XXXXVII Panzer Corps had already reached the line they were supposed to be reaching only two days after the beginning of the operation. 'If the panzer divisions had kept rolling, we might have reached the objective Kursk – the enemy was completely taken by surprise and still weak. Valuable time was lost, which the enemy used to move his reserves forward.'[43] At first glance, this statement might seem like one of the idealized misrepresentations of 'missed chances' typical for the post-war period, but it can be corroborated by contemporary records such as the combat report of the I Battalion of the 74th Panzer Artillery Regiment. The battalion directly supported the attack of the 505th Heavy Panzer Battalion with self-propelled artillery and, together with the *Tigers* and the assault guns of the 245th and the 904th Battalion, it pushed east of Podolyan towards Step. In the area south and southeast of Saborovka, Soviet formations were sighted around noon, among them 25-30 tanks, several lorries with infantry and four multiple rocket launchers. Apparently, these were the units Lieutenant-General Pukhov had deployed from the reserve to the forward area of the 15th Rifle Division to fill the gap in the frontline at Bobrik, namely the 237th Tank Regiment, a self-propelled artillery regiment and an artillery brigade. The Germans began shelling the Soviet assembly area, reported its destruction and then prepared to follow up the enemy. Yet, as a report of the 74th Panzer Artillery Regiment remarked succinctly: 'Nothing is following from the rear.'[44] Whether this comment was referring to the supply of ammunition and petrol, or meant that the infantry of the 6th Infantry Division had failed to catch up, remains unclear. Major Bernhard Sauvant, commander of the 505th

42 NARA, T315/220/273, Kriegstagebuch der 4. Panzerdivision, Führungsabteilung, vom 1.7.-31.7.1943, Anlage C, vol. 1, Operationsakten.

43 Horst Großmann, *Geschichte der rheinisch-westfälischen 6. Infanterie-Division 1939-1945* (Bad Nauheim, 1958), p. 164.

44 Walter Heinlein, *Vom Fahnenjunker zum Abteilungsführer*, ed. Ingo Möbius (Chemnitz, 2nd edn, 2007), p. 111.

Heavy Panzer Battalion, consequently decided to withdraw his exposed battalion to the area southeast of Podolyan.

However, this was not the last chance for the Germans to cross the Svapa River southwards on 5 July, because in the evening, the 20th Panzer Division managed to capture the settlement of Saborovka and establish a bridgehead south of the Svapa. Major-General Mortimer von Kessel, commander of the 20th Panzer Division, tried to convince Lemelsen that the division had found an enemy 'weak spot' and should seize the opportunity this presented. Kessel believed his division could push through as far as the Soviet positions on the dominating ridge between Tëploe and Olkhovatka. Lemelsen refused because the 20th Panzer Division already had a long open flank in the west, as the attack of the XXXXVI Panzer Corps, which was responsible for the flank protection of the XXXXVII Panzer Corps, had come to a halt north of Gnilets. Since Lemelsen could not spare any units for flank protection, the 20th Panzer Division had to handle the protection of its western flank on its own and thus refrain from advancing further southwards.

It is difficult to assess whether a great opportunity was squandered in the sector of the XXXXVII Panzer Corps on 5 July, and to what extent this had an effect on the ensuing battles. On the one hand, it should not be forgotten that Model – correctly, in fact – expected strong Soviet counterattacks to be launched the following day, which would best be met from secure positions. On the other hand, Großmann failed to recognize in his assessment that the German tanks never even had the option simply to 'roll on through' to Kursk, as the operational and tactical situation at the time would not have allowed it. In the evening of 5 July, the XXXXVII Panzer Corps had not broken through all Soviet defensive positions, nor had it been forced to fight the Soviet operational reserves. On its own, the 20th Panzer Division probably would not have succeeded in taking the heavily fortified heights between Tëploe and Olkhovatka and defending them against Soviet counterattacks. The only possibility to turn the tactical success of the 20th Panzer Division into a larger-scale opportunity would have been the immediate deployment of those panzer divisions held in reserve, intended for the second wave; but Model had not planned to deploy them on the first day of the attack. When he realized in the afternoon of 5 July how surprisingly well the attack of the XXXXVII Panzer Corps had proceeded, he ordered the 2nd and 9th Panzer Division to be brought forward at once. However, it was too late for their employment on that day. Model hoped to achieve a breakthrough of the Soviet positions the following day.

In the meantime, General Rokossovskiy, commander of the Central Front, decided to mount a counteroffensive against the front of the Ninth Army on 6 July – just as Model had expected. Its objective was to throw the German attack forces back to their initial positions of 5 July. The main thrust was to be undertaken by the Soviet 2nd Tank Army commanded by Lieutenant-General Aleksey Grigor'evich Rodin, with the 3rd and 16th Tank Corps as well as the 11th Guards Tank Brigade. In addition, the 19th Tank Corps was brought up from the front reserves. Pukhov's 13th Army was to join the counterattack as well, along with the 17th Guards Rifle Corps, the 4th Breakthrough Artillery Corps and parts of the 15th and the 29th Rifle Corps.

But these units were not ready to conduct an operational counterattack so soon. So, on the Soviet side, too, many things did not go according to plan. Neither the 3rd Tank Corps nor the 11th Guards Tank Brigade, or the 19th Tank Corps, were able to complete their assembly for the attack. Of the 650 tanks and self-propelled guns intended for the assault, only 220 tanks and self-propelled guns of the 16th Tank Corps, commanded by Major-General Vasiliy Efimovich Grigor'ev, were actually available on the morning of 6 July.

As would happen repeatedly during the Battle of Kursk, the Red Army did not concentrate its operational counterattacks on one of the flanks of the German attack wedge. Instead, the 16th Tank Corps made a frontal attack against the formations of the German main attack corps, with the 107th Tank Brigade commanded by Lieutenant-Colonel Nikolay Matveevich Telyakov taking the lead. Most Soviet tank brigades had an authorized strength of 53 tanks, of which 32 were medium T-34 and 21 were light T-70 or T-60 machines. Telyakov's brigade was slightly below its authorized strength, having 51 operational tanks available on the morning of 6 July 1943. At Step, these pushed into the combat sector of the German 6th Infantry Division, where they encountered the *Tigers* of the 505th Heavy Panzer Battalion and the self-propelled guns of the 245th Assault Gun Battalion. Within a short time, Telyakov's brigade was all but annihilated, losing 47 of its tanks, 41 of which were totally destroyed.

Further west, the two other armoured formations of the Soviet 16th Tank Corps, the 109th and the 164th Tank Brigade, attacked the German 20th and 2nd Panzer Division, which by now had been brought up. They, too, were repulsed, and lost 42 tanks. On the German side, it was the 20th Panzer Division which had to bear the brunt of the fighting. After it had been fending off the Soviet 16th Tank Corps and 17th Guards Rifle Corps throughout the day, it was hit by the attack of the Soviet 19th Tank Corps in the evening. The 19th Tank Corps, led by Major-General Ivan Dmitrievich Vasil'ev, was supposed to attack together with the 16th Tank Corps in the morning. However, since it had not finished preparations for the attack in time, it began its thrust towards Podolyan only during the evening of 6 July. Subordinate to Vasil'ev's corps were the 79th, the 101st and the 202nd Tank Brigade with 187 tanks in total. Advancing from the area of Saborovka, the 79th and the 101st Tank Brigade came up against the 20th Panzer Division from the south. This German division managed to fend off the Soviet attacks fairly quickly. The tanks of the 202nd Tank Brigade, by contrast, succeeded in breaking through the western flank of the division and pushing as far as Bobrik. After a fierce fight with some German tanks, assault guns and *Marder* tank destroyers, the Soviet tanks eventually had to withdraw – the attack of the 19th Tank Corps had therefore failed as well. The corps had to write off 52 tanks as total losses on that day. The 202nd Tank Brigade's thrust on Bobrik, however, highlights the danger the Soviet operational counterattack might have presented if it had been concentrated against the flanks of the German spearhead. In fact, the Red Army suffered many more bitter defeats until it learned to direct counterattacks against the enemy's weak points rather than send its soldiers to the slaughter in fruitless frontal attacks. After the defeat of 6 July, General Rokossovskiy gave the order to dig in the tanks of the 16th and the 19th Tank Corps and, for the time being, employ them defensively to bring the attack forces of the Ninth Army to a halt. In the case of counterattacks, the Soviet tank soldiers were only to engage German light tanks.

On 6 July 1943, the Soviet forces in the northern sector of the Kursk salient suffered a major defeat not only on the ground but in the air as well. On that day, Lieutenant-General Rudenko, the commander of the Russian 16th Air Army, planned to begin the counterattack of the Soviet ground forces with a massive air strike against the XXXXVII Panzer Corps. However, a few Soviet fighters appeared over the battlefield too soon, thereby alerting the fighters of the German 51st *Jagdgeschwader*, which arrived over the combat zone at exactly the same time as Rudenko's main attack forces, inflicting considerable losses on the Soviet attackers. A violent air battle raged all day, particularly in the sector of the XXXXVII Panzer Corps. The 16th Air Army lost 91 aircraft and, after two days of heavy fighting, its fighter formations had suffered so badly that Rudenko had to ask the Soviet high command to bring up the 234th Fighter Aviation Division of the 15th Air Army as reinforcements from the Bryansk Front.

Fierce air battles also took place in the southern sector of the Kursk salient on 6 July, during which the Soviet 2nd and the 17th Air Armies lost 80 planes. In total, including the losses of the 16th Air Army, the number of lost aircraft amounted to 171. In addition, this number should include the losses suffered by the 15th Air Army, which flew about 400 sorties on 6 July; unfortunately, no casualty reports are available for this army. All in all, the Red Army Air Forces probably lost no less than 180 aircraft in the Kursk salient on 6 July 1943. In turn, the Soviet pilots reported 217 German aircraft shot down on 6 July alone. This number was a gross exaggeration. In reality, the 1st Air Division lost 10 aeroplanes in the northern sector of the Kursk salient, the VIII Air Corps lost 12, most of which were in fact shot down by anti-aircraft fire.

Even though the Luftwaffe held the upper hand in the following days, the attack of Model's Ninth Army in the northern sector of Kursk hardly made any progress. The reason for this deadlock was primarily the massive concentration of artillery Rokossovskiy had at his disposal to counter the German attack. An after-action report from the 656th Heavy Tank Destroyer Regiment, which advanced on Ponyri together with the 86th and the 292nd Infantry Division, stated that the attack of its infantry was broken up by heavy Soviet artillery fire. The report claimed that of the 19 *Ferdinands* which had to be written off as complete losses during the first days of the attack, most had been destroyed by direct artillery hits on the ventilations grilles above the engine compartment. This is in fact not correct, as Soviet records demonstrate. When examining the damaged or destroyed *Ferdinand* tanks left on the battlefield of Ponyri, the Soviets discovered that only one *Ferdinand* had been destroyed by a direct hit from a heavy artillery shell – which had penetrated the roof of the fighting compartment, not the engine compartment. Another *Ferdinand* had been wrecked by a direct hit by a bomb from a Soviet combat aircraft. Most of the other tank destroyers had hit mines or booby traps prepared by Soviet engineers, using captured German artillery shells and aerial bombs.

Despite the deep minefields, the soundly constructed positions and the murderous Soviet artillery fire, the 86th Infantry Division succeeded in breaking through the second Soviet defence line north of Ponyri on 6 July. On the morning of 7 July, the 292nd Infantry Division, with the support of the 654th Heavy Tank Destroyer Battalion and the 244th Assault Gun Battalion, began its attack on Ponyri. This settlement had been turned into a veritable fortress by the Soviet 307th Rifle Division under the command of Major-General Mikhail Aleksandrovich Enshin. In addition, Enshin's division was provided with more support than any other division in the Second World War: artillery formations with 380 guns in total, anti-tank and engineer units as well as the tanks and self-propelled guns of the 27th Guards Tank Regiment, the 103rd and 129th Tank Brigade and of the 1442nd Self-Propelled Artillery Regiment. Still, on the morning of 7 July, the German 292nd Infantry Division managed to enter the northern area of Ponyri and, by the evening, advance to the centre of the village. Enshin's 307th Rifle Division had to withdraw to the southern part of Ponyri, where rear positions had been prepared earlier. Here, the attack of the XXXXI Panzer Corps came to a definite standstill. Even though the battle in the southern part of Ponyri still continued for a few days, neither side had any resounding successes.

However, Model was not yet prepared to give up Operation Citadel. On the one hand, he still had reserves at his disposal which he could throw into battle – on 7 July he decided to bring up the 4th Panzer Division in order to reinforce the attack of the XXXXVII Panzer Corps. The 12th Panzer Division, in turn, was to be deployed with the XXXXVI Panzer Corps to renew the corps' attack. In the case of the XXXXI Panzer Corps, Model planned to relieve the battle-weary 292nd Infantry Division with the 10th Panzergrenadier Division. On the other hand, he did not want to admit defeat because he did not consider the attack of the XXXXI Panzer Corps at Ponyri as important as the advance of the XXXXVII Panzer Corps. And it is true that the latter made good progress on 7 July. The 6th Infantry Division successfully broke through the second army defence belt in the sector of the Soviet 75th Guards Rifle Division and reached Hill 257.0 east of Kashara. The fierce resistance of the Soviet soldiers is described in the war diary of the 6th Infantry Division: 'Our own losses are high … In close combat every trench and every sap has to be taken.'[45]

The 9th Panzer Division, which advanced east of the 6th Infantry Division, even got as far as Hill 260.0, and so broke into the third Soviet defence belt – in spite of strong resistance by the Soviet 6th Guards Rifle Division. However, the 9th Panzer Division lacked the strength to break through the Soviet positions completely; by then, it had only 11 operational tanks left. The division's Quartermaster Department remarked: 'About two thirds of the tanks are – except for two total losses – temporarily

45 BA-MA, RH 26-6/47, Kriegstagebuch Nr. 7 der 6. Infanterie-Division vom 1.1.-30.9.1943, no pagination.

out of action. Most losses are caused by anti-tank rifles. The tank skirts [which have been] introduced proved very successful.'[46]

The strongest unit of the XXXXVII Panzer Corps, the 2nd Panzer Division, attacked with the 505th Heavy Panzer Battalion from west of Kashara towards the south. When the division began assembling in the morning of 7 July in completely open terrain and the commanders gathered for a last briefing, Soviet bombers attacked, dropping their bombs directly on the assembly area. Many soldiers were killed, including the commander of the 304th Panzergrenadier Regiment, Colonel Wilhelm von Goerne. The number of wounded was high, as the report on the deployment of the division's medical services illustrates: 'Great number of wounded (*schwerster Verwundetenanfall*). Heavy bombing raids.'[47] The attack had to be launched afresh. At Kashara, the Germans managed to break through the second Soviet defence line, pushing back the Soviet 70th Rifle Division and capturing the locality of Kashara. Here, however, the German tanks came up against numerous well-camouflaged anti-tank guns of the Soviet 3rd Anti-Tank Artillery Brigade; the tanks of the Soviet 16th Tank Corps were also dug in in this area. Even though the 2nd Panzer Division received strong support from *Stuka* dive bombers, it could not push through to the third Soviet defence line. 'In the course of the day, the enemy tenaciously held his defensive sector, using all available weapons', the division reported. 'Particularly strong and systematic is the artillery support and the anti-tank defence as well as occasional attacks by the [Soviet] Air Forces with bombers and ground-attack aircraft.'[48]

The Russian defenders inflicted serious casualties on the 2nd Panzer Division, but they also suffered heavy losses themselves. The 16th Tank Corps, which had lost 89 tanks in its failed frontal attack against the XXXXVII Panzer Corps, reported another 35 lost tanks on 7 July, even though by that time it had dug in its tanks for the defence. The 19th Tank Corps, which on 6 July had fought the 20th Panzer Division and lost 52 tanks, had to write off another 49 tanks as total losses the next day. The German 2nd Panzer Division, by contrast, had to write off only eight tanks as destroyed beyond repair during those two days of action, even though a large number of their tanks needed maintenance and repair due to battle damage, and the division's combat effectiveness had suffered considerably.

Since the start of the offensive, two of the 31 *Tigers* of the 505th Heavy Panzer Battalion had become complete losses, while 25 were under repair due to battle damage or technical defects. On 8 July, the battalion's newly activated 3rd Company arrived from Germany with 14 *Tigers*. In addition, the recently arrived 4th Panzer Division was available for the attack on the third Soviet army defence line on 8 July.

46 NARA, T315/543/996, Kriegstagebuch Nr. 5, 9. Panzerdivision, Abteilung Ib, 1.5.-31.10.1943.

47 NARA, T315/97/9, Tätigkeitsbericht der Abteilung IVb der 2. Panzerdivision für die Zeit vom 1.7.-30.9.1943, Einsatz der Sanitätsdienste.

48 NARA, T315/95/641, Tätigkeitsbericht der 2. Panzerdivision, Abteilung Ic, Einsatz Russland (Fortsetzung), 5.3.-20.9.1943.

This panzer division was one of the most powerful divisions of the Wehrmacht; with its help, Colonel-General Model hoped to force the breakthrough towards the south on 8 July.

On 8 July, the 4th Panzer Division was not employed *en masse* for the attack. The panzer battalions of the 2nd and the 4th Panzer Division as well as the 505th Heavy Panzer Battalion were grouped into a strong panzer battle group (*Kampfgruppe*) and subordinated to Panzer Brigade Staff Burmeister, named after its commander, Colonel Arnold Burmeister. The objective of the panzer brigade was the high ground position southwest of Olkhovatka, which dominated the terrain with its highest elevation, Hill 274.5. To its west, in the direction of Tëploe, the 4th Panzer Division launched the attack without its tanks but with the support of the 904th Assault Gun Battalion. Tëploe was defended by the Soviet 140th Rifle Division. In an intense battle, the Germans managed to push back the Soviet infantry and occupy Tëploe in the early afternoon. The 140th Rifle Division withdrew to the south, thereby leaving a gap in the Soviet frontline, which had to be plugged by the 70th Guards Rifle Division and the 175th Rifle Division. The 4th Panzer Division's attack nevertheless halted a few hundred metres south of Tëploe because the Soviet troops dominated the area with their artillery from the heights south and southeast of Tëploe. In addition to that, the 79th Tank Brigade of the Soviet 19th Tank Corps had occupied defensive positions on the ridge south of Tëploe. Their tanks, which were dug in up to the gun barrel, could not be combated from the foot of the ridge because they offered much too small a target for the German gunners. In the afternoon it started to rain, so the German Luftwaffe could no longer join the battle and bomb the Soviet positions.

Panzer Brigade Burmeister, thrusting towards Hill 274.5, did not fare any better. Apart from the fact that its tanks could not effectively engage the Soviet troops dug in on the ridge, the brigade was under constant fire from Soviet artillery and the dug-in tanks of the 16th Tank Corps – and in the open terrain, the German tanks were sitting ducks. Adding to these problems, errors in command and control were identified, which were criticized in the war diary of the Ninth Army Headquarters: 'Because the German panzer forces were just standing around for hours – undeniably the brigade commander's mistake! – they have regrettably suffered considerable losses, also of *Tigers*, from the high ground position firing from all barrels.'[49] When Brigade Burmeister disengaged from the enemy in the early evening, the Soviet 11th Guards Tank Brigade launched a counterattack, causing a panic among the soldiers of the 2nd Panzer Division, who were in the midst of withdrawing. To make things worse, the brigade's withdrawal opened up the eastern flank of the 4th Panzer Division. To avoid being out-flanked and cut off by Soviet tanks, the 33rd Panzergrenadier Regiment of the 4th Panzer Division was forced to give up the hard-won Tëploe on the morning of 9 July.

49 NARA, T312/317/7886152-4, Kriegstagebuch Nr. 8, Armee-Oberkommando 9, Führungsabteilung, 26.3.-18.8.1943.

The failure of 8 July angered Colonel-General Model; he not only blamed Colonel Burmeister and the commander of the 2nd Panzer Division, Lieutenant-General Vollrath Lübbe, but also the Headquarters of the XXXXVII Panzer Corps: without an advanced command post, Lemelsen and his staff had been taking uninformed decisions, in essence lacking an accurate picture of the situation. For a moment, Model considered relieving Lübbe and Burmeister of their command, but in the end he left Lübbe the command of his division. The Brigade Staff Burmeister, however, was re-designated 'Staff General von Esebeck', named after Lieutenant-General Hans-Karl von Esebeck.

After consultation with General Lemelsen, the Commanding General of the XXXXVII Panzer Corps, Model decided to give the exhausted troops a break on 9 July; the attack on the heights between Tëploe and Olkhovatka was not to be renewed until the following day. Nonetheless, Model no longer expected a quick success. On 9 July, a briefing was held at the headquarters of the XXXXVII Panzer Corps about the continuation of Operation Citadel; apart from Model, Field-Marshal von Kluge was also present. Model explained that it would take four to five days to break through the Soviet positions located on the high ground at Olkhovatka. He suggested that the attack be carried out by the XXXXVII Panzer Corps, with the 2nd, 4th, 9th and 20th Panzer Division as well as the 6th Infantry Division – not in the form of a 'panzer raid', however, but as alternating, partial attacks. Model figured that the offensive would proceed slowly even after conquering the ridge and breaking through the third Soviet army defence belt, so the final objective of Kursk would not be reached quickly. 'The battle has the novel character of a 'rolling battle of material attrition', it is a question of men, material and ammunition; without their constant and ample supply Operation Citadel cannot be brought to a close.'[50] This was nothing less than admitting that Operation Citadel as originally planned had failed. Field-Marshal von Kluge agreed, though he pointed out that it was necessary to continue the operation in order to destroy the Red Army's reserves, which were becoming stronger by the day. On 10 July, Kluge visited the headquarters of the XXXXVI Panzer Corps. When its commanding general Hans Zorn explained to him that the objective set for the attack could not be attained with the available forces, Kluge replied that 'the pessimism emerging in various places has to be rejected and opposed most vigorously as there really is no basis for it.' Kluge called the pessimists 'scaremongers' (*Miesmacher*) and stated that 'an immense battle of attrition is in progress, which will get even worse and in whose course our envisaged intensions will be fulfilled.'[51]

Why Model was not as optimistic as Kluge about the further course of the operation becomes clearer from an entry in the war diary of the Ninth Army Headquarters.

50 NARA, T312/317/7886158, Kriegstagebuch Nr. 8, Armee-Oberkommando 9, Führungsabteilung, 26.3.-18.8.1943.

51 BA-MA, RH 24-46/91, Generalkommando XXXXVI. Panzerkorps, Ia, Kriegstagebuch Nr. 7 vom 1.6.-15.8.1943, fol. 83-4.

On 9 July it reads that the Ninth Army would actually have to 'expect increasing enemy resistance. It remains a hard fact that so far the enemy has fought with fanatical determination. Intercepted radio messages again and again confirm this conclusion: 'Change of position [is] forbidden, hold out until death."[52] Besides, General Rokossovskiy, the commander of the Central Front, still had reserves at his disposal, among them Major-General Semën Il'ich Bogdanov's 9th Tank Corps with 168 tanks. The Red Army had also reinforced the front sector opposite the German XXXXVI and XXXXVII Panzer Corps with the 162nd Rifle Division, the 40th Tank Regiment and the 251st Tank Regiment.

On 10 July at 0700, General von Esebeck's panzer assault group launched its attack on the third Soviet army defence belt at Tëploe. *Stuka* formations supported the thrust, and the German artillery tried to obstruct the view of the Soviet defenders in the high ground position by firing smoke barrages. The 2nd, 4th and 20th Panzer Division as well as the 505th Heavy Panzer Battalion were to join the attack, whilst the 9th Panzer Division remained on the defensive that day. Yet again, delays and mishaps occurred from the very beginning. The 20th Panzer Division, which was tasked with covering the western flank, began the attack at 0800, one hour later than scheduled. The 2nd Panzer Division, attacking Hill 274.5 from Kashara, was soon stalled by heavy Soviet defensive fire. The 4th Panzer Division, which attacked in the centre, thus had to advance with two open flanks. Still, it succeeded in reaching Tëploe fairly quickly. At 1015, however, one of the German planes accidentally bombed the command post of the 4th Panzer Division, killing the commander of the 4th Panzer Reconnaissance Battalion, Captain Lothar Schmidt, and wounding the division's Operations Officer (Ia), Lieutenant-Colonel Hans Lutz. It would take several hours before his deputy, Captain Eike Middeldorf, arrived at the command post. In the meantime, another accident took place. Around noon, the commander of the 4th Panzer Division, Lieutenant-General Dietrich von Saucken's command tank crashed through a bridge spanning a ravine in the western area of Tëploe. The ravine was exposed to observation by Soviet troops – two officers of the 4th Panzer Division were killed in the attempt to rescue the divisional commander from his unfortunate predicament. Saucken could do nothing but stay put and hold out in his trapped tank. Hence, it was all but impossible for him to command his division, even if communication by radio was still possible. Due to the absence of both its commander and the Operations Officer, the 4th Panzer Division was temporarily leaderless – and at a critical moment, too. After extensive *Stuka* and artillery preparations, the *Tigers* of the 505th Heavy Panzer Battalion arrived on Hill 253.5 south of Tëploe. They took the Soviet tanks, dug in on the ridge, under heavy fire. Soon panic broke out among the Soviet infantry, who abandoned their positions and fled the heights. Luckily for the Soviets, the German infantry and the tanks of the 4th Panzer Division did not realize

52 NARA, T312/317/7886159, Kriegstagebuch Nr. 8, Armee-Oberkommando 9, Führungsabteilung, 26.3.-18.8.1943.

the opportunity this offered and did not follow up. Instead, the commander of the I Battalion of the 35th Panzer Regiment, Major Hans-Detloff von Cossel, first asked the division commander for permission to continue the attack – a blatant disregard of the principle of autonomous leadership demanded repeatedly by the Wehrmacht. In fact, Cossel in particular should have been familiar with this principle, as he had been awarded the Knight's Cross of the Iron Cross on 8 September 1941. This was the highest German decoration for bravery – and it was explicitly only awarded for achievements in battle if the said feat had been accomplished on the recipient's 'own initiative' (*aus eigenem Entschluss*). As on 10 July neither Cossel's tanks nor the panzergrenadiers of the 4th Panzer Division followed the *Tigers* of the 505th Heavy Panzer Battalion to Hill 253.5; as a result, the latter eventually had to withdraw. Consequently, the Soviet soldiers gained time, overcame their panic and returned to their former positions.

In the late afternoon, Lieutenant-General von Saucken launched a new attack on Hill 253.5 – and the men of the 33rd Panzergrenadier Regiment actually managed to take the ridge once more. Major von Cossel, however, failed again. A report of the II Battalion of the 33rd Panzergrenadier Regiment states:

> The tanks [of the I Battalion of the 35th Panzer Regiment] were supposed to roll on through to the height at once, as had been decided in the briefing. Shortly before the assault, the height is once more bombed by a formation of *Stukas*. The attack proceeds surprisingly well in the heavy, flanking enemy fire. Only on the crest does exceptionally fierce close combat ensue. The Russians have to be literally pulled out of every foxhole. Unfortunately, the tanks have stayed at the foot of the ridge and have not moved. During the mopping up of the hilltop, a Russian counterattack began, supported by tanks. The remainder of the rifle companies, who carried out this hard attack with admirable spirit in spite of the great physical and mental strains of the previous three days, are, when they realize that their own tanks are offering no support, no longer able to fend off the attack carried out by fresh Soviet troops. The height, which for three days was bitterly fought for, taking a bloody toll of countless lives, now has to be given up once again. It would never have been retaken by the Russians if just a few tanks had positioned themselves on the reverse slope of the hill, to at least morally support the utterly exhausted and depleted battalion against an enemy tank attack. But when smoke signal after smoke signal went out and no tank began to move and bring help, the battalion again had to withdraw to the village outskirts [of Tëploe], albeit with a bloody [sic!] heart.[53]

53 BA-MA, N 460/14, Nachlass Gerlach von Gaudecker, Tätigkeitsbericht des Panzergrenadier-Regiments 33 vom Juni 1941-März 1944, pp. 54-5.

It is hardly surprising that no mention is made of these accidents, mistakes and examples of negligence in the war diary of the 4th Panzer Division. Major von Cossel, who on that day failed twice in crucial situations, was killed in battle on 22 July 1943. A month later, he was posthumously awarded the Oak Leaves to the Knight's Cross 'for his actions during Operation Citadel.'[54] To the soldiers of the 33rd Panzergrenadier Regiment, this must have seemed like a slap in the face.

After the failure of 10 July, disillusionment spread at the Ninth Army Headquarters. The war diary reads: 'Despite organizing and regrouping the attack forces, despite bringing up all available artillery, despite the concentrated deployment of the air force, the main effort did not manage to reach its objectives today … The hard fact cannot be ignored that for the moment, the German main attack has come to a halt.'[55] When Model learned on 11 July that Hill 253.5 had been lost again in the evening of the previous day, he realized that further attacks of the XXXXVII Panzer Corps against the Soviet high ground position between Tëploe and Olkhovatka would be futile and that the Ninth Army would probably not succeed in breaking through to Kursk. Therefore only minor attacks with limited objectives were to be carried out; doing so would minimize their own losses while inflicting maximum casualties on the enemy. Model planned to launch the first assault with the XXXXVI Panzer Corps, which would be reinforced with those parts of the 12th Panzer Division which had not yet been deployed in the offensive, the 4th and the 20th Panzer Division, as well as the 36th Infantry Division which had just been brought up to the front. On 14 July it was to begin the attack in the direction of Nikol'skoe. But things turned out differently, as on 12 July the Red Army began its offensive against the Orël salient. Because of this, the Ninth Army had to discontinue all its attacks and withdraw to the initial positions of 5 July. The number of casualties it had suffered in one week of heavy combat was high: 3,869 soldiers had been killed, 17,510 wounded and 822 were missing – 22,201 casualties in total. According to official Soviet figures, the Red Army Central Front lost by contrast 33,897 men in total, 15,336 killed and missing, and 18,561 wounded. However, various Russian historians suspect that these numbers are far too low, estimating the losses of the Central Front during the defensive phase from 5-11 July 1943 at about 63,000 or even 92,600.[56]

How many tanks the Ninth Army lost in Operation Citadel is difficult to reconstruct because there are insufficient contemporary records available. On 17 July 1943, the Army High Command's liaison officer at the Ninth Army Headquarters reported

54 Neumann, *4. Panzerdivision*, vol. 2, p. 72.
55 NARA, T312/317/7886160, Kriegstagebuch Nr. 8, Armee-Oberkommando 9, Führungsabteilung, 26.3.-18.8.1943.
56 Lev N. Lopukhovsky and Boris Kavalerchik, *The Price of Victory: The Red Army's Casualties in the Great Patriotic War* (Barnsley, 2017), p. 63 (63,000); and, Boris V. Sokolov, *Tsena voiny: Lyudskie poteri Rossii/SSSR v XX–XXI vv.* (Moscow, 2017), p. 173 (92,600). Contradicting such high figures is Vladimir V. Litvinenko, *Lyudskie poteri na frontakh Velikoy Otechestvennoy: Krasnaya armiya protiv vermakhta* (Moscow, 2015), pp. 114-122.

that the Ninth Army had lost 87 tanks, assault guns, assault tanks and heavy *Ferdinand* tank destroyers during Operation Citadel.[57] However, this number is too low. What is missing are the light tanks and command tanks as well as the *Marder* tank destroyers and the self-propelled artillery pieces; furthermore, some tanks which later had to be written off as total losses are not included in this number, either. According to the report to the Army High Command, the 656th Heavy Tank Destroyer Regiment, for instance, lost 19 *Ferdinand* tank destroyers during Citadel. Yet after the Germans' withdrawal, Soviet troops found 21 destroyed or damaged *Ferdinands* on the battlefield of Ponyri. Apart from that, the 656th Heavy Tank Destroyer Regiment lost at least three Panzer III tanks, which had been assigned to the regiment for the duration of the attack on Kursk. These losses, too, were excluded from the Army High Command's record.

The 4th Panzer Division lost six tanks during Citadel according to the report sent to the Army High Command – but the available tank situation reports in the divisional records indicate 14 tanks completely destroyed. Similarly, the OKH report registered 11 tanks lost for the 18th Panzer Division, whereas the divisional records list 13. Three more tanks were so badly damaged that they had to be sent to Magdeburg for repair and refitting. Unfortunately, no records of the other panzer units of the Ninth Army have survived; the total of tanks lost during Operation Citadel can therefore only be guessed at rather than reconstructed – it probably amounts to about 120 tanks and self-propelled guns.

The losses of the Soviet Central Front, by contrast, are listed in a report by Colonel Dmitriy Ivanovich Zaev, the Deputy Chief of Staff of the Armoured and Mechanized Forces of the Red Army, drawn up on 19 July 1943: In the period of 5-15 July 1943, the Central Front lost 651 tanks (self-propelled guns not included) in total, 526 of which had to be written off as completely destroyed.[58] This number apparently only takes those tanks into account which were lost during the defensive phase from 5-11 July 1943; it is almost exactly the number that Russian historian Boris Vadimovich Sokolov calculated. Without knowing Zaev's report, Sokolov estimated that the Central Front lost a total of 530 tanks and 28 self-propelled guns during the defensive phase.[59]

The total number of Soviet aircraft lost cannot be determined, as long as no figures are available for the 15th Air Army and the local air defence of Kursk. From 5-11 July, the 16th Air Army, which had to bear the brunt of combat action on the Soviet side, had 439 fighters, ground-attack aircraft and bombers as total losses; 323 of these were shot down in aerial combat and 57 by anti-aircraft fire, 11 aircraft were destroyed in

57 BA-MA, RH 10/65, Pz-Lage 'M' Zitadelle, 7.7.-17.7., fol. 4.

58 Spravka o poteryakh tankovykh voysk frontov, poteryakh, nanesënnykh imi protivniku, i vyvody o deystviyakh tankovykh voysk protivnika v operatsiyakh s 5-go po 15-e iyulya 1943 goda, copy from the document collection ('Materialsammlung') of the ZMSBw.

59 Boris V. Sokolov, *Marshal K.K. Rokossovsky: The Red Army's Gentleman Commander* (Solihull, 2015), p. 263.

accidents and 48 were damaged so badly in battle that they could not be repaired. Added to this must be a number of shot down liaison and reconnaissance planes. Overall, the 16th Air Army probably lost about 450 aircraft, while the total number of Soviet aircraft lost in the northern sector of Kursk roughly amounts to 500. In the same period, the German 1st Air Division had to write off only 66 aircraft, which were either destroyed by enemy action, in accidents and due to technical defects or damaged so badly they were beyond repair. These numbers clearly illustrate how high the price was which the Red Army had to pay for its victory in the northern sector of Kursk. Even though many authors repeatedly – and sometimes snidely – point out that the German forces attacking in the north only managed to advance 10-15 kilometres, it cannot be ignored that they still managed to inflict many times more losses on the Russian troops than they themselves suffered, not to mention that they managed to reach the third Soviet defence line. That Model's Army gained only a little terrain was understandable due to the fact that the Soviet defensive belts were much closer together than in the southern sector.

The Assault of Army Detachment Kempf East of Belgorod

On 5 July 1943, five German Corps of Manstein's Army Group South launched the assault on Kursk from the area of Belgorod in the south. The main attack was carried out by the Fourth Panzer Army under the command of Colonel-General Hermann Hoth. It was attached the LII Army Corps led by *General der Infanterie* Eugen Ott, the XXXXVIII Panzer Corps led by *General der Panzertruppe* Otto von Knobelsdorff and the II SS Panzer Corps led by SS *Obergruppenführer* Paul Hausser. East of the Fourth Panzer Army, Army Detachment Kempf joined the attack with two corps: the III Panzer Corps commanded by *General der Panzertruppe* Hermann Breith and the Corps Raus under the command of *General der Panzertruppe* Erhard Raus. Breith's III Panzer Corps had orders to provide offensive cover for the Fourth Panzer Army's right flank towards the east, so that Hoth's units could fully concentrate on the advance northwards. Four divisions were assigned to the III Panzer Corps Headquarters. The 6th Panzer Division was to advance on the far left (west), next to the right flank of the II SS Panzer Corps. To its right, the 168th Infantry Division, the 19th Panzer Division and the 7th Panzer Division joined the assault. The task of protecting the right flank of the III Panzer Corps fell to Corps Raus, with the 106th and the 320th Infantry Division.

The plan of manoeuvre for Army Detachment Kempf had one serious tactical flaw: all six divisions first had to attack across the Donets at the beginning of the offensive. The river, however, was exposed to observation from the Soviet side of the front. This is why in order to maintain the element of surprise no bridges could be built on the day before the attack. Since it was essential for the army detachment to have several military bridges, their construction would begin in the night of 4-5 July. The tanks and self-propelled guns were scheduled to cross the finished bridges just in time for the beginning of the attack on 5 July at 0225 and support the infantry's advance on the eastern side of the Donets. As all three panzer divisions of the III Panzer Corps was assigned a company of the 503rd Heavy Panzer Battalion with 14 *Tigers* each, it was planned that at least two bridges would be built for each panzer division, which could carry the weight of tanks: one 60-tonne bridge for each *Tiger* company and a 24-tonne bridge for the light and medium tanks of each panzer battalion. The 7th Panzer Division was one of the few divisions which had two panzer battalions at its disposal for the attack on Kursk, namely I and II Battalion of the 25th Panzer Regiment. Thus, as many as three military bridges had to be built for this division: two 24-tonne bridges for the panzer battalions and a 60-tonne bridge for the *Tigers*. In fact, two 60-tonne bridges would have been needed, as the 3rd Company of 503rd Heavy Panzer Battalion assigned to the 7th Panzer Division was divided for the attack: two platoons and the company headquarters with 10 *Tigers* in total were to support the II Battalion of the 25th Panzer Regiment, whereas one platoon with four *Tigers* should lead the attack of the I Battalion. After reconnoitring the area, however, the platoon leader of these four *Tigers*, Lieutenant Richard von Rosen, reckoned his tanks could ford the Donets instead.

On the day of the attack, almost nothing went according to plan. The Mikhaylovka bridgehead, whence the 6th Panzer Division and the 168th Infantry Division were to carry out their assault northeastwards against the heavily fortified Staryy Gorod, was under heavy Soviet artillery fire from 0200. The nearly completed 60-tonne bridge for the *Tigers* of the 1st Company of the 503rd Heavy Panzer Battalion supporting the attack on Staryy Gorod was destroyed by a direct hit. The second 24-tonne bridge was supposed to be used by the assault guns of the 228th Assault Gun Battalion and later by the tanks of the 11th Panzer Regiment of the 6th Panzer Division to cross the Donets. But when the first assault gun was driving over the bridge, a pile broke and the bridge became impassable. Since the Soviet artillery fire on the bridge sites did not cease after the beginning of the attack, the bridges could not be repaired. The tanks of the 6th Panzer Division were, therefore, re-routed to the sector of the 19th Panzer Division further south. But this division, too, had bad luck with its bridges. Construction works for the 60-tonne bridge for the *Tigers* of the 2nd Company of the 503rd Heavy Panzer Battalion could not be concluded by the time the attack began; as Soviet artillery kept shelling the bridging site, work had to be temporarily suspended. The second bridge, with a payload of 24 tonnes, was designated for the light and medium tanks of the 27th Panzer Regiment of the 19th Panzer Division. However, one of the *Tiger* commanders, *Feldwebel* Willibald Krakow, apparently did not want to wait idly on the western side of the Donets River while the infantrymen of the 19th Panzer Division, armed only 'with hand grenades and submachine guns' had to struggle their way 'into the still completely intact defensive positions' of the Soviet 81st Guards Rifle Division, suffering heavy casualties.[60] So Krakow attempted

60 Adalbert Wasner, *Inf.- und Pz.-Gren.-Regiment 74: Erinnerungen an den Weg des Regiments durch Polen, Holland, Belgien, Frankreich und Russland 1939–1945* (Hanover, 1970), p. 161.

to cross the 24-tonne bridge with his *Tiger* – it collapsed under the tank's weight of 57 tonnes. It is no surprise that this mishap was not recorded in the war diaries. The tanks of the 27th Panzer Regiment of the 19th Panzer Division also now had to be re-routed, namely to the sector of the 7th Panzer Division.

At first, the infantrymen of the 7th Panzer Division did not have armoured support, either. Since the Donets was exposed to observation from the eastern side, and because the first Soviet defensive positions were set up right behind the river, bridge construction was only to commence once the infantry had established bridgeheads on the eastern bank of the Donets. It was planned, however, that at least the soldiers of the 7th Panzergrenadier Regiment would be supported by Lieutenant von Rosen's four *Tigers* from the very beginning of the attack. As soon as the infantry had crossed over the river in rubber dinghies, engineers blew up the eastern riverbank so that the *Tigers* could drive to the opposite river shore. The tanks did indeed succeed in crossing the Donets, but when the first *Tiger* reached the damaged riverbank, it became bogged down in the mud and had to be pulled back. Rosen's platoon thus had no other choice but to wait for the construction of the 60-tonne bridge – which would not be completed before 1115.

In the northern part of Solomino, by contrast, the engineers of the 674th Engineer Regiment managed to finish building the first 24-tonne bridge shortly after 0600. Advancing over it, the tanks of the 25th Panzer Regiment of the 7th Panzer Division were the first to cross the Donets River. Soon they were followed by the tanks of the 27th Panzer Regiment of the 19th Panzer Division, which used the same bridge to get across the river. At 0815, the engineers in the sector of the 19th Panzer Division completed the first 60-tonne bridge, whose construction had been interrupted by Soviet artillery fire the night before. This allowed the *Tigers* of the 1st and 2nd Company of the 503rd Heavy Panzer Battalion, and the tanks of the 11th Panzer Regiment of the 6th Panzer Division, finally to get across the Donets River. Still, the attack of the 6th and 19th Panzer Division did not make much progress. The 19th Panzer Division was held back by marshy terrain, mines and heavy Soviet mortar fire. Of the 14 *Tigers* of the 2nd Company of the 503rd Heavy Panzer Battalion, which supported the attack of the 19th Panzer Division, 13 were put out of action; nine of these hit mines; some *Tigers* were in fact knocked out by German mines which had not been cleared. The attack of the 6th Panzer Division on Staryy Gorod, on the other hand, came to a halt because of the determined resistance of the Soviet 81st Guards Rifle Division and heavily mined terrain, and neither the *Tigers* of the 1st Company of the 503rd Heavy Panzer Battalion nor the assault guns of the 228th Assault Gun Battalion were able to carry the 6th Panzer Division's attack forward. The war diary of the III Panzer Corps noted: 'On the whole corps front the enemy offers fierce resistance in deeply echeloned positions reinforced with wide minefields and fortified in exemplary fashion.'[61] At 1600,

61 BA-MA, RH 24-3/78, Kriegstagebuch des Stabes Generalkommando III. Panzerkorps, 1.7.-22.7. 1943, fol. 221.

Major-General Walther von Hünersdorff, commander of the 6th Panzer Division, reported that he had ordered the attack on Staryy Gorod to be broken off, arguing that the casualties which would be sustained in another frontal attack would not justify the success. A battle group of the 168th Infantry Division, which supported the attack of the 6th Panzer Division, had also gained only little ground and was thrown back to its initial start-line by a Soviet counterattack.

Bridge construction was delayed in the sector of Corps Raus as well. The corps, which attacked south of Solomino, could only begin working on the bridges once the infantry had established bridgeheads on the eastern bank of the Donets. The attacks of the 106th and 320th Infantry Division initially progressed well, even though they had no support from heavy weapons. The war diary of Corps Raus states: 'At 0225, as planned, the attack began on the entire width of the Donets. The moment took the foe by surprise, so the crossing was at first made without any major difficulties.'[62] The spearheads of the two divisions reached the railway embankment of the Belgorod–Kupyansk line after about an hour, but there resistance from the Soviet 72nd and 78th Guards Rifle Division stiffened. Throughout the day, parts of the 106th Infantry Division were engaged in fierce house-to-house fighting in Nizhniy Ol'shanets with units of the 78th Guards Rifle Division. Further south, in Maslova Pristan, other elements of the 106th Infantry Division succeeded in encircling and nearly wiping out the 229th Guards Rifle Regiment of the 72nd Guards Rifle Division. Only 17 soldiers of the regiment managed to break out from Maslova Pristan in the evening of 5 July.

In the meantime, the leading units of the 320th Infantry Division had advanced as far as Bezlyudovka south of Maslova Pristan. They had to get by without heavy weapons, though, as the construction of military bridges had been severely hampered by Soviet artillery. As soon as a bridge was completed, it was damaged again by enemy artillery fire. Later on, another accident occurred: around 1100, a 20-tonne military bridge was operational, on which the 905th Assault Gun Battalion was supposed to cross the Donets in order to support the attack of the 320th Infantry Division. However, on the other side of the river there was a ditch about 10 metres wide, which had not been noticed before; the assault guns therefore had to wait until an emergency bridge with a load rating of 20 tonnes had been built. Before the bridges for the 320th Infantry Division could be completed, units of the Soviet 72nd Guards Rifle Division and the 213th Rifle Division, reinforced by the 27th Guards Tank Brigade, launched a counterattack in the afternoon, which struck the 320th Infantry Division hard. As the soldiers of the 587th Grenadier Regiment had neither assault guns nor heavy anti-tank guns at their disposal, they were powerless against the Soviet tanks. Suffering heavy casualties, they had to withdraw. In fact, the division was lucky that the 27th Guards Tank Brigade's counterattack was not carried out with more vigour and force.

62 BA-MA, RH 24-11/67, Kriegstagebuch des Generalkommandos z.b.V. Raus, ab 20.7.43: Generalkommando XI. Armeekorps, Ia, 1.1.-30.9.1943, fol. 149.

The Germans managed to repel it that same evening after knocking out six tanks – but the 27th Guards Tank Brigade actually had 52 tanks available that day.

On the German side, the 320th Infantry Division was so battered that for the moment it could not be employed further in major offensive missions. The division lost almost 1,700 men on 5 July. Above all, the lack of air support had proved to be a significant disadvantage, since all bomber, dive bomber and ground-attack formations of the VIII Air Corps were assigned to the Fourth Panzer Army that day. Army Detachment Kempf only received fighter support during daytime, and it was not until the evening that ground-attack aircraft and *Stukas* appeared over the front sector of the 320th Infantry Division, though by that time the division had already repelled the Soviet attacks so that air support was no longer needed.

Of all divisions of Army Detachment Kempf, the 7th Panzer Division made the best progress on 5 July. It was commanded by Lieutenant-General Hans von Funck, whose soldiers came upon the Soviet 78th Guards Rifle Division led by Major-General Aleksandr Vasil'evich Skvortsov. With its 84 4.5cm, 7.6cm and 12.2cm guns, Skvortsov's division boasted considerable firepower. The 7th Panzer Division, however, could deploy its panzer regiment in the morning, which had crossed the Donets on the newly completed 24-tonne bridge at Solomino shortly after 0600. The division managed to break through the defensive positions of the 225th Guards Rifle Regiment fairly quickly and advance as far as Razumnoe. Consequently, the Commanding General of the Soviet 25th Guards Rifle Corps, Major-General Ganiy Bekinovich Safiullin, launched a counterattack with the 167th Tank Regiment. In a report from the III Panzer Corps it is stated: 'A counterattack from Generalovka against Razumnoe with more than 30 T-34 tanks was repelled. 10 T-34 were put out of action.'[63] In fact, the 167th Tank Regiment lost as many as 24 of the 32 tanks employed during the encounter, 20 T-34s and four T-70s.[64]

In the afternoon of 5 July, the headquarters of Army Detachment Kempf decided to shift the point of main effort to the 7th Panzer Division, whose attack had made the best progress. The Soviet forces at Staryy Gorod would be flanked and attacked from behind rather than from the front again. No doubt this was a sensible decision, but it also resulted in a gap between the III Panzer Corps and the II SS Panzer Corps. Both corps therefore had to advance with an open flank, and the II SS Panzer Corps was now responsible for protecting its own right (eastern) flank – which is exactly the situation which the III Panzer Corps had been supposed to prevent.

That first day of the attack certainly did not yield the expected results for Army Detachment Kempf – and, from the German point of view, it cast a shadow on the entire future course of the offensive. Viewed objectively, however, the overly

63 BA-MA, RH 20-8/99, Kriegstagebuch Nr. 2, Armee-Oberkommando 8, Ia Morgen- und Tagesmeldungen, Ic Morgen- und Tagesmeldungen, sonstige taktische Meldungen unterstellter Verbände, 1.7.-31.7.1934, Ia-Tagesmeldung vom 5.7.1943, no pagination.

64 Lawrence, *Kursk*, p. 408.

pessimistic tenor of both German records and unit histories must be taken with a pinch of salt. Even though all records and subsequent accounts confirm that every attack unit suffered heavy losses, one must consider the enormous difficulties and the adverse tactical conditions the attackers had to deal with from the very beginning of the operation. There was almost no support from the Luftwaffe, terrain was hardly suitable for an attack and the infantry were without heavy weapons because these could not be brought across the Donets. Another serious problem was the staunch Soviet defence, which relied on deep minefields, superbly fortified positions, as well as a superior artillery whose excellent observation gave them command over the terrain. Finally, the Red Army Air Forces dominated the air-space over this sector of the front. It is therefore remarkable that, in spite of these aggravating factors, the German formations still managed to break through the first Soviet defensive sector on that day. The 6th and 7th Panzer Division suffered relatively few casualties (contrary to what the war diaries and unit histories concluded): the 6th Panzer Division lost 78 men in total, including 11 dead and four missing, whilst the 7th Panzer Division had 96 casualties, including 10 dead. Only the 19th Panzer Division (497 casualties) and particularly the 106th Infantry Division (1,183 casualties) and the 320th Infantry Division (1,663 casualties) suffered heavy losses. The 168th Infantry Division, which, together with the 6th Panzer Division, had carried out an unsuccessful attack on Staryy Gorod in the morning, lost 201 soldiers, including nine dead.

On the second day of the operation, 6 July 1943, the III Panzer Corps advanced from the area between Generalovka and Krutoy Log towards the northeast. The main effort of the attack lay with the 7th Panzer Division, which pushed towards Batratskaya Dacha. The soldiers of the Soviet 73rd and 78th Guards Rifle Division offered bitter resistance. They were reinforced by several anti-tank regiments, which had been brought up on the orders from Lieutenant-General Shumilov, the commander of the 7th Guards Army. Additionally, two Soviet tank regiments and a regiment of self-propelled guns joined the battle, and the pilots of the 17th Air Army flew numerous raids against the 7th Panzer Division. The 7th lost 135 men which, considering the fierce and bloody combat, was a relatively low number of casualties.

In view of the severity of the combat, the 7th Panzer Division also lost a relatively small number of tanks. It is unclear how many tanks the division lost on each day, but in the first three days of the attack, it only had to write off seven tanks as completely destroyed. By contrast, the 167th Tank Regiment, which had already lost 24 tanks on the previous day, suffered another 11 tanks as casualties on 6 July – of its 40 tanks only five remained. The 262nd Tank Regiment lost 16 of its 37 tanks.

That same day, the 3rd Company of the 503rd Heavy Panzer Battalion, which was supporting the attack of the 7th Panzer Division, had its first encounter with the new Soviet SU-122 self-propelled guns. These belonged to the 1438th Self-Propelled Artillery Regiment, which attacked the *Tigers* from an advantageous direction, to the rear of the German tanks. The SU-122 knocked out two *Tigers*, but the regiment had to pay for this success with the loss of eight SU-122 and three SU-76 machines.[65]

The fierce Soviet resistance notwithstanding, the 7th Panzer Division succeeded in breaking through the second Soviet army defence line and advanced into the region west of Batratskaya Dacha on 6 July. This achievement also assisted the 6th Panzer Division's attack, which by the end of the day had managed to link up with the 25th Panzer Regiment of the 7th Panzer Division west of Batratskaya Dacha. As part of that day's success, the 6th Panzer Division also reported the destruction of seven Soviet tanks; this is exactly in accordance with Soviet records, which confirm that the 148th Tank Regiment did indeed lose seven tanks in the battle against the 6th Panzer Division.

By contrast, the 19th Panzer Division, led by Lieutenant-General Gustav Schmidt, received only criticism from both the headquarters of the III Panzer Corps and the commanders of Army Detachment Kempf. On 6 July, the division was repeatedly urged finally to 'get [the attack] going.'[66] In the morning, though, the division's advance came to a halt in a deep minefield. 14 of its tanks were put out of action by mines, four more were knocked out by enemy fire. When the division renewed its attack in the afternoon, it soon found itself trapped in another Soviet minefield – it would not be before the evening that a lane could be cleared through it. The 73rd Panzergrenadier Regiment of the 19th Panzer Division suffered particularly bloody losses. Whereas the bulk of the division had already crossed the Belgorod–Kupyansk railway line north of Razumnoe, the regiment was still stuck in the first Soviet defence line east of Belgorod. In the afternoon, the company commander Lieutenant Herbert Krögel finally managed to push the regiment's assault forward. By doing so, Krögel offered a good example of how the actions of individual officers could often decide the outcome of an engagement. Still, the 73rd Panzergrenadier Regiment lost about 180 men that day, including numerous officers.

Despite the success of the 7th Panzer Division, Field-Marshal von Manstein was not satisfied with the progress of the III Panzer Corps' attack. In the afternoon, he reminded Army Detachment Kempf that it was its task to link up with the right wing of the Fourth Panzer Army. In a telephone call with General Kempf in the evening, Manstein complained he had the impression that in the III Panzer Corps everyone was doing as they pleased. As it was already becoming apparent that Corps Raus was too weak to cover the right flank of Army Detachment Kempf, Manstein decided to bring up the 198th Infantry Division as reinforcements. It took two days until the

65 BA-MA, RH 20-8/83, Kriegstagebuch Nr. 2 (vol. 1) des Armee-Oberkommandos 8, Ia (Armee-Abteilung Kempf) vom 1.7.-31.7.1943, fol. 29; BA-MA, RH 20-8/99, Kriegstagebuch Nr. 2, Armee-Oberkommando 8, Ia Morgen- und Tagesmeldungen, Ic Morgen- und Tagesmeldungen, sonstige taktische Meldungen unterstellter Verbände, 1.7.-31.7.1934, Ia-Tagesmeldung vom 5.7.1943, no pagination; Lawrence, *Kursk*, p. 481.

66 BA-MA, RH 24-3/88, Anlagen zum Kriegstagebuch Generalkommando III. Panzerkorps, Ia, Nr. 8004 bis 8307 für die Zeit vom 5.7.-16.7.1943 (= vol. X), fol. 29, 31.

division could be employed for flank protection though and, during that time, the III Panzer Corps was alone responsible for protecting its eastern flank.

On 7 July, the 7th Panzer Division took control of Batratskaya Dacha and Myasoedovo, but then it had to halt because the 106th Infantry Division was unable to catch up and relieve the 7th Panzer Division. On 8 July, the main effort lay, therefore, in the hands of the 6th Panzer Division, which, supported by elements of the 19th Panzer Division, advanced as far as Melikhovo. Meanwhile, the 73rd Panzergrenadier Regiment of the 19th Panzer Division was still engaged at the Soviet defensive positions east of Belgorod, stubbornly defended by the 81st Guards Rifle Division under the command of Major-General Ivan Konstantinovich Morozov. 'In his well-fortified positions, the enemy lets himself be beaten to death', the war diary of Army Detachment Kempf noted.[67] The last Soviet position would only be captured by the 73rd Panzergrenadier Regiment in the evening of 9 July – after they had been attacked by *Stukas* and flamethrower tanks. The days of heavy fighting east of Belgorod had taken their toll on the regiment; it had lost more than 1,000 soldiers and had nearly been bled white – by 10 July, it was down to a frontline strength of 85 men.

On the same day, the 168th Infantry Division captured the fiercely contested Staryy Gorod, while the 6th Panzer Division advanced on Shishino, forcing the Soviet formations east and northeast of Belgorod to withdraw northwards in order to escape the impending encirclement. Once the III Panzer Corps had eliminated the threat to its left (western) flank, it continued its attack towards the north on 11 July. By now, however, the divisions of Army Detachment Kempf were so depleted that General Kempf wondered if it was at all possible to proceed with the assault. He at least wanted to replace the particularly worn out 19th Panzer Division with a fresh panzer formation, but there was none that Manstein could offer him.

In comparison, General Breith, the Commanding General of the III Panzer Corps, remained optimistic. When the 6th Panzer Division and the 503rd Heavy Panzer Battalion made a successful thrust from Melikhovo via Shlyakhovoe to Kazachye, he believed that his Corps had broken through the last Soviet defensive belt. Even after the war he was convinced that the III Panzer Corps had actually achieved the operational breakthrough on 11 July, which would have offered the possibility to 'operate in open space' (*im freien Raum*).[68] In truth, the corps had only penetrated the second Soviet army defence line. A daring surprise attack carried out in the night of 11-12 July got the 6th Panzer Division as far as Rzhavets – but with that final assault, the advance of the III Panzer Corps came to a halt for the time being. There was still a large gap between the Fourth Panzer Army and Army Detachment Kempf. Much worse, however, was the fact that the III Panzer Corps still could not fulfil its task of

67 BA-MA, RH 20-8/83, Kriegstagebuch Nr. 2 (vol. 1) des Armee-Oberkommandos 8, Ia (Armee-Abteilung Kempf) vom 1.7.-31.7.1943, fol. 44.

68 BA-MA, ZA 1/1601, Hermann Breith, Durchbruch eines Panzerkorps durch ein tief gegliedertes feindliches Stellungssystem in der Schlacht bei Charkow im Juli 1943, p. 9.

protecting the eastern flank of the Fourth Panzer Army against attacks by the 'strategic reserves' of the Red Army. So, on 12 July 1943, the strongest of these reserves, the 5th Guards Tank Army, did not encounter the III Panzer Corps at Prokhorovka but rather the spearhead of the Fourth Panzer Army.

The Tank Battle at Prokhorovka, 12 July 1943

Following the preliminary attacks of 4 July 1943, the Fourth Panzer Army began the actual Citadel attack in the early morning hours of 5 July. On the far right (eastern) side, the II SS Panzer Corps moved forward with the three SS Panzergrenadier Divisions: *Leibstandarte SS Adolf Hitler*, *Das Reich* and *Totenkopf*. To the left, the XXXXVIII Panzer Corps attacked with the 3rd Panzer Division, the Panzergrenadier Division *Großdeutschland* and the 11th Panzer Division. The boundary between the II SS Panzer Corps and the XXXXVIII Panzer Corps was assigned to the 167th Infantry Division, while the LII Army Corps, which was tasked with securing the left flank of the Fourth Panzer Army, was deployed at the far left (western) side of the axis of advance. In the initial days of the attack, the Fourth Panzer Army was facing the 6th Guards Army, led by Lieutenant-General Ivan Mikhaylovich Chistyakov, and the 1st Tank Army, commanded by Lieutenant-General Mikhail Efimovich Katukov.

The main German attack was delivered by the II SS Panzer Corps, which was involved in heavy fighting from the very first day of the assault. The Soviet 52nd Guards Rifle Division, commanded by Major-General Ivan Mikhaylovich Nekrasov, put up particularly fierce resistance in the village of Berëzov. Major-General Friedrich Fangohr, Chief of Staff of the Fourth Panzer Army, noted: 'The enemy infantryman fights well; contrary to the previous assumption that these are weak trench divisions (*schlechte Stellungsdivisionen*) it must be remarked that this foe knows how to fight and how to die.'[69]

Around noon, the SS divisions broke through the first Soviet defence line. A short time later, after bitter fighting and a concentrated air strike from dive bombers, *Das Reich* captured Berëzov and continued its northwards advance. The first encounter with enemy tanks took place in the afternoon at Bykovka, where the Soviet 230th Tank Regiment launched a counterattack against the spearheads of the *Leibstandarte* and *Das Reich*. The Soviet tank regiment was equipped with 32 American tanks, M3 Lees and M3 Stuarts, which did not stand a chance against the German tanks. They were knocked out before the German tanks even came into range of their guns.

On 6 July, Hausser's II SS Panzer Corps penetrated the second Soviet defence line. The *Das Reich* Division pushed as far as Kalinin, whilst the *Leibstandarte* reached Teterevino (North). The SS division's attack lost momentum, however, because both

69 BA-MA, RH 21-4/106, Chefnotizen (Abschriften) zum Kriegstagebuch des Panzerarmee-Oberkommandos 4, Ia, 1.1.-31.7.1943, fol. 175.

its neighbouring corps – the XXXXVIII Panzer Corps in the west, the III Panzer Corps in the east – could not advance fast enough, exposing the flanks of Hausser's corps even further. The Soviet troops put up a strong defence, but they also suffered horrific losses. The 51st Guards Rifle Division, for instance, lost more than 5,000 of its 8,400 soldiers in three days, most of them on 6 July, and the 5th Guards Tank Corps, led by Major-General Andrey Grigor'evich Kravchenko, lost 110 tanks during its counterattack against *Das Reich* on 6 July. On the same day, the *Das Reich* Division, by comparison, had to write off only one tank, destroyed by a Soviet anti-tank gun – a serious loss nevertheless, as in the tank SS *Hauptscharführer* and Knight's Cross holder Karl-Heinz Worthmann, one of the most experienced tank commanders and platoon leaders of *Das Reich*'s Panzer Regiment, was killed.

General Vatutin, the commander of the Voronezh Front, was shocked that the Germans had managed to break through the particularly strong army main defence belt on the very first day of their attack. He hurriedly ordered the deployment of his most important reserve, the 1st Tank Army, for a major counterattack on 6 July. But during the night of 5-6 July, Stalin forbade the counterattack as it went completely against the Soviet defensive concept: in essence, that the German armoured formations should first be critically weakened in the Soviet defensive positions before operational counterattacks were to be launched. Indeed the failed counterattack of the Soviet 2nd Tank Army against the spearhead of Model's Ninth Army in the northern sector of the Kursk salient on 6 July was to demonstrate the fatal consequences a precipitate counterattack could lead to.

When the II SS Panzer Corps broke through the second defensive belt in the morning of 6 July, Vatutin's nervousness increased. He ordered the 6th Guards Army and the 40th Army to launch a massive counterattack on the same day. Yet neither the army nor the corps headquarters were able to mount an organized counteroffensive on such short notice. This meant that on 6 July, the Soviet troops would make only uncoordinated attacks. Vatutin, in turn, came under increasing pressure as Stalin and the *Stavka* blamed him for failing to halt the German advance.

In the course of the next two days, the tank battle in the southern sector of the Kursk salient reached its first climax. Vatutin now deployed his armoured reserves for counterattacks. On 8 July, the German Fourth Panzer Army was facing seven Soviet tank and mechanized corps: the 3rd Mechanized Corps and the 6th Tank Corps in the sector of the XXXXVIII Panzer Corps and, in the sector of the II SS Panzer Corps, the 10th Tank Corps, the 31st Tank Corps, the 2nd Guards Tank Corps, the 5th Guards Tank Corps and the 2nd Tank Corps. On 8 July, the 2nd and 5th Guards Tank and the 2nd Tank Corps launched a counterattack in an attempt to encircle the II SS Panzer Corps. The war diary of Hausser's corps commented on this as follows: 'At noon, with newly brought up armoured formations… the enemy mounts relentless massed tank attacks with unprecedented force against the eastern and northeastern front of the *Das Reich* Division, as well as against the strongpoints of the *Leibstandarte SS Adolf Hitler* division with tank forces advancing from the northwest; he thereby forces the corps to fierce defensive combat, which has to be carried out with the very last reserves.'[70] On the German side, it was *Das Reich* which had to carry the brunt of the fighting that day. It reported the destruction of 190 enemy tanks while losing only one assault gun to a direct hit in an encounter with Soviet tanks at Kalinin.

In total, Vatutin's formations lost 343 tanks and self-propelled guns on this day, about two thirds of which were totally destroyed, whereas Hoth's Fourth Panzer Army only suffered complete write-offs of about 20 tanks and self-propelled guns. Yet Vatutin's troops had at least succeeded in bringing Hoth's panzer army to a halt. The war diary of the II SS Panzer Corps recorded: 'After the initially successful break-through through the 2nd [Soviet] position, the operation stalled; enemy operational reserves have to be destroyed in harsh defensive fighting.'[71] But Vatutin's Voronezh Front had paid a high price for its success. Since the beginning of the fighting, 527 of its tanks had been knocked out; 372 of these were destroyed completely. By contrast, the number of losses suffered by the Fourth Panzer Army since the beginning of the attack only amounted to roughly 70 tanks and self-propelled guns. Since Vatutin had not been able to eliminate the risk of a German breakthrough to Kursk, in spite of deploying all his operational reserves, the Red Army was forced to draw on its 'strategic reserves', whose deployment had to be authorized by the *Stavka*. On that same day, 8 July, the Soviet command gave orders to bring up the 5th Guards Army, led by Lieutenant-General Aleksey Semënovich Zhadov, and the 5th Guards Tank Army under the command of Lieutenant-General Pavel Alekseevich Rotmistrov from the Steppe Military District in order to reinforce the Voronezh Front.

On 9 July, the German XXXXVIII Panzer Corps broke through the first section of the third Soviet army defence line. This third rearward army defensive belt ran west of the Belgorod–Prokhorovka railway line in two sectors some distance apart from each other. The first sector extended from the area southwest of Prokhorovka in a nearly straight line to the west, while the second sector curved to the northwest, following the course of the Psël River (Map 5). In order to reach Kursk, the German formations advancing west of the Belgorod–Prokhorovka railway line therefore had to break through seven defensive sectors in total.

When the Germans broke through the first section of the third defensive belt, this shook the Soviet command, the more so as the defensive positions were less fortified in the rear than at the front. Within five days, the XXXXVIII had therefore penetrated the three strongest Soviet defensive sectors. In the afternoon of 9 July, the Panzergrenadier Division *Großdeutschland* advanced as far as Hill 244.8 north of Novoselovka – the furthest north the XXXXVIII Panzer Corps reached during Operation Citadel. Here, however, the advance northwards had to be halted because the corps' western flank was menaced by strong Soviet forces. During the days that followed, the fighting concentrated on the area around Hill 258.5 and the Tolstoe forest.

70 Stadler, *Offensive*, p. 65.
71 Ibid., p. 65.

The II SS Panzer Corps, on the other hand, continued its thrust approaching the north and northeast towards Prokhorovka. On 9 July, the *Totenkopf* Division succeeded in breaking through the first sector of the third Soviet army defence line, too, and pushing into the area of Kochetovka and Krasnyy Oktyabr at the Psël River. As a result of this advance, the 5th Guards Tank Army received orders to advance into the Prokhorovka area and prepare for counterattacks.

On 10 July, the *Totenkopf* Division attempted to establish a bridgehead across the Psël at Kozlovka (Map 6). The soldiers of the Soviet 95th Guards Rifle Division put up determined resistance, but in the afternoon they were forced to withdraw. The decisive factor was that, following a thunderstorm, the weather cleared up in the afternoon, allowing for the employment of the Luftwaffe. '[The] Russian runs from *Stukas*', the *Totenkopf* Division reported at 1800.[72] Soon afterwards it captured Hill 226.6; now, the third Soviet defensive belt north of the Psël River was completely overrun.

On the following day the *Leibstandarte SS Adolf Hitler*, too, penetrated the last Red Army defence line southwest of Prokhorovka and advanced as far as Hill 252.2. However, the division now had two open flanks and therefore discontinued the advance for the moment. The next day, on 12 July, the *Totenkopf* Division was to carry the attack forward on its own and close the open left flank of the *Leibstandarte*. As it transpired, on 12 July, the soldiers of the *Leibstandarte* would be involved in one of the bloodiest tank battles of Operation Citadel, although they did not yet know that in the early hours of the day, as German reconnaissance had failed to recognize that the Soviet 5th Guards Tank Army had been brought up to the front. According to SS *Obersturmführer* Rudolf von Ribbentrop and other witnesses, the German panzer soldiers were 'deeply asleep' when the 5th Guards Tank Army mounted its attack on the morning of 12 July.[73] During the morning of 12 July, Ribbentrop, son of the Reich Minister for Foreign Affairs Joachim von Ribbentrop, was leading that panzer company of the *Leibstandarte* which the tanks of the Soviet 5th Guards Tank Army first encountered.

Five corps with a total number of 860 operational tanks and self-propelled guns were under Lieutenant-General Rotmistrov's command that day: the 18th Tank Corps, the 29th Tank Corps, the 5th Guards Mechanized Corps, the 2nd Tank Corps and the 2nd Guards Tank Corps; the latter two had already joined the battle a few days earlier and suffered heavy losses, whereas the other three corps were fresh reserves. Four of the five corps began their assault against the two Waffen-SS Divisions *Leibstandarte SS Adolf Hitler* and *Das Reich* with 514 tanks and self-propelled guns at their disposal. The 18th Tank Corps, which had 149 tanks, and the 29th Tank Corps, equipped with 219 tanks and self-propelled guns faced the *Leibstandarte*, the 2nd Tank Corps (52 tanks) and the 2nd Guards Tank Corps (94 tanks) attacked in the sector of *Das Reich*.

72 Ibid., p. 88.
73 Rudolf von Ribbentrop, *Mein Vater Joachim von Ribbentrop: Erlebnisse und Erinnerungen* (Graz, 2008), p. 342.

Both SS divisions in total had 218 tanks, assault guns and *Marder* tank destroyers at their disposal.[74]

At the same time as the 5th Guards Tank Army launched its attack, the 1st Tank Army, the 6th Guards Army and parts of the 5th Guards Army further west began their assault against the German XXXXVIII Panzer Corps and the SS Division *Totenkopf*. The Soviet command aimed at destroying the whole German Fourth Panzer Army in a converging attack. The main attack was to be carried out towards the southwest by the 18th and the particularly strong 29th Tank Corps on a front of only about 5 kilometres between the Psël River and the Prokhorovka–Belgorod railway line (Map 6). However, the Soviet command made some grave errors when preparing for the attack, beginning with the choice of where to launch the attack. In the evening of 11 July, Marshal Vasilevskiy, Chief of the Soviet General Staff, arrived at the 5th Guards Tank Army's headquarters in order to coordinate the counterattack. Immediately he went on a tour of inspection with Lieutenant-General Rotmistrov to explore the initial positions for the assault of the 29th Tank Corps. The corps' advance was to be launched from the third army defence line. To their consternation, however, Vasilevskiy and Rotmistrov realized that the Germans had already broken through that defensive belt and the area envisaged as the start-line was already in German hands. Vasilevskiy thus gave the order to mount the attack that very evening at 2100 Moscow time rather than at 1000 on the following day, as had initially been planned – but as the preparations for the operation could not possibly be concluded in so short a time, the time for the attack was postponed to 0300. During the night of 12 July, the 29th Tank Corps had thus to occupy the newly assigned assembly area just west and southwest of Prokhorovka. Yet when changing the plan of the attack, no commander took into consideration that as part of the third Soviet army defence line, which the 29th Tank Corps was to cross from the rear when counterattack, there was an anti-tank ditch, which was impassable from either direction.

Another fatal mistake was that Rotmistrov instructed the Soviet tank crews to attack the German armoured formations at full speed, in order to seek 'close combat' with the German tanks. Rotmistrov issued this order because the Soviet tank guns were too weak to penetrate the frontal armour of the *Tiger* and because he was convinced that the two SS Divisions *Leibstandarte* and *Das Reich* had 110 *Tigers* at their disposal – in reality, they only had five operational *Tigers* in the morning of 12 July.

At 0300 (Moscow time), the Soviet tankers tensely waited for the signal to attack. But none came. It was not before 0400 that the fatigued soldiers were informed the attack had been postponed until 0830. According to Soviet combat reports, Rotmistrov radioed the signal to attack at 0830, whereupon the 18th and 29th Tank

74 For the numbers of Soviet tanks and SP guns at Prokhorovka, see Zamulin, *The Battle of Kursk: Controversial and Neglected Aspects*, p. 375; for the German figures, see Roman Töppel, 'Kursk – Mythen und Wirklichkeit einer Schlacht', *Vierteljahrshefte für Zeitgeschichte*, 57 (2009), pp. 349-84, here, 374-5.

Corps at once began their advance. However, this is unlikely, as German combat messages reported that the first Soviet tanks reached Hill 252.2 only at 1015 Moscow time, which, in turn, is in agreement with a report from the Soviet 31st Tank Brigade advancing behind the 32nd Tank Brigade, which states: 'At 1030 the tanks reached the area of the Oktyabrskiy *Sovkhoz*.'[75] It seems absurd that it took the Soviet tanks almost two hours to drive the few kilometres from their assembly area at Prokhorovka to the forward German lines at said *Sovkhoz* (on Hill 252.2). It is more likely that the Soviet commanders wanted to allow their soldiers some rest before the operation and then launched the attack at 1000 Moscow time, as initially scheduled.

The Soviet 29th Tank Corps, commanded by Major-General Ivan Fëdorovich Kirichenko, attacked along the Prokhorovka–Belgorod railway line. It was composed of three tank brigades, one motorized rifle brigade and one self-propelled artillery regiment. Kirichenko's tank brigades were unusually strong; instead of an authorized strength of 53 tanks per brigade, which was still standard then, they each had an authorized strength of 65 tanks. Additionally, the 32nd Tank Brigade – unlike all other tank brigades of the 5th Guards Tank Army – was equipped exclusively with T-34 medium tanks and had no light tanks. This is why this brigade took the lead. It advanced in a front about 900 metres wide right next to the railway line (northern side) towards Hill 252.2. The 31st Tank Brigade, the second wave, followed directly behind it. The two brigades arrived on Hill 252.2 with roughly 130 tanks; at full speed they broke through the forward positions of the 2nd Panzergrenadier Regiment of the *Leibstandarte SS Adolf Hitler*. Behind the hill – and out of sight – the *Leibstandarte*'s panzer battalion was in a rest position. The German panzergrenadiers fired purple smoke signals, the designated sign for 'tank warning', to warn the panzer crews of the approaching Soviet tanks.[76] Unaware of the strength of the Soviet attackers, SS *Obersturmführer* von Ribbentrop drove onto the height with seven Panzer IV to intercept the enemy tanks. In the skirmish which followed, four of the seven Panzer IV were knocked out. Yet the Soviet tank crews did not concern themselves with the remaining three tanks; instead, they continued across the height at high speed. As a result, Ribbentrop's remaining three tanks not only managed to get back to their own lines unscathed, but Ribbentrop actually turned his tank around and drove back to the German lines undetected in the midst of the enemy tank formation, using up all his anti-tank ammunition on the tanks around him. After the battle he was credited with the destruction of 14 Soviet tanks. Even though this was but a small part of the attacking force, the noise of battle as well as Ribbentrop's radio messages alerted the remainder of the *Leibstandarte*'s panzer battalion: 'I was just standing next to the

75 Otchët o boevykh deystviyakh 29 tankovogo korpusa za period s 7.7. po 24.7.1943 g. [Report on the operations of the 29th Tank Corps, 7 July to 24 July 1943], p. 4, copy from the document collection ('Materialsammlung') of the ZMSBw.

76 BA-MA, RH 21-4/122, Anlagenband zum Kriegstagebuch des Panzerarmee-Oberkommandos 4, Ia, Operation 'Zitadelle', 15.5.-9.7.1943, fol. 196-7.

cannon doing a few squats when frantic shouts of alarm abruptly chased away my sleepiness', a tanker of battalion headquarters later wrote.[77] At full speed the tanks of the Soviet 32nd and 31st Tank Brigade drove down the southwestern slope of Hill 252.2 to tear into the German formations. Now, however, their own anti-tank ditch became their undoing. A number of tanks toppled into the ditch, because the tank commanders did not recognize the obstacle ahead. Other tanks tried to 'jump over' the ditch at full speed – those few which succeeded were knocked out right away. Most Soviet tank commanders had their tanks turn southwards to reach the only crossing over the ditch, which was situated on the road next to the railway line. This decision turned out to be even more disastrous, however, as now the Soviet tanks became jammed at the crossing. One by one they were knocked out by the tanks of the *Leibstandarte*, which were well positioned behind the anti-tank ditch. Without losing another tank, the *Leibstandarte* completely smashed the two Soviet tank brigades.

By now, however, more Soviet tanks were arriving on the battlefield at Hill 252.2, namely the 170th Tank Brigade and parts of the 181st Tank Brigade, both attached to the 18th Tank Corps commanded by Major-General Boris Sergeevich Bakharov. As Bakharov's tanks advanced north of the anti-tank ditch, some of them managed to get as far as the Komsomolets *Sovkhoz*. However, there they were knocked out – some by artillery fire, some by infantry with close-range weapons. Two Soviet tanks, which reached the railway embankment south of the *Sovkhoz*, encountered two German *Tigers* just arriving from the workshop and were also knocked out.

Things were hardly better for the soldiers of the Soviet 25th Tank Brigade, which was assigned to the 29th Tank Corps and attacked south of the embankment. In its combat report the brigade stated: 'When the tanks reached the forward edge of the enemy defences, they were ambushed from the forest northwest of Storozhevoe and east of the outskirts of Storozhevoe and taken under heavy fire from *Tigers*, self-propelled artillery and anti-tank guns. The infantry was cut off from the tanks and had to seek cover. After the in-depth breakthrough of the defence, the tanks suffered heavy losses.'[78] In fact, the tanks of the 25th Tank Brigade were not facing *Tigers* but encountered parts of the tank destroyer battalion and the assault guns of the *Leibstandarte*. Four *Marder* self-propelled guns were supporting the Waffen-SS panzergrenadiers at the Stalinsk *Sovkhoz* northeast of Storozhevoe. Without suffering any losses, they knocked out 24 Soviet tanks and self-propelled guns. To the north of Storozhevoe, the remaining tanks of the 25th Tank Brigade come upon the assault gun battalion of the *Leibstandarte*, which was not expecting to see action that morning: 'We were held in reserve (*Eingreifreserve*) and were only employed when our spearhead troops were

77 Wilhelm Roes, *Freiwillig in den Krieg: Auf den Spuren einer verlorenen Jugend*, ed. Jörn Roes (Berlin, 2005), p. 93.

78 Otchët o boevykh deystviyakh 29 tankovogo korpusa za period s 7.7. po 24.7.1943 g. [Report on the operations of the 29th Tank Corps, 7 July to 24 July 1943], p. 6, copy from the document collection ('Materialsammlung') of the ZMSBw.

retreating', a gun commander of the battalion later recalled.[79] But within just a short time, the assault guns were ready for combat. Repelling the Soviet tank attack, they mounted a counterattack to eliminate the threat to the *Leibstandarte*'s flank and close the gap between their own division and its neighbouring division, *Das Reich*. Again, the battalion inflicted significant losses on the Soviet 25th Tank Brigade – two hours after the beginning of the attack, only 21 of 69 tanks remained of the brigade. The 1446th Self-Propelled Artillery Regiment, which was attacking south of the railway embankment as well, also suffered appalling losses in just a short time; 19 of its 20 SU-76s and SU-122s were destroyed, 14 of which were complete write-offs.

The Soviet attacks not only failed in the sector of the *Leibstandarte*; the Divisions *Das Reich* and *Totenkopf* as well as the XXXXVIII Panzer Corps managed to break all the Soviet attacks on 12 July 1943, too. So the Soviet operational counterattack, which was supposed to destroy the Fourth Panzer Army, ended with a devastating defeat for the Red Army. Rotmistrov's 5th Guards Tank Army alone lost 3,908 soldiers in total on 12 July; 1,827 of them were either killed in battle or taken prisoner, the others were wounded. It also lost 382 tanks, including 223 completely destroyed. The war diary of the Fourth Panzer Army noted: 'On 12 July, [the] enemy attacked the Fourth Panzer Army on its entire front with at least parts of nine armoured and mechanized corps and several rifle divisions. [The] main effort of the enemy's attacks [was directed] against both flanks at and north of Kalinin, west of Prokhorovka and west of Verkhopen'e. To this end, the enemy committed two new tank corps to the area of Prokhorovka today.... All attempts by the enemy to penetrate the flanks of the Panzer Army were foiled in fierce defensive combat.'[80]

That same day, 12 July, Field-Marshal von Manstein personally convinced himself of the success of the Fourth Panzer Army: 'In all headquarters visited [by Manstein] that day, the commanders expressed their confidence about the situation after the fierce but successful early battles, as the enemy was beginning to show clear signs of incipient weakness.'[81] As a consequence, Manstein was certain that the operational breakthrough of his forces was imminent and that victory in the battle of Kursk was within grasp. In the southern sector of the Kursk salient, the Red Army had already suffered about 1,200 total losses of tanks and self-propelled guns, whereas Manstein's attack formations had lost only about 200 tanks and self-propelled guns. On 13 July, however, Manstein was summoned to the *Führerhauptquartier Wolfsschanze* (Wolf's Lair) near Rastenburg in Eastern Prussia, where Hitler informed him of his decision to abandon Operation Citadel.

79 Letter from Fritz Henke to the author, 3 November 1999.
80 BA-MA, RH 21-4/104, Kriegstagebuch des Oberkommandos der 4. Panzerarmee, Ia, 25.3.-31.7.1943, fol. 155.
81 Private Archive of Rüdiger von Manstein, Handakte des Oberbefehlshabers der Heeresgruppe Süd, Juli 1943, note for the war diary, 12 July 1943, no pagination.

Field Marshal Erich von Manstein (foreground, right) during an exercise in the vicinity of Khar'kov on 26 June 1943 on the occasion of a visit from Turkish Colonel-General Cemil Cahit Toydemir (centre). Manstein's disappointment with the shooting demonstration is reflected in his face. On account of his skills he was considered an operational genius at that time already. (Private collection)

Russian farmers constructing field fortifications in the sector of the Soviet Central Front north of Kursk on 2 July 1943. Both the Soviets and the Germans employed the local population for construction work on a large scale. According to Soviet sources, the Red Army called on 300,000 civilians to build the elaborate defensive system in the Kursk salient. (Russian State Archive of Film and Photo Documents, hereafter RGAKFD)

Panzerkampfwagen VI Tiger of the 2 Coy of the 503rd Heavy Panzer Battalion. This company had a stroke of bad luck on the first day of Operation Citadel: it lost 13 of its 14 *Tigers*, nine of which were damaged by mines. All in all, however, the company only had to write off two *Tigers* as total losses during the attack on Kursk. (Private collection)

Brand-new *Panzerkampfwagen V Panthers*, version D, are loaded for rail transport. It was at Kursk that the *Panther* was first deployed at the front. During Operation Citadel, 200 *Panther* tanks were used by Panzer Regiment 39, 58 of which were destroyed – mostly due to incorrect tactical employment. (Open source)

Panzerkampfwagen IV with side-skirts. The pictured vehicle is the tank of the CO of the Panzer Regiment of the *Leibstandarte SS Adolf Hitler*; originally, it was a regular version G vehicle, which was then converted to a command tank featuring an additional radio set. (Private collection)

StuG III version G assault gun of the SS Panzergrenadier Division *Totenkopf*. For the attack on Kursk, the *Totenkopf* Division had 35 assault guns at its disposal. The vehicles were generally well-liked by the troops. One of its advantages was its low profile, making it difficult for the enemy to target the vehicle. (Private collection)

A *Ferdinand* of the 653rd Heavy Tank Destroyer Battalion. The battalion had 44 *Ferdinands* at its disposal, six of which were destroyed during the attack on Kursk. Due to their heavy armour and superior guns, the *Ferdinands* were considered a 'veritable life insurance policy' by their crews. (Private collection)

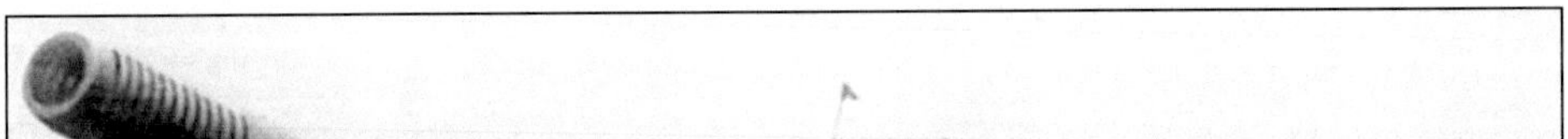

Soviet self-propelled gun SU-152, armed with a 152mm howitzer ML-20S. The SU-152 was used as heavy assault gun and tank destroyer by the Red Army. It was a dangerous opponent for the German tanks and self-propelled guns. However, at the beginning of the Battle of Kursk, the Red Army only had 37 SU-152 at its disposal. (Private collection)

A *Marder II* tank destroyer of the SS *Totenkopf* Panzergrenadier Division during Operation Citadel in July 1943. Even though these light self-propelled tank destroyers played an important role in the battles around Kursk, they are not usually included in discussions of strength comparison in scholarship. (Private collection)

Soviet self-propelled gun SU-76 driving through the village of Staritsa north of Orël in August 1943. The SU-76 was the Soviet equivalent of the German *Marder* tank destroyer, even though its armament was no match for the heavy German tanks and self-propelled guns. (RGAKFD)

Wespe self-propelled gun of the *Leibstandarte SS Adolf Hitler* during Operation Citadel. The *Wespe* was armed with a 10.5cm light field howitzer, which was also effective against armoured targets. On 12 July 1943 at Prokhorovka, *Wespe* howitzers of the *Leibstandarte* destroyed several tanks of the Soviet 29th Tank Corps by direct fire. (US National Archives and Records Administration, hereafter NARA)

Soviet gun crew loading a 152mm howitzer M1937 (ML-20) in the sector of the Central Front in July 1943. Unlike the Wehrmacht, the Red Army did not have any 'armoured artillery', but it did have a quantitatively far superior and technically superb field artillery. The ML-20 was one of the best artillery pieces of World War Two. (RGAKFD)

Armoured personnel carriers and tanks of the *Leibstandarte SS Adolf Hitler* advancing on Teterevino (North) on 6 July 1943. Together with other armoured units of the *Leibstandarte*, the medium tank companies and the APC battalion of the division formed the *Panzergruppe LAH*, which pushed further north than all other attacking formations on that day. (Private collection)

T-34 M1943 destroyed during a Soviet counter-attack against the *Panzergruppe LAH* on 6 July 1943. The distinctive shape of the turret indicates that this vehicle was produced in the Tractor Plant in Chelyabinsk ('Tankograd'). At Kursk, the Soviet armoured formations were employed in combat in a tactically inept and piecemeal manner and suffered enormous losses. (Private collection)

This armoured command vehicle (*Panzerbefehlswagen Ausf H*) of the *Leibstandarte* hit a mine on 6 July 1943, damaging the running gear. This was the division's only command vehicle that was equipped with a dummy gun only; all others were regularly armed. The *Leibstandarte*'s Panzer Regiment staff used it as a 'mobile orderly room'. (Private collection)

Soviet 12cm mortar crew in the sector of the Voronezh Front in July 1943. The Red Army had large numbers of mortars available at Kursk, inflicting heavy losses on the German infantry. General Field Marshal von Kluge was convinced that the Ninth Army's attack at Kursk failed only because of the Soviet artillery and mortar fire. (RGAKFD)

Air support during Operation Citadel: German Junkers Ju 87 *Stuka* flying over the armoured vanguard of the SS *Totenkopf* Division. Even though this division was one of the privileged armoured divisions of the Waffen-SS, half of its panzer regiment consisted of outdated *Panzerkampfwagen III*, some of which can be seen in the above photograph. (Private collection)

Soviet ground-attack aircraft Ilyushin Il-2 Shturmovik. The famous aircraft also acquired its legendary reputation from the fact that their crews grossly exaggerated their successes. The Il-2 was heavily armoured and therefore fairly impervious to enemy fire. Still, the Soviet ground-attack regiments lost hundreds of Il-2 during the first days of the Battle of Kursk. (Open source)

Messerschmitt Bf 109 G-6 fighter of the I Group of *Jagdgeschwader* 52 on a frontline airstrip at Belgorod in July 1943. The G-6 version was the most produced version of the Bf 109 and the German *Luftwaffe*'s standard fighter in 1943/44. In summer 1943, it was superior to the Soviet fighter aircraft with regards to speed and climb performance. (Private collection)

Soldiers of the *Leibstandarte SS Adolf Hitler* examine a Soviet Yak-7B fighter aircraft, which had to make an emergency landing after a dogfight in the first days of the Battle of Kursk. At Kursk, the Soviet fighter formations were far inferior to their German opponents in terms of tactics; many Soviet pilots were also inexperienced and badly trained. (NARA)

A Soviet 76mm divisional gun M1942 (ZiS-3) firing in the sector of the Voronezh Front in July 1943. Because of its characteristic sound, the gun was called 'Ratsch-Bumm' by the Germans. Apart from the 4.5cm anti-tank guns, the ZiS-3 formed the backbone of the Soviet anti-tank defence. (RGAKFD)

Crew of a 57mm anti-tank gun M1943 (ZiS-2) of the Soviet 2nd Anti-Tank Artillery Brigade ready to open fire. The ZiS-2 had a considerably higher muzzle velocity than the 76mm ZiS-3, and its shells had a much higher penetrating power. However, at Kursk, the Red Army only had a handful of ZiS-2 available. (RGAKFD)

Preparation of the German retreat from Orël. On 3 August 1943, the crew of a 75mm anti-tank gun Pak 40 is observing the demolition of the brewery opposite. The Germans destroyed all military and economically important buildings before withdrawing from Orël on 5 August. (NARA)

Tigers of the 3rd Company of the 503rd Heavy Panzer Battalion in front of the Three Saints Church in Khar'kov on 5 June 1943. Khar'kov changed hands three times in 1943, until the city was finally liberated by the Red Army on 23 August, ending the Battle of Kursk – after exactly 50 days. (Private collection)

Additional images of German armour from private collections

A well-camouflaged *StuG III* version G assault gun of the 244th Assault Gun Battalion. (Private collection)

A *Ferdinand* Tank Destroyer of the 653rd Heavy Tank Destroyer Battalion. (Private collection)

Panzerkampfwagen IV of the *Leibstandarte SS Adolf Hitler* undergoing maintenance. (Private collection)

A *Panzerkampfwagen III* of the reconnaissance platoon, regimental staff, Panzer Regiment of the *Leibstandarte SS Adolf Hitler*. (Private collection)

The only tanks the *Leibstandarte*'s Panzer Regiment was allowed to keep before being transferred to Italy were these vehicles of the regimental staff. (Private collection)

Tanks of the regimental staff of the *Leibstandarte*'s Panzer Regiment after their arrival in Northern Italy. (Private collection)

Panzerkampfwagen IV of the SS Panzergrenadier Division *Totenkopf*. (Private collection)

A *Panzerkampfwagen VI* of the SS Panzergrenadier Division *Totenkopf*. (Private collection)

The Abandonment of the German Offensive against Kursk

As well as Erich von Manstein, Field-Marshal Hans Günther von Kluge, Commander-in-Chief of Army Group Centre, was also present at the briefing in the *Führerhauptquartier* on 13 July. According to Manstein's private war diary, Hitler began his discussions with the observation that the situation in Sicily was quite serious. On 10 July, the Anglo-Americans had landed on the island and the Italian soldiers had hardly offered any resistance. Hitler remarked that Sicily would probably soon be lost. The Western Allies' next step could be a landing in southern Italy or in the Balkans; the formation of new armies in Italy and in the western Balkans had therefore become a priority – and this was possible only by pulling troops away from the Eastern Front. Consequently, Operation Citadel would have to be abandoned.

Manstein quoted Hitler on this subject nearly word for word in his 1955 memoirs; this has led generations of military historians to regard the Allied landing on Sicily as the main reason for breaking off Operation Citadel. In reality, not a single unit was actually deployed from the Eastern Front to Italy during the following two weeks. Only when the Italian dictator Benito Mussolini was ousted on 25 July 1943, did Hitler see the need for action and had the *Leibstandarte SS Adolf Hitler* transferred to Italy. The division, however, was not to be employed against the Anglo-American forces on Sicily or in southern Italy. Instead it was tasked with securing the key transport route through the Brenner Pass and – in the event of Italy's withdrawal from the Axis – disarming the Italian troops in northern Italy. All other divisions that had taken part in Operation Citadel remained at the Eastern Front.

So, why did Hitler, in the presence of Manstein, emphasize the particular importance of the situation on Sicily if in truth it hardly had an impact on his decision to cancel Operation Citadel? A careful study of Manstein's diary and his personal papers from 1943 offers an explanation. Hitler was particularly worried about the Soviet offensives threatening the Donets Basin and the Orël salient. However, in front of Manstein, he focused on the strategic situation in Italy so he would not have to discuss the operational options on the Eastern Front with him. When it came to the conduct of operations, Manstein not only usually had a different opinion to Hitler, he was also able to marshal superior arguments. Hitler, for his part, used to point out technical, economical or broader strategic aspects on which Manstein had no insight. By first discussing the situation in the Mediterranean during the briefing of 13 July, Hitler thus took the wind out of Manstein's sails at the beginning of the meeting.

According to Manstein's diary, it was Field-Marshal von Kluge's turn to speak after Hitler. He explained that the attack of Model's Ninth Army was not progressing at all and that the Ninth Army had so far lost as many as 20,000 soldiers. Kluge also had to withdraw 'all mobile forces' of the Ninth Army to clear up 'the three deep penetrations the Russian has achieved in the offensive against [the] Second Panzer Army launched the previous day.' The Ninth Army's attack could not therefore be continued. In fact, Kluge needed even more troops from other front sectors to block the Soviet offensive against the Orël salient. Manstein, on the other hand, declared 'that the battle has reached its crucial point. There is hope that, having suffered as many casualties, the Russian will soon collapse.' Yet without the assistance of the Ninth Army the offensive could not be continued, as the striking power of the attack forces of Army Group South would 'at best' get them 'as far as the sector south [of] Kursk.' It had to be assumed, Manstein continued, that the Red Army was soon going to launch an attack against the Sixth Army and the First Panzer Army in the Donets Basin. 'But we always had to expect this. If we let the Russian go now, he will have complete freedom.' If the Ninth Army could not renew its attack, Manstein said, 'I would at least have to try and clean up south of the Pssel [Psël] River through [a] push towards the west and get some breathing room, unless [the] development in the Donets area calls for an immediate discontinuation.' This last sentence is remarkable insofar as Manstein admitted that a crisis in the Donets region might actually require calling off all further attacks at Kursk.[82]

The fact that Hitler called off Operation Citadel has resulted in numerous legends surrounding the decision. Johann Adolf Graf von Kielmansegg, who after the Second World War continued his career as a high-ranking NATO officer, was a general staff officer in the Operations Section of the army in the summer of 1943, and responsible for one of the myths. At a military history conference in Ingolstadt in 1993, he came up with the story that, together with the Chief of Staff Kurt Zeitzler and Lieutenant-General Adolf Heusinger, then chief of the Operations Section, he attempted to bypass Hitler: 'Hitler issued the order to call off Citadel, that is the attacks, to the two Field-Marshals [Kluge and Manstein] on that day, 13 July … However, I did not pass this order on until 16 July. Here you have an example of 'delaying tactics.' Why? Because Heusinger and Zeitzler were still hopeful about obtaining permission for operation plan 'Roland' within the next two days, of whose prospect of success we were convinced.'[83] Operation Roland was the limited objective attack with which Manstein intended to destroy the Soviet formations still located in the western flank of Hoth's Fourth Panzer Army. However, the claim that Zeitzler, Heusinger and Kielmansegg employed 'delaying tactics' in order to gain Hitler's consent for Roland can be refuted by Manstein's contemporary records. As a matter of fact, Hitler gave Manstein permission for the limited objective attack south of the Psël River during the briefing of 13 July: 'The *Führer* basically approved these proposals, emphasizing

82 Private Archive of Rüdiger von Manstein, Erich von Manstein, persönliches Kriegstagebuch Nr. 5, März 1943-1.4.1944, no pagination.

83 Johann Adolf Graf von Kielmansegg, 'Bemerkungen eines Zeitzeugen zu den Schlachten von Char'kov und Kursk aus der Sicht des damaligen Generalstabsoffiziers Ia in der Operationsabteilung des Generalstabs des Heeres', in Roland G. Foerster (ed.), *Gezeitenwechsel im Zweiten Weltkrieg? Die Schlachten von Char'kov und Kursk im Frühjahr und Sommer 1943 in operativer Anlage, Verlauf und politischer Bedeutung* (Hamburg, 1996), pp. 137-48, quote, 146.

that naturally the possibilities depended on how the situation developed in the Donets region.'[84]

Hitler had consented to Operation Roland, but Manstein was nevertheless disappointed that Operation Citadel would not be continued. Frustrated, he noted in his private war diary: 'Result: Kluge discontinues attack. Supposed to free reserves by giving up Orël salient. Nothing happened that was not to be expected. So one should have attacked in May! If Citadel was to be aborted as soon as any crisis occurred, on other fronts or in the Mediterranean, it should not have been launched in the first place.'[85]

Nonetheless, on 13 July, Hitler told his generals that he was satisfied with the outcome of Operation Citadel: 'Even if the attack Citadel has not achieved its initial objective so far, it has still accomplished its purpose insofar as it destroyed considerable offensive forces of the Russian.'[86] Hitler now directed his attention primarily to the Donets Basin where the Red Army was preparing for the assault. In the north of the Donbas, at the Donets River, four armies of the Soviet Southwestern Front under the command of General Rodion Yakovlevich Malinovskiy were to attack the German First Panzer Army commanded by Colonel-General Eberhard von Mackensen. At the same time, the Soviet Southern Front, commanded by Colonel-General Fëdor Ivanovich Tolbukhin, was to thrust at the Mius River from the east into the Donets basin. On the German side, *General der Infanterie* Karl-Adolf Hollidt's Sixth Army by itself was facing Tolbukhin's five armies (Map 7).

The Soviet offensive in the Donbas pursued two objectives. First, the economically important Donets Basin had to be regained. Second, the Germans had to be forced to withdraw their forces from the Belgorod–Kursk front sector and, by doing so, facilitate the Red Army's counteroffensive in this area. In order to achieve this, units of Tolbukhin's Southern Front had begun to assemble troops for the attack in full view of the Germans since 10 July: 'Since the early afternoon, infantry and motorized troop movements have begun in front of the XXIX and XVII Army Corps to an extent which already on the following day left no doubts about the build-up of enemy troops', a report from the Sixth Army states.[87] Observers of the First Panzer Army, too, detected 'increased enemy movements in the area of Izyum.'[88] At first

84 Private Archive of Rüdiger von Manstein, Erich von Manstein, Rückblick auf 'Zitadelle', 18.7.1943, p. 17, in Handakte des Oberbefehlshabers der Heeresgruppe Süd, Juli 1943, no pagination.

85 Private Archive of Rüdiger von Manstein, Erich von Manstein, persönliches Kriegstagebuch Nr. 5, März 1943-1.4.1944, no pagination.

86 Private Archive of Rüdiger von Manstein, Erich von Manstein, Rückblick auf 'Zitadelle', 18.7.1943, p. 16, in Handakte des Oberbefehlshabers der Heeresgruppe Süd, Juli 1943, no pagination.

87 BA-MA, RH 20-6/303, Kriegstagebuch des Armee-Oberkommando 6, Nr. 5, 17.7.-17.8.1943, fol. 4.

88 BA-MA, RH 21-1/94, Kriegstagebuch des Panzerarmee-Oberkommandos 1, Ia, Nr. 11, 1.5.-31.8.1943, fol. 82.

the German command believed this was merely a feint. On 12 July, Minister of Propaganda Joseph Goebbels, who was informed daily and in detail about the military situation, wrote in his diary: 'In the Mius sector the enemy is trying to simulate some larger movements by driving his columns back and forth in various directions. This ruse, however, has been detected.'[89] Hitler did not see any imminent danger either and, on 12 July, he ordered the XXIV Panzer Corps with the 23rd Panzer Division and the SS Panzergrenadier Division *Wiking* to advance in the area west of Belgorod to employ it in the Battle of Kursk.

But in the days that followed it became more and more evident that the Red Army was not just carrying out deceptive manoeuvres at the Donets and Mius but would, in fact, be attacking soon. By 11 July, the command of the Sixth Army had recognized that the main concentration area of the Soviet Southern Front was the area east of Kuybyshevo and around Dmitrievka. Three days later the First Panzer Army reported 'a Soviet concentration of forces in the area of Izyum.'[90] Subsequently, Hitler withdrew his order of releasing the XXIV Panzer Corps for combat action at Kursk, instead reassigning it to the First Panzer Army. Furthermore, the VIII Air Corps was tasked with combating the Soviet assembly at Izyum. First Lieutenant Rainer Mulzer, a member of the 23rd Panzer Division, noted in his diary: 'In the afternoon [of 15 July] we drive straight back through the dark evening, on the same road we had come. At Izyum the enemy is said to be making massive preparations for a breakthrough attack. Continuous bomber formations are flying from the airfields around Khar'kov towards this town.'[91] In the evening of 15 July, Manstein made a phone call to Mackensen and Hollidt. Both army commanders expressed their view 'that the enemy has finished assembling [his troops] and is in a position to launch his attack tomorrow.'[92]

On 16 July, Hitler ordered the withdrawal of the II SS Panzer Corps from the front, so it could be positioned west of Belgorod. On the same day, Manstein telephoned Zeitzler and noted, referring to the conversation, 'that the *Führer* is on the one hand afraid that we will be too late in the Donets area, but in the case of the first penetrations this will happen anyway as the attack there is likely to be launched tomorrow. If one had wanted to avoid this, one should not have begun Citadel on 5 July. Above all, however, he wants to obtain reserves for [Army Group] Centre.'[93] Where he wanted to send the II SS Panzer Corps, Hitler did not disclose at first. When Manstein called Zeitzler the next day to inquire about what had been planned for the corps, the Chief

89 Goebbels, *Tagebücher*, pt. II, vol. 9, p. 85.

90 BA-MA, RH 21-1/94, Kriegstagebuch des Panzerarmee-Oberkommandos 1, Ia, Nr. 11, 1.5.-31.8.1943, fol. 86.

91 Diary of Rainer Mulzer, 22.6.1942-18.7.1943, original privately owned, copy in author's possession.

92 Private Archive of Rüdiger von Manstein, Handakte des Oberbefehlshabers der Heeresgruppe Süd, Juli 1943, no pagination.

93 Private Archive of Rüdiger von Manstein, Erich von Manstein, persönliches Kriegstagebuch Nr. 5, März 1943-1.4.1944, no pagination.

of the General Staff replied: 'With the SS Corps the *Führer* wants to be able to drive around the entire globe. Its next employment might be just as well in the Donets area as at Orël or at some other spot.'[94]

On 16 July, Soviet prisoners confirmed what the Germans had already realized – not least because of the apparently 'very careless' behaviour of the Soviet troops: Tolbukhin's Southern Front had assembled an attack formation in the area of Dmitrievka and another in the area of Kuybyshevo.[95] The captured Red Army soldiers also disclosed that the Soviet assault would begin on 17 July. On the evening of 16 July, the three German corps stationed in this front sector were hence notified about the imminent Soviet attack.

On the morning of 17 July the formations of the Soviet Southwestern and Southern Front indeed began their offensive. The main thrusts of Tolbukhin's Southern Front were – inexplicably – carried out exactly where the Soviet troops had so demonstratively assembled in the previous days, namely at Dmitrievka and Kuybyshevo. It is possible that the Soviet command believed the Germans would interpret this as a feint and thus not expect any attacks from this very direction, but this cannot be confirmed by Soviet sources. Only one thing is certain – the Soviet command let their soldiers walk right into the trap.

Even though the Germans had expected and prepared for the Soviet attacks, the momentum of the Soviet offensive at the Mius still far exceeded their fears. A member of the 210th Assault Gun Battalion wrote in his diary on 17 July:

> I wake up in the morning at 2.30 hours. A dull grumbling, banging, whining and cracking makes me sit up ... Never before have I heard such a heavy barrage, even the 'old Russia hands' among us could not remember one like it ... Soon a loud humming and hissing follows. The familiar sound of heavy bombs. In a flash we are out of our tent and do not believe our eyes. The whole sky is filled with Russian ground-attack aircraft ... At 7.30 hours the alarm sounds. The Russian has begun a large-scale attack on the entire Mius front. In various places, our infantry positions have already been breached by the enemy.[96]

West of Dmitrievka, the 210th Assault Gun Battalion found itself in the midst of battle – right in the path of the Soviet main attack which was carried out by the 5th Shock Army under the command of Lieutenant-General Vyacheslav Dmitrievich Tsvetaev. It was supported by the bulk of the 8th Air Army, which had more than 800 aircraft at its disposal. The heavy Soviet artillery fire caused 'considerable losses in

94 Private Archive of Rüdiger von Manstein, Handakte des Oberbefehlshabers der Heeresgruppe Süd, July 1943, no pagination.
95 BA-MA, RH 20-6/286, Kriegstagebuch des Armee-Oberkommandos 6, Nr. 4, 1.6.-16.7.1943, fol. 108.
96 Karlheinz Münch, *StuG.Abt./Brig. 210* (Katowice 2007), p. 22.

personnel and material' among the German XVII Army Corps' front line battalions, and the Soviet Air Forces, which had air superiority, 'severely [hit] many of the positions' in the German defence system.[97] Only when the German Luftwaffe joined the battle with its dive bomber formations in the late afternoon were the Germans able to bring the Soviet advance to a temporary halt.

Whereas the pushes by the Soviet Southwestern Front could all be fended off in the sector of the German XXX Army Corps on the first day of the battle, the units of the Soviet 8th Guards Army, led by Lieutenant-General Vasiliy Ivanovich Chuykov, succeeded in establishing several bridgeheads in the sector of the German XXXX Panzer Corps southeast of Izyum. On the orders of the First Panzer Army Headquarters the 17th Panzer Division and the SS Panzergrenadier Division *Wiking* began counterattacking in the morning of 18 July, but after some initial success their attacks soon bogged down.

At the Mius, the German counterattacks also remained fruitless on 18 July. The Soviet 5th Shock Army was able to expand its bridgehead west of Dmitrievka to a depth of roughly 10 kilometres. Furthermore, by capturing Hill 213.9, the Soviet troops managed to occupy a key tactical position of this front sector, albeit suffering enormous casualties. The war diary of the German Sixth Army Headquarters noted that in a single regimental sector 510 dead Red Army soldiers were counted after a counterattack, whilst 110 prisoners were taken and 56 machine guns as well as 13 anti-tank rifles were captured. 'According to intercepted radio messages, the enemy commanders had been threatened with execution, should the high ground position not be seized on 18 July.'[98] The Germans, too, suffered terrible losses. Throughout the course of the day, the 513th Grenadier Regiment (294th Infantry Division) and the 581st Grenadier Regiment (306th Infantry Division) lost about two thirds of their combat strength. In addition to the commander and his aide, the latter regiment lost all its battalion commanders.

The Germans soon realized that at both the Mius and at the Donets additional units were needed to bring the Soviet offensive to a definitive halt and to eliminate the enemy bridgeheads. On 18 July, Manstein therefore called the Operations Section of the General Staff of the Army and requested the deployment of the II SS Panzer Corps to the Donets region – a request which Hitler acceded to on the same day.

On 19 July, the Soviet forces at both the Donets and the Mius continued their fierce attacks. They sustained further heavy losses, but the German forces, too, were suffering. The war diary of the First Panzer Army reports: 'The army thins out the less threatened front sectors as much as possible in order to deploy the last available troops to the XXXX Panzer Corps. Weakening the two flank corps even further is not possible.'[99]

97 BA-MA, RH 20-6/303, Kriegstagebuch des Armee-Oberkommandos 6, Nr. 5, 17.7.-17.8.1943, fol. 9.

98 BA-MA, RH 20-6/303, Kriegstagebuch des Armee-Oberkommandos 6, Nr. 5, 17.7.-17.8.1943, fol. 42.

99 BA-MA, RH 21-1/94, Kriegstagebuch des Panzerarmee-Oberkommandos 1, Ia, Nr. 11, 1.5.-31.8.1943, fol. 101.

At the Mius River, the 23rd Panzer Division and the 16th Panzergrenadier Division attempted to recapture Hill 213.9 that same day, but did not succeed. The 23rd Panzer Division lost 28 tanks, including 10 completely destroyed. In the evening, the division had only 25 operational tanks at its disposal; the 16th Panzergrenadier Division had only five tanks left. The war diary of the Sixth Army states: 'The course of 19 July has proved that, due to the Russian superiority in material and personnel, future counterattacks can only be carried out if our own forces are considerably stronger.'[100]

The following day, Manstein sent an estimate of the situation to the Army High Command, declaring that 'the danger of a breakthrough at the two hot spots still remains [i.e., with Sixth Army west of Dmitrievka and First Panzer Army in the area south of Izyum]. The only effective countermeasure is a successive strike in both areas. For this [the] SS Panzer Corps and [the] III Panzer Corps will be required.'[101] Manstein therefore clearly acknowledged that he, too, thought the threat of a Soviet breakthrough to the Donets Basin could only be prevented with formations which had previously been employed in Operation Citadel. In this respect, Hitler and Manstein both shared the same view. During the midday situation briefing taking place in the *Führerhauptquartier Wolfsschanze* on 25 July, Hitler announced his intention of further reinforcing Manstein's forces in the Donets Basin – if necessary even through redeployments from Army Group Centre: 'There is no other way; he [Manstein] needs a number of divisions. They must come in anyhow, there is no way around it.'[102] For some time Hitler even entertained the idea of employing the *Leibstandarte SS Adolf Hitler* for a counterattack at the Mius River before its planned relocation to Italy, but later abandoned it. As replacement for the departing *Leibstandarte*, the II SS Panzer Corps was assigned the 3rd Panzer Division of the army. Together with the XXIV Panzer Corps as well as parts of the XVII and XXIX Army Corps, the II SS Panzer Corps mounted its counterattack on 30 July to eliminate the Soviet Mius bridgehead. Following particularly bloody fighting, the Germans succeeded in re-taking their old positions at the Mius on 2 August. The Donets bridgehead, too, was eliminated by the German First Panzer Army two days later. After relatively small initial successes, but at horrendous cost, the Soviet offensive aiming at recapturing the Donets Basin had thus failed. Still, the Red Army had reached one of its goals: the Germans had withdrawn the II SS Panzer Corps and the XXIV Panzer Corps, that is, two of their most powerful formations, from the area of Khar'kov, where on 3 August, the Soviet Voronezh and Steppe Front mounted their offensive. With this, the last phase of the Battle of Kursk began.

100 BA-MA, RH 20-6/303, Kriegstagebuch des Armee-Oberkommandos 6, Nr. 5, 17.7.-17.8.1943, fol. 57.

101 BA-MA, RH 2/3060, Kriegstagebuch der Operationsabteilung des Generalstabs des Heeres, 9.3.-31.7.1943, fol. 257.

102 Heiber, *Conferences*, p. 171.

Operation *Kutuzov*: The Soviet Offensive at Orël

As early as April 1943, the Soviet planning for the summer battles of that year was aiming at launching massive counteroffensives once the German Operation Citadel had successfully been halted. In the north of the Kursk salient, the Soviet Western, Bryansk and Central Front were given the task of preparing an assault against the Orël salient. The *Stavka*'s objective was not to encircle the enemy in a pincer movement, as the Germans had tried with Citadel at Kursk. Rather, the Red Army was to split up the German forces in the Orël salient with converging attacks from various directions and destroy them in individual groups. The main attack was entrusted to the Bryansk Front, which was to advance from Novosil′ straight westwards and reach Orël as quickly as possible. The Bryansk Front was commanded by Colonel-General Markian Mikhaylovich Popov, who at the beginning of the battle had about 470,000 soldiers, 1,525 tanks and self-propelled guns, in addition to the 10,200 guns and mortars at his disposal.

The Soviet Western Front, led by Colonel-General Vasiliy Danilovich Sokolovskiy, was to thrust into the Orël salient from the north. Sokolovskiy's Front consisted of nearly 250,000 men, roughly 1,740 tanks and self-propelled guns and 5,800 guns and mortars. The attacks by the Bryansk and the Western Front were initially directed solely against the German Second Panzer Army, whose actual commander, Colonel-General Rudolf Schmidt had fallen from grace and been on leave since April 1943 due to politically incriminating letters. On 10 July 1943, he was transferred to the Officer Reserve (*Führerreserve*) of the Army High Command, until he was discharged from the Wehrmacht on 30 September 1943. Since 24 April, the deputy commander-in-chief *General der Infanterie* Erich-Heinrich Clößner was responsible for the Second Panzer Army. He had 120,000 men and 940 guns and mortars available. In contrast to the 3,260 tanks and self-propelled guns of the Bryansk Front and the Western Front, the Second Panzer Army only had about 550 tanks and self-propelled guns, including reserves and those vehicles still in transit to the front.

Even though the German command was expecting Soviet counteroffensives, they had no clear idea of the strength of the Soviet troops, or of the force of the attacks. However, as early as June 1943, Field-Marshal von Kluge announced that in the case of a Soviet counteroffensive at Orël, Colonel-General Model, commander of the Ninth Army would, in addition to his own army, also take over the Second Panzer Army. Model was considered particularly energetic and stable. His taking over the command of the two armies would ensure a consistent and simplified command in the Orël salient; Model himself was all in favour of this decision.

In view of the overwhelming numerical superiority of the Soviet Bryansk and Western Front over the German Second Panzer Army, it was obvious that the latter would not be able to hold the Orël salient against the Soviet offensive on its own. Both the personnel and tank strength ratio was 6:1 in favour of the Soviets, in artillery it was as much as 17:1. Besides, as soon as the Germans were forced to transfer formations from the Ninth Army to the Second Panzer Army, General Rokossovskiy's Central Front would join the offensive against the Orël salient as well.

On 11 July, the Bryansk and the Western Front carried out limited, local reconnaissance thrusts which aimed at capturing German combat outposts. The command of the German Second Panzer Army considered these probing assaults to be mere holding attacks, but also saw them as the beginning of the Soviet counteroffensive against the Orël salient. According to the Soviet view, however, Operation *Kutuzov* only began on 12 July. After a nearly three-hour long artillery preparation, the two Soviet Fronts mounted their attack against the Second Panzer Army at three sectors of the Orël salient. East of Orël, at Novosil′, the 3rd Army (Lieutenant-General Aleksandr Vasil′evich Gorbatov) and the 63rd Army (Lieutenant-General Vladimir Yakovlevich Kolpakchi) moved against the front of the German XXXV Army Corps (*General der Infanterie* Lothar Rendulic), where they faced the 56th and 262nd Infantry Division. The main attack was made by Kolpakchi's 63rd Army, which advanced with four rifle divisions, one breakthrough artillery corps and five tank regiments. They were supported by the nearly 1,000 planes of the 15th Air Army under Lieutenant-General Nikolay Fëdorovich Naumenko. West of Novosil′, the Soviet troops came upon well-fortified German positions. On the first day of the attack they made only small gains in territory; and, at the high price of 60 tanks.

The second Soviet point of concentration was at Bolkhov, north of Orël. There the Soviet 61st Army (Lieutenant-General Pavel Alekseevich Belov) attacked the German 208th Infantry Division with four rifle divisions. By the evening, the Soviet troops had managed to advance five to six kilometres. The most dangerous situation for the Germans, though, developed further northwest, at Ulyanovo. In this sector of the Soviet Western Front, the Soviet 11th Guards Army (Lieutenant-General Ivan Khristoforovich Bagramyan) – with six divisions, one breakthrough artillery corps and two guards tank regiments – achieved a deep penetration at the boundary between the German 211th and 293rd Infantry Division. In order to exploit the success, break through the German Front completely and penetrate in depth, Bagramyan deployed the 5th Tank Corps with about 185 tanks and self-propelled guns in the afternoon. His formations succeeded in advancing 10-12 kilometres and reaching Ulyanovo. Since all available German air forces were committed at the Bryansk Front, the Soviet 1st Air Army (Lieutenant-General Mikhail Mikhaylovich Gromov) dominated the air space with its 1,320 aircraft.

Army Group Centre hurriedly brought up Major-General Ernst Faeckenstedt's 5th Panzer Division, so far held in reserve, to repulse the Soviet formations at Ulyanovo. General Clößner, the deputy commander of the Second Panzer Army, had the division mount a counterattack in the evening of 12 July; the attack was unsuccessful, whereupon Clößner and Faeckenstedt blamed each other for the failure.

For the soldiers of the 5th Panzer Division, 13 July turned out to be the 'blackest day of the entire Russian Campaign.'[103] Even before sunrise, the division began the

103 Anton Detlev von Plato, *Die Geschichte der 5. Panzerdivision 1938-1945* (Regensburg, 1978), p. 274.

assault against the units of the Soviet 11th Guards Army northwest of Ulyanovo. The bulk of the division, the II Battalion of the 31st Panzer Regiment and the 14th Panzergrenadier Regiment, attacked over a commanding height and ran into parts of the Soviet 16th Guards Rifle Corps, which itself was just getting ready for an attack with strong armoured support. Since the German attack was carried out from the west towards the east, the German panzer soldiers were driving directly towards the rising sun and therefore failed to see that they were only a few hundred meters away from a Soviet tank formation when the latter opened fire, catching them by surprise. 'At such a short distance, the disadvantage of the thinner armour and the box-like, square shape of the Panzer IV became particularly evident', a soldier of the 31st Panzer Regiment wrote. 'Additionally, the enemy was in the still low but rising sun, blinding our boys whilst illuminating our tanks like an open barn door for the enemy. So from the first minutes, the noise of the continuous firing from our guns blended with the bang of the hits.'[104]

Within a short time, the German attack was decimated by the Soviet tanks. The II Battalion of the 31st Panzer Regiment had 45 tanks completely destroyed – even in the entire course of Operation Citadel, no panzer battalion had suffered as many losses. After the German tanks had been knocked out, the Soviet formations in turn launched their attack, inflicting heavy casualties on the 14th Panzergrenadier Regiment. On 13 July, the 5th Panzer Division lost 855 soldiers in total, including 126 killed and 315 missing. In the afternoon of the same day, Lieutenant-General Bagramyan deployed both the 1st Tank Corps with over 200 tanks and self-propelled guns and the 1st Guards Rifle Division in order to destroy the badly battered division and achieve an operational breakthrough. The Soviet formations tore a gap more than 20 kilometres wide in the German front, behind which there were no longer any significant German forces. However, the Soviet command did not recognize the opportunity to thrust southwards and encircle the German forces in the area of Orël. Instead of letting the 11th Guards Army advance at full tilt towards Khotynets further south, the strong Soviet formations turned southeast in order to destroy the German forces in the area of Bolkhov.

On the morning of 13 July, the Germans realized that the Soviet assaults were 'not holding attacks, but attacks with [a] further objective.'[105] In the afternoon of 13 July, as initially planned, Colonel-General Model took over command of the Second Panzer Army as well, and called the army's commanding generals, informing them that the 'operational situation [has changed] since this morning. The aim is not to regain the old main line of resistance anymore but to stop the breakthrough of the Russian forces at a suitable line and to free forces for counterattacks at operationally crucial places. Tactical gains or losses in territory no longer play a decisive role.'[106] Still, on 13 July,

104 Ibid., p. 273.
105 NARA, T313/153/7407419, Kriegstagebuch Nr. 3, Panzerarmee-Oberkommando 2, Ia, 1.6.-13.8.1943.
106 NARA, T313/153/7407421, Kriegstagebuch Nr. 3, Panzerarmee-Oberkommando 2, Ia, 1.6.-13.8.1943.

and during the following night, the 2nd, 18th and 20th Panzer Division, elements of the 12th Panzer Division and three assault gun battalions were withdrawn from the front of the Ninth Army and transferred to the sector of the Second Panzer Army. More panzer formations followed in the ensuing days. Even though most of these units were assigned to the XXXV Army Corps to block the Soviet advance east of Orël, and even though the Soviet forces hardly made any progress there, the *Stavka* adhered to its original operations plan. It reinforced the attack west of Novosil′ with additional reserves, instead of shifting the point of main effort to the 11th Guards Army at Ulyanovo, where the Soviet troops kept broadening the gap in the German frontline and pushing southwards.

Hitler realized that the advance of the 11th Guards Army was a significant threat to the German troops in the Orël salient; so, on 14 July, he ordered the 1st Air Division to join the battle 'with all available planes [in the] area of Ulyanovo.'[107] At that moment, Model did not have any more reserves he could have employed against the 11th Guards Army at Ulyanovo, thus, on 15 July, he decided gradually to shorten the front of the LV and LIII Army Corps in order to free up forces.

On the same day, Rokossovskiy's Central Front launched its offensive south of Orël. After having suffered such bloody losses during the defence against Operation Citadel, the formations of the Central Front first had to be replenished; though when they began the offensive on 15 July, they were still at partial strength – the 2nd Tank Army, for instance, only had 358 tanks at its disposal. Yet, all in all, Rokossovskiy's troops represented a considerable force: 675,300 men, more than 12,000 guns, mortars and rocket launchers, nearly 1,500 tanks and self-propelled guns and more than 700 planes. If the bulk of these forces had been employed in the sector of the Soviet 65th or 70th Army, they could easily have broken through the weak German frontline there. For the Red Army, this would have offered no less than an opportunity for a pincer movement like the one the Germans had failed to achieve in their attack on Kursk. But eschewing this opportunity, the Central Front continued to carry out its main assaults frontally against the attack forces of the German XXXXVII and XXXXI Panzer Corps still southeast of Kromy. According to Soviet accounts, the main effort was with the 16th and 19th Tank Corps attacking at Tëploe. There, Rokossovskiy's troops encountered the German 4th and 9th Panzer Division, as well as the *Tigers* of the 505th Heavy Panzer Battalion. Having been forewarned through intercepted Soviet radio messages and by Red Army soldiers who had deserted, the Germans inflicted heavy casualties on the Soviet troops.

The Ninth Army Headquarters registered the strongest Soviet attacks not at Tëploe, but at Ponyri, where the Soviet 18th Guards Rifle Corps and the 55th Rifle Division were attacking, the latter having been brought up from the area of the 60th Army. The Soviet formations at Ponyri were provided with armoured support by the

107 NARA, T313/153/7407884-5, Panzerarmee-Oberkommando 2, Ia, Anlagen-Band 2, Ferngespräche O.B., Chef, Ia (Juli-Kämpfe), 12.7.-29.7.1943.

3rd and 9th Tank Corps. On the German side, the 10th Panzergrenadier Division, the 86th Infantry Division and parts of the 292nd Infantry Division were at Ponyri on 15 July. Two assault gun battalions as well as the 654th Heavy Tank Destroyer Battalion were assigned to the 86th Infantry Division, which had to bear the brunt of the fighting that day. The daily report from the XXXXI Panzer Corps states: 'The 15 July was characterized by a tank battle of unprecedented scale. Repeatedly the enemy tried to break through our main line of resistance by sending forward numerous tanks, followed by dense masses of infantry.'[108] In fact, the Soviet troops succeeded in breaking through the German frontline at various places, but by the evening the Germans had managed to plug nearly all the breaches and knock out more than 100 Russian tanks. Nevertheless, the German forces also suffered heavy losses, and by now they were under serious pressure from the Central Front's attacks. But Model still wanted to disengage more units from the front of the Ninth Army and transfer them to the Second Panzer Army. In the evening of 15 July, therefore, he ordered the formations of the Ninth Army to commence the withdrawal to the initial position of 5 July. Up until 18 July, the Germans withdrew in three stages, giving up the terrain they had seized during Operation Citadel.

In the weeks which followed, Model reacted to crises and imminent Soviet breakthroughs with flexible withdrawal tactics in other front sectors of the Orël salient as well – and Hitler had no objections to it. In fact, for the dictator, who was usually known for his halt orders, the evacuation of the entire Orël salient could not happen fast enough. After all, he needed reserves for other front sectors and did not consider the area of Orël and the city itself as important as, for example, the Donets Basin or Khar'kov. On 26 July 1943, Hitler announced in a meeting with Field-Marshal von Kluge in the *Führerhauptquartier Wolfsschanze* that he wanted to clear the Orël salient to free forces for other front sectors. Kluge replied that he did not want to withdraw to the so-called Hagen line – the position at the base of the Orël salient that the German troops were to occupy after the final evacuation from the entire area of Orël – before the beginning of September (Map 8). Hitler's answer to this was: 'That's impossible. Completely impossible, Herr Field-Marshal!' After some back-and-forth Kluge conceded: 'In my opinion, the earliest we could move into the Hagen position would be in approximately – today is the 26th – four weeks; if we take the earliest calculation, in 3 to 4 weeks. That's the absolute earliest.' To this, Hitler replied: 'We can't wait that long. Forces have to be freed up before then, or it's no use.'[109]

The defensive combat actions of the Ninth Army and the Second Panzer Army were not only facilitated by the fact that Hitler gave Model free reign to operate, but also due to the Red Army dispersing its forces. On 18 July, the Soviet command committed the fresh 25th Tank Corps with about 200 tanks and self-propelled guns

108 BA-MA, RH 24-41/84, Generalkommando XXXXI. Panzerkorps, Ia, Tagesmeldung, 15.7.1943, no pagination.
109 Heiber, *Conferences*, pp. 257, 259.

to battle in the sector of the 11th Guards Army at Ulyanovo. Yet, the bulk of the corps did not attack towards the south and thrust into the still open gap in the front between the German LV and LIII Army Corps. Instead, most tanks were deployed for the assault towards Bolkhov in the southeast. By doing so, the Soviet high command had missed a great opportunity, as became apparent the following day. Some tanks of the 162nd Soviet Tank Brigade under Colonel Ignatiy Antonovich Volynets, which were moving southwards, succeeded in advancing as far as the Bryansk–Orël railway line at Khotynets. This railway line was of crucial importance for all German forces in the Orël salient because it was the main traffic corridor and the only railway line which led into and out of the salient. But as no further troops or supplies followed the Soviet tank unit, they had to content themselves with blowing up the railway line in numerous places before withdrawing once again. The Germans repaired the line the very next day.

Rather than exploiting the weak spot south of Ulyanovo, the *Stavka* continued to do all it could to ensure the breakthrough of the Bryansk Front east of Orël. On 19 July, the Soviet command threw one of its most powerful reserves into battle against the German XXXV Army Corps: the 3rd Guards Tank Army under the command of Lieutenant-General Pavel Semënovich Rybalko. The army had 730 operational tanks and self-propelled guns at its disposal; at first, about 450 of these were deployed with the 12th and 15th Tank Corps. Rybalko's forces encountered the German 36th Infantry Division and the 2nd and 8th Panzer Division, inflicting heavy casualties on these units. Even though the Germans managed to bring the Soviet thrust to a halt after roughly 12 kilometres, by the afternoon the XXXV Army Corps had to report to the Second Panzer Army Headquarters that 'we no longer have the means to plug the torn-open frontline.' Consequently, Model ordered the retirement to a line 'which has to be held for a few more days.'[110]

On the following day, Rybalko deployed the 2nd Mechanized Corps with more than 200 tanks and, on 21 July, his reserve, the 91st Tank Brigade, which had 72 tanks. But they also failed to break through the German frontlines east of Orël. One by one, Model's units withdrew in an orderly manner as soon as they were in danger of being surrounded or destroyed; then they dug in at the next defensive line, offering fierce resistance and, at the same time, preparing to disengage and withdraw to the next rearward positions.

On 26 July, the 11th Guards Army continued its attack from the area west of Bolkhov towards the south to advance into the region west of Orël and, thus, into the rear of the German forces still positioned at Orël. It was reinforced by the 4th Tank Army under the command of Lieutenant-General Vasiliy Mikhaylovich Badanov; this formation, which had been held back in reserve until that moment, had about 750 tanks and self-propelled guns at its disposal. In addition, the 2nd Guards Cavalry

110 NARA, T313/153/7407460, Kriegstagebuch Nr. 3, Panzerarmee-Oberkommando 2, Ia, 1.6.-13.8.1943.

Corps was also employed. Yet the opportunity to break through to the south and to encircle the German forces in the area of Orël, which had been open to the 11th Guards Army a week earlier, no longer existed. Model's troops had managed to close the gap in the frontline north of Khotynets and to some degree stabilize the situation; this was not least of all thanks to the appearance of the Panzergrenadier Division *Großdeutschland*, which had been transferred from Army Group South. Now the Soviet forces had to fight their way towards the south, thereby suffering heavy losses. The 11th Tank Corps, for instance, which was assigned to Badanov's 4th Tank Army, lost 119 of its 214 tanks and self-propelled guns within two days.

On 28 July, Model finally gave the order to prepare to retire to the Hagen position. The so-called 'Hagen movement' was to be carried out during the period from 31 July to 17 August in four stages. Nothing was to be left for the Red Army but 'scorched earth', although the city of Orël was fortunate under the circumstances. On 29 July, Field-Marshal von Kluge let the Second Panzer Army Headquarters know that he 'places no importance on the destruction of the entire city of Orël in the case of its evacuation. [The] destruction of larger buildings, however, should be carried out.'[111] According to a report from the German Garrison Headquarters Orël, only buildings of military and economic importance were destroyed before the Germans evacuated the city on 5 August. On the following day, Bagramyan's 11th Guards Army renewed its attack on Khotynets, but could not reach the Bryansk–Orël railway. It was not before 10 August, after the German formations had withdrawn further west and abandoned Khotynets, that the Soviet troops retook the settlement. In the following days, the forces of the Bryansk Front attempted to break through to Karachev. But, again, they only succeeded in capturing the city once the Germans had withdrawn further westwards. Karachev was not as fortunate as Orël; already on 3 August the headquarters of the Second Panzer Army noted in its war diary: 'On Army order, the town of Karachev has to be destroyed by burning down and blowing up all important objects. As the place is in the forefront of the Hagen position, the importance of the thorough destruction is particularly emphasized.'[112] A week later, the war diary of the Ninth Army noted the following about the 'scorched earth' tactics: 'While ahead the front withstands the onslaught of the pursuing enemy, the villages behind go up in flames; in the rear, everything that cannot be taken is burned and destroyed.'[113]

On 18 August, the last German formations which had withdrawn from the Orël salient reached the Hagen position. At the same time, a few hundred kilometres to the south, Field-Marshal Erich von Manstein was battling to secure Hitler's permission to evacuate the city of Khar'kov. The last act of the great Battle of Kursk had begun.

111 NARA, T313/153/7407515, Kriegstagebuch Nr. 3, Panzerarmee-Oberkommando 2, Ia, 1.6.-13.8.1943.
112 NARA, T313/153/7407536, Kriegstagebuch Nr. 3, Panzerarmee-Oberkommando 2, Ia, 1.6.-13.8.1943.
113 NARA, T312/317/7886221, Kriegstagebuch Nr. 8, Armee-Oberkommando 9, Führungsabteilung, 26.3.-18.8.1943.

Operation *Polkovodets Rumyantsev*: The Soviet Offensive at Khar'kov

The Soviet offensive at Khar'kov was the Red Army's main attack in summer 1943; it had been planned and prepared since the spring. In fact, the prelude to this operation would have been the attack of the Soviet 5th Guards Tank Army, the 1st Tank Army as well as the 5th and 6th Guards Army on 12 July 1943. Operation *Polkovodets Rumyantsev* (Commander Rumyantsev) in the south of Kursk should therefore have begun at the same time as Operation *Kutuzov* at Orël. However, during the battle of Prokhorovka, the 5th Guards Tank Army suffered a devastating defeat by the II SS Panzer Corps, which smothered the Soviet counteroffensive. The units of the Voronezh Front under General Vatutin and the troops of the Steppe Front, commanded by Colonel-General Konev, needed time before they could renew the offensive.

On 24 July 1943, the *Stavka* announced on Moscow radio that on the previous day, that is, 23 July, the German summer offensive had finally been defeated. The Soviet troops had not only repelled all German attacks but also pushed the Germans back to their start lines from where they had launched Operation Citadel on 5 July. Soviet historiography later adopted the line that on 23 July 1943 the troops of the Voronezh Front reached the positions of 5 July. The defensive phase in the south of Kursk had thereby found its point of closure; following it, it suggested, was a lull in the fighting until 3 August 1943.

In truth, this was just a propaganda claim, and wrong in two respects. For one thing, the Germans had already concluded their attack in the south of Kursk by 16 July. During the night of 18-19 July, the Fourth Panzer Army began withdrawing to an 'intermediate position'; on 19 July, Army Detachment Kempf joined the withdrawal. The 'intermediate position', however, was not identical to the initial positions of 5 July 1943 but was situated further north (Map 8). Manstein's formations withdrew to the initial position of 5 July only in early August. As another point, there was no pause in the fighting between 23 July and 3 August. In fact, Soviet formations kept attacking the Fourth Panzer Army and Army Detachment Kempf during this time. On 28 July, for instance, the war diary of the Fourth Panzer Army Headquarters reported: 'At the LII Army Corps, the enemy all day carries out attacks in regimental strength with tanks against the entire front of the 167th Infantry Division, the 332nd Infantry Division and the 255th Infantry Division. All assaults can be repelled or thrown back by counter-attacks.'[114]

The break of 23 July 1943 is therefore entirely arbitrary, as this day did not mark any turning point for either the Soviet or the German troops. In actual fact, Manstein's soldiers would have liked to have withdrawn to the initial positions of 5 July, as these had been well prepared and fortified during the preparation phase of the battle of Kursk. The 'intermediate position', by contrast, was merely an improvised defensive

114 BA-MA, RH 21-4/104, Kriegstagebuch des Oberkommandos der 4. Panzerarmee, Ia, 25.3.-31.7.1943, fol. 212.

line, which offered inadequate protection against the very effective Soviet artillery and mortar fire. Colonel-General Hoth, the commander of the Fourth Panzer Army, called Manstein on 30 July, and explained: 'I believe a new major attack of the enemy against the front of the Fourth Panzer Army is imminent. I think it is time to fall back to the old position.' To this, Manstein replied that he was not yet expecting a large-scale Soviet attack and that he only wanted to withdraw to the old position in the case of 'an actual major attack.'[115]

That attack came four days later. On the morning of 3 August, the formations of the Voronezh and the Steppe Front launched their offensive after more than two hours of artillery preparatory fire. At the beginning of the fighting, the two fronts could muster about 1 million soldiers, 2,440 tanks and self-propelled guns as well as 1,520 planes in total, whereas the German Fourth Panzer Army and Army Detachment Kempf were considerably weakened after the cancellation of Operation Citadel and the transfer of panzer formations to the Donets Basin and the Orël salient. Therefore, in the area of Khar'kov, the Soviet troops were initially facing only about 210,000 German soldiers – a personnel ratio of 5:1. On paper, the units of the Fourth Panzer Army and of Army Detachment Kempf still had 640 tanks and self-propelled guns at their disposal. However, many of these had been damaged during the attack on Kursk and the ensuing defensive battles and were being repaired in workshops; the fact that the Wehrmacht had a chronic shortage of spare parts as well as mechanics only lengthened the time for maintenance and repair work. In early August, a mere 270 tanks and self-propelled guns were operational. This was a strength ratio of about 9:1. In terms of aerial power, the situation was slightly less disadvantageous for the Germans, as *Luftflotte* 4 had about 1,140 planes, roughly 800 of which were operational – a strength ratio of 2:1. This air fleet had to cover the entire southern sector of the Eastern Front, however. Furthermore, the Soviet 17th Air Army (Southwestern Front) joined the combat at Khar'kov after a few days as well, so the relative strength in the air became even more favourable for the Soviet side.

On the ground, the Red Army at first deployed five armies, the 5th Guards Army, the 6th Guards Army, the 53rd Army, the 69th Army and parts of the 7th Guards Army. The main attack of the first wave was carried out by the 5th Guards Army under the command of Lieutenant-General Zhadov. It attacked Hoth's Fourth Panzer Army frontally – Stalin had forbidden operational envelopment with the argument that the Soviet forces were too weak for such a manoeuvre. Zhadov's troops broke through the positions of the German LII Army Corps in the sector of the 332nd Infantry Division and the 167th Infantry Division; both divisions suffered heavy losses. In the afternoon, the Soviet command deployed the 1st Tank Army and the 5th Guards Tank Army in the sector of the 5th Guards Army to achieve the operational breakthrough. Both these armies had been rebuilt after the

115 Private Archive of Rüdiger von Manstein, Handakte des Oberbefehlshabers der Heeresgruppe Süd, Juli 1943, no pagination.

horrific losses sustained during the defensive phase; at the beginning of Operation *Polkovodets Rumyantsev* they had about 74,000 men and 1,050 operational tanks and self-propelled guns in total. The Germans could neither physically nor psychologically measure up to such a mass of troops; among the soldiers of the 167th Infantry Division, which had proved itself very well during Operation Citadel, panic broke out, and the Soviet 5th Guards Tank Army managed to advance more than 25 kilometres in this sector. In other areas of the front, the Soviet formations succeeded in penetrating the German lines more than eight kilometres in depth. Only the attack of the 69th Army and the 7th Guards Army remained unsuccessful because the Soviet soldiers could not cross the Donets River.

Initially, the Germans only had three panzer divisions at their disposal for counterattacks: the 6th, the 11th and the 19th Panzer Division, which together had about 180 operational tanks and self-propelled guns. Even though their counterattacks slowed down the Soviet advance, they could not bring it to a halt. In the evening of 3 August, both the Fourth Panzer Army Headquarters and the Headquarters of Army Detachment Kempf as a result ordered their troops to withdraw to the initial positions of Operation Citadel.

It is more than likely that the Soviet forces could have achieved even greater successes on the first day of the battle, had the Luftwaffe not intervened as effectively, despite its inferiority in numbers. The war diary of the Fourth Panzer Army commented on its effort as follows: 'All day, particularly in the afternoon, strong formations of the Luftwaffe (*Stukas* and bombers) have lent the most valuable help. At first they were employed as support for the 332nd Infantry Division, then mainly to combat concentrations of enemy troops in the gap [in the frontline].'[116] But the Russian Air Forces, too, joined the battle in great strength. The air armies of the Voronezh and the Steppe Front flew nearly 2,400 sorties on the first day of the battle. They lost 40 planes, compared to seven planes lost by the Luftwaffe.

The following day, the Luftwaffe again played a decisive role during the battle. On 4 August, the two Soviet tank armies continued pushing through the gap that Zhadov's 5th Guards Army had forced open the previous day at the boundary between the Fourth Panzer Army and Army Detachment Kempf. A counterattack by the German panzer divisions to close the gap failed, and Manstein had no more ground troops he could have deployed against the Soviet formations which had broken through; the Russians could thus only be countered by German aircraft; and, once more, it became apparent that the Luftwaffe was still tactically superior to the Red Army Air Forces. Whereas *Luftflotte* 4 had seven completely destroyed and four planes badly damaged, the Soviets suffered at least 62 total losses that day.

On 5 August, Vatutin deployed the fresh 27th Army for an attack southwards. It was to link up with the units of the 1st Tank Army and the 5th Guards Tank Army

116 NARA, T313/372/8658841, Panzerarmee-Oberkommando 4, Ia, Kriegstagebuch, vol. 1, vom 1.8.-30.9.1943.

east of Grayvoron, thereby encircling the German troops which were still putting up stubborn resistance northeast of Grayvoron and holding up the advance of the 5th and 6th Guards Army. They nearly succeeded. The 27th Army pushed 13 kilometres ahead, and the formations of the German LII Army Corps had to beat a hasty retreat to escape encirclement. However, the 19th Panzer Division failed to pull back in time, was cut off, failing to break out and reach the new defensive line before the next day, and with heavy losses. In the meantime, the Soviet command kept throwing new units into battle. Apart from the 27th Army, the 40th Army joined the offensive on 5 August. Its attack tore a large gap in the German frontline between the XXXXVIII Panzer Corps and the LII Army Corps. Only the counterattacking 7th Panzer Division was able to stop the Soviet thrust temporarily.

In the sector of Army Detachment Kempf, the troops of the Soviet Steppe Front began their attack on Belgorod on 5 August. While the 53rd Army bypassed west of Belgorod towards the south, the 69th Army and the 7th Guards Army attacked the city from the north and east. In the area of the 7th Guards Army, Soviet soldiers finally managed to bridge the Donets. The German soldiers were no longer able to check the advance of the Russian troops. In the afternoon of 5 August, the XI Army Corps[117] reported to Army Detachment Kempf: 'Enemy has broken through in the eastern part of Belgorod. The troops' state of exhaustion is so great that any serious resistance is out of the question. The commander [of the] 168th Infantry Division reported that the men are so apathetic that they do not even react to threats at gunpoint anymore.'[118]

To avoid being trapped the Germans evacuated Belgorod in the evening. As the Wehrmacht gave up Orël on the same day, the *Stavka* could announce a notable victory, which above all possessed a symbolic value. Since the beginning of the Great Patriotic War, the Red Army had never beaten the Wehrmacht in one of the great summer battles. This had now changed. For the first time, Stalin ordered a victory salute in Moscow. At midnight, 124 guns fired 12 salvoes in an interval of 30 seconds to celebrate the liberation of Orël and Belgorod from the Germans.

On the following day, 6 August, the Soviet armoured spearhead thrust as far as Bogodukhov. In other sectors of the front around the area of Khar'kov the Germans also had to withdraw. This time, however, the LII Army Corps failed to disengage quickly enough and was encircled. The next day, supported by supplies delivered by air, it fought its way back towards the southwest against the resistance of the Soviet 27th Army and parts of the 1st Tank Army. Katukov's 1st Tank Army meanwhile captured Bogodukhov, while Konev's armies advanced further towards Khar'kov, which prompted the Germans to begin evacuating materiel from the city.

Finally, the impetuous thrust of the Soviet tank armies had passed its culmination point. By this point, the Germans had brought up the 3rd Panzer Division from the

117 Corps Raus had been renamed XI Army Corps on 20 July 1943.

118 NARA, T312/54/7569807, Kriegstagebuch Nr. 2 (vol. 2) des Armee-Oberkommandos 8, Ia (bis 16.8.43: Armee-Abteilung Kempf), 1.8.-31.8.1943.

Donets area, which successfully stopped the advance of the 5th Guards Tank Army in the evening of 7 August. At Bogodukhov the next morning, the spearheads of Katukov's 1st Tank Army encountered the SS Division *Das Reich*, which had also been brought up again, and were repelled. The LII Army Corps managed to break out of the encirclement on the same day, reaching the German lines at Akhtyrka. Furthermore, more German units were now being brought into the threatened area: the Panzergrenadier Division *Großdeutschland* from the area of Orël, the Waffen-SS Divisions *Totenkopf* and *Wiking* from the Donets Basin and the 355th Infantry Division from the Crimea.

Vatutin now shifted the point of main effort to the area of Bogodukhov and brought up the 5th and 6th Guards Army to reinforce his 1st Tank Army. At the same time, he had the 27th Army attack in the direction of Akhtyrka to protect the western flank of the 1st Tank Army. He also employed large, fresh formations. On 8 August, the Soviet 38th Army attacked in the sector of the German VII Army Corps, which was by now subordinate to the Fourth Panzer Army. The next day, the 57th Army attacked east of Khar'kov against the XXXXII Army Corps of Army Detachment Kempf. Two days later, on 10 August, it took Chuguev. The same day, the Germans were faced with a crisis to the northeast of Khar'kov as well. Parts of the Soviet 7th Guards Army successfully breached the German frontline around the 282nd Infantry Division to a width of seven kilometres and pushed towards Khar'kov, thereby forcing Army Detachment Kempf to withdraw to a new main line of resistance. The headquarters of XXXXII Army Corps reported that the crisis had arisen because the green 282nd Infantry Division had failed mostly 'due to inept leadership.'[119] Consequently, the division commander, Major-General Wilhelm Kohler was relieved of his command and transferred to the Officer Reserve of the Army High Command.

The next day, 11 August, the formations of the Steppe Front were only about 10-15 kilometres away from the city of Khar'kov. In the sector of the Voronezh Front, the point of main effort was in the area south and southwest of Bogodukhov. There attacks by the Soviet 1st Tank Army and the 5th Guards Tank Army alternated with counterattacks by German panzer formations. Manstein saw the greatest danger in a Soviet thrust from the area of Kolomak towards Poltava and in the blocking of the Poltava–Khar'kov railway line, which is why he deployed his strongest panzer units to the region of Bogodukhov, Kolomak and Valki. On 15 August, the SS Division *Totenkopf* succeeded with a flanking thrust in intercepting an attack on Poltava by the Soviet 6th Guards Army, which was supported by parts of the 1st Tank Army. The Soviet formations suffered heavy losses and had to withdraw towards the north. In the evening of 15 August, Katukov's 1st Tank Army only had about 100 operational tanks in the field. Nonetheless, in the following days, the fighting at Bogodukhov continued with undiminished ferocity.

119 NARA, T312/54/7569852-4, Kriegstagebuch Nr. 2 (vol. 2) des Armee-Oberkommandos 8, Ia (bis 16.8.43: Armee-Abteilung Kempf), 1.8.-31.8.1943.

For Army Group South, Poltava was a particularly crucial logistical centre, whereas Manstein considered the city of Khar'kov to be of minor importance. On 11 August, the Chief of Staff of Army Detachment Kempf, Major-General Hans Speidel, told Manstein's Chief of Staff, Major-General Theodor Busse, that Army Detachment Kempf intended to give up Khar'kov. Busse replied: 'We don't care about that backwater, either.'[120] Yet, on 13 August, Hitler gave orders to hold Khar'kov at any price. On the same day, Manstein was told that the Army High Command planned to replace General Werner Kempf, whose situation reports had become increasingly pessimistic, with *General der Infanterie* Otto Wöhler. In 1942/43, Wöhler had been Chief of Staff of Manstein's 11th Army and had just proved himself as Commanding General of the I Army Corps in the third battle south of Lake Ladoga; he had been mentioned in the Wehrmacht report the day before. According to his diary, Manstein had no objections against Kempf being replaced by Wöhler, and, on 15 August, the latter took over the command of Army Detachment Kempf, which was renamed the Eighth Army on 16 August.

In fact, Hitler attached political significance to the city of Khar'kov. He feared that both Germany's allies and the neutral powers would take the evacuation of this important Soviet industrial city as a sign that the fortunes of war had now irrevocably turned against the Germans. In the evening of 14 August, the Chief of the Army General Staff, General Zeitzler, informed Manstein in a telephone call: 'The *Führer* has told me once more to make *Herrn Feldmarschall* particularly aware of the necessity that Khar'kov must be held. During these days, meetings are taking place with the Bulgarians and the Turks.'[121]

As for Manstein, his focus was still on the sector of the front where the Fourth Panzer Army was involved in fierce combat with Vatutin's Voronezh Front. Manstein could not afford to withdraw strong forces from this sector to deploy them to Khar'kov, as Vatutin kept bringing up fresh troops to renew the offensive *Polkovodets Rumyantsev*. Not only did the Soviet tank formations constantly receive replacements, but fresh formations also joined the attack. Along with the 38th and 40th Army, the 47th Army, which had been held back in reserve until that moment, launched an attack from the south of Sumy towards Lebedyn on 17 August. The spearhead of the attack was the 3rd Guards Mechanized Corps with more than 200 tanks. The sheer force of the Soviet attack hit the combat morale of the already totally exhausted German troops hard. The war diary of the Fourth Panzer Army noted: 'The 57th Infantry Division fails completely and in some instances retreats without a fight. Only the Commanding General of the LII Army Corps manages through personal commitment… to detain

120 NARA, T312/54/7569861, Kriegstagebuch Nr. 2 (vol. 2) des Armee-Oberkommandos 8, Ia (bis 16.8.43: Armee-Abteilung Kempf), 1.8.-31.8.1943; and, see also, NARA, T312/54/7569869.

121 Private Archive of Rüdiger von Manstein, Handakte des Oberbefehlshabers der Heeresgruppe Süd, August 1943, no pagination.

considerable parts of the division again and deploy them for a counterattack towards the east.'[122] Shortly after 1000, Colonel-General Hoth radioed the 57th Infantry Division: 'Not one step back. Hold commanders accountable.'[123] The Soviet assault would eventually be brought to a halt after 12-15 kilometres by the fierce resistance of the 68th Infantry Division and a counterattack by the 11th Panzer Division. However, on the next day, 18 August, the Soviet formations continued their offensive towards Lebedyn and Gadyach, all but destroyed the 112th Infantry Division, and inflicted further heavy casualties on the 57th Infantry Division.

From Akhtyrka further south, the Division *Großdeutschland* on the same day advanced almost 25 kilometres southeastwards. The units of the Soviet 27th Army, which had pushed into the area of Kotelva, were therefore in danger of becoming encircled. In the following days, they had to fight their way back towards the north. For Manstein's troops this was the only glimmer of light on that day. Meanwhile, the armies of Konev's Steppe Front tightened the ring around Khar′kov. At least Hitler was not insisting anymore that the city had to be held at all costs. On 18 August, Zeitzler told Manstein that on behalf of Hitler he had to point out once more to Manstein how important it was to hold Khar′kov. But the *Führer* also admitted that German formations must not be encircled in Khar′kov. If the worst came to worst, Hitler preferred giving up the city.

Khar′kov was nonetheless of considerable importance to Hitler. This was highlighted by a phone call he made personally to Manstein on 20 August. This happened only on rare occasions. Usually, the commanders of the Eastern Front's army groups only indirectly communicated with Hitler through the Chief of the Army General Staff. Hitler told Manstein on the phone that it was a psychological and military necessity to hold Khar′kov. Manstein was able to convince Hitler that the city had to be given up or else the German forces would be trapped in the city; still, Hitler ended the conversation with the instruction 'to hold if in any way possible.'[124]

Just like Manstein himself, his most important opponent at that time, General Vatutin, was under considerable pressure as well. On 21 August, he ordered the 40th and 47th Army, which in the days before had captured Lebedyn and advanced to the Psël River at Gadyach, to turn southwards and push towards Zen′kov so as to renew the stalled assault towards Poltava. The Soviet 2nd Tank Corps, which was assigned to the 40th Army, reached the outskirts of Zen′kov but was then repelled by the newly arrived 10th Panzergrenadier Division. The following night, Stalin reprimanded Vatutin for having split his attack forces. The Voronezh Front's main task, according to Stalin, was to beat the German forces in the area of Akhtyrka. At once,

122 NARA, T313/372/8658906, Panzerarmee-Oberkommando 4, Ia, Kriegstagebuch, vol. 1, 1.8.-30.9.1943.
123 NARA, T313/372/8658907, Panzerarmee-Oberkommando 4, Ia, Kriegstagebuch, vol. 1, 1.8.-30.9.1943.
124 Private Archive of Rüdiger von Manstein, Handakte des Oberbefehlshabers der Heeresgruppe Süd, August 1943, no pagination.

Vatutin reacted to this admonishment by having his formations attack Akhtyrka once again on the morning of 22 August. The Soviet troops succeeded in breaking through the German frontlines and, by noon, the situation for the German XXXXVIII and XXIV Panzer Corps was becoming critical. Still, in the afternoon, the Divisions *Totenkopf* and *Großdeutschland* launched counterattacks, undoing the earlier Soviet success.

On the same day, General Wöhler had to order the units of his Eighth Army (the former Army Detachment Kempf) to evacuate Khar'kov. At 2000, the Germans began withdrawing from the city, and the following morning, Soviet troops moved in. The fourth and last battle for Khar'kov was thus over – and, according to Soviet historiography, so was the Battle of Kursk. The highest price for the victory at Khar'kov had been paid by the Soviet tank troops. Most of the 2,440 tanks and self-propelled guns with which the Red Army had begun Operation *Polkovodets Rumyantsev* had been knocked out. Katukov's 1st Tank Army lost 1,042 tanks, including 753 completely destroyed, during the offensive at Khar'kov. On 23 August, the 1st Tank Army had a mere 120 operational tanks available. By 25 August, Rotmistrov's 5th Guards Tank Army had lost almost three quarters of its officers and had only 50 operational tanks at its disposal. It took the army two months until it was once again ready for employment in battle.

3

A Battle of Attrition: Consequences of the Summer Battles in 1943

The Outcome of the Battle of Kursk and the Tally of Losses

The Battle of Kursk ended in defeat for the Germans. None of the objectives the German command had set for the summer of 1943 were achieved. First, during the first few days of Operation Citadel, it was intended that the German formations would break through the Soviet positions and encircle the troops in the area of Kursk. They did not succeed. Second, the liquidation of the Kursk salient should have resulted in a considerable shortening of the frontline, which in turn would have allowed the Germans to free up formations to form a new reserve. This goal was not achieved either. According to Hitler, victory at Kursk should have served, third, as a signpost for both sides. This hope, though, was likewise in vain. The fourth objective was that the Wehrmacht would take as many Russian soldiers prisoner as possible, as they were needed as workers for the German war economy. In 1941, the Wehrmacht had captured about 665,000 Soviet soldiers during the Battle of Kiev and the double encirclement of Vyazma and Bryansk, respectively. By contrast, only about 40,000 Soviet soldiers were taken prisoner during the attack against Kursk in July 1943; this was not going to alleviate the shortage of workers in the German Reich. The fifth objective of the German offensive at Kursk was to break the Soviet offensive strength in order to give the German *Ostheer* a much-needed respite for the remainder of the year 1943. This was not achieved either. While the Germans did inflict horrific losses on the Red Army at Kursk and weakened their enemy, the Soviet Union had so many military reserves in 1943 that, in spite of severe setbacks, it was still able to have its armies launch offensives along the entire German-Soviet front from July 1943.

However, the success of the 1943 Soviet summer and autumn offensives was not thanks to tremendous and irreplaceable losses inflicted on the Wehrmacht during Operation Citadel, even though this legend is still perpetuated. Its origin does not only lie in Soviet propaganda, but also in the memoirs of German generals, who after the war claimed that the German formations had bled out in Operation Citadel. Until today, such statements by Guderian, Mellenthin or Warlimont can be found especially in Russian historiography on the subject, buttressing the assertion that the Red Army inflicted a crushing defeat on the Wehrmacht in Operation Citadel.

If the contemporary Soviet reports of success had been true, then Citadel would indeed have been a disaster for the Wehrmacht. On 24 July 1943, Stalin announced that in the time from 5-23 July, the Red Army had killed more than 70,000 German soldiers, destroyed almost 3,100 German tanks and self-propelled guns and shot down approximately 1,400 aircraft. In fact, the figures offered by the *Stavka* were thought to be underestimates as, all told, the victories reported by the individual Soviet fronts were considerably higher than the total numbers as reported by the Soviet high command!

According to German records, the Wehrmacht and Waffen-SS did not suffer 70,000 dead during the Red Army's defensive phase, that is, the number used in the Soviet version, from 5-23 July 1943. Their approximate losses were 10,000 dead, 46,000 wounded and 2,000 missing. Had the Red Army in the same period of time actually destroyed 3,100 German tanks and self-propelled guns, then Model's, Hoth's and Kempf's armies would not have had any tanks at all by the end of July. In truth, the Germans only had about 350 total losses in tanks and self-propelled guns during the Soviet defensive phase; this is not a rough estimate but the number calculated from all available contemporary records. The number of 1,400 allegedly destroyed German planes is also far from the truth. In fact, the German aerial forces deployed in the battles at Kursk lost in total 240 aircraft during Operation Citadel, including losses due to technical problems or accidents. After Operation Citadel was broken off, the German VIII Air Corps only flew a few sorties at Kursk and therefore suffered practically no losses. Until 23 July 1943, the Germans therefore cannot have lost more than 250 planes. At the same time, the Soviet Air Forces (not including the long-range aviation) lost about 1,200 aircraft in the area of Kursk. The loss ratio was thus at roughly 1:5.

On 24 July 1943, the Voronezh Front reported that its formations had suffered total losses of 1,571 tanks and 57 self-propelled guns between 4 and 22 July; the Central Front had to write off 526 tanks and 28 self-propelled guns as destroyed beyond repair during the defensive phase in the north of Kursk. The Germans, for their part, lost 350 tanks and self-propelled guns, compared to no fewer than 2,182 Soviet ones – a ratio of 1:6 in the Wehrmacht's favour.

Unlike the losses in materiel, it is much more difficult to assess how many casualties the Red Army suffered during the defensive phase. In 1993, a Russian group of scientists led by the military historian and former Colonel-General of the Red Army Grigoriy Fedorovich Krivosheev published a book titled *Grif sekretnosti snyat* (The 'Classified' Seal Is No Longer Valid). It was the first summary of the losses the Red Army sustained in the wars of the 20th century based on Soviet military records. The book was translated to English in 1997 as *Soviet Casualties and Combat Losses in the Twentieth Century*, while a revised Russian edition was published with a new title in 2001.[1] However, the numbers of casualties the Red Army suffered in the Battle of

1 Gregoriy F. Krivosheev (ed.), *Rossiya i SSSR v voynach XX veka: Poteri vooruzhennykh sil: Statisticheskoe issledovanie* (Moscow, 2001).

Kursk was not revised – they are considered the 'official' number of Soviet losses, and most military historians who research the Battle of Kursk continue to rely on them. Yet many aspects of the statistics in *Grif sekretnosti snyat* are verifiably false. According to the official figures, the Voronezh Front, for instance, lost roughly 74,000 soldiers, including 27,500 'irrevocable losses' (killed or taken prisoner) in the period of 5-23 July, although the report by the Voronezh Front from 24 July 1943 quoted above states that by 22 July the front had already suffered approximately 101,000 casualties, including 20,500 killed and 26,000 missing. In other words, the losses reported on 24 July are about a third higher than the official numbers. What also needs to be taken into account is that on 23 July intense fighting took place – however, the losses of that day are not included in the following day's report. The total losses sustained by the Voronezh Front were, therefore, even higher, amounting to at least 40 percent more than the official statistics.

For the two other fronts involved in the defensive phase, the Central and the Steppe Front, no other numbers are available than those in *Grif sekretnosti snyat.* Some Russian historians assume that the losses of the Central Front were twice or three times higher than what is presented in *Grif sekretnosti snyat.* Even if one adds but 40 percent to the official casualty numbers of the Central and the Steppe Front (analogous to the Voronezh Front), the total number of losses for the defensive phase amounts to roughly 250,000. When compared to Wehrmacht losses, the ratio of casualties is therefore at 1:4.

Estimated Losses during the Red Army's Defensive Phase at Kursk

	Wehrmacht	Red Army	Loss Ratio
Men	58,000	250,000	1:4.3
Tanks and SP Guns	350	2,200	1:6.3
Aircraft	250	1,200	1:4.8

Other than the official information given in *Grif sekretnosti snyat* – which are incorrect – there are almost no accurate numbers available to calculate the total losses the Red Army suffered in the entire Battle of Kursk. According to *Grif sekretnosti snyat,* the Soviets had approximately 863,000 casualties, whereas Russian historians critical of the official report estimate losses ranging from 910,000 to 2.3 million men. Adding another 40 percent to the official casualty statistics (as with the estimates of losses during the defensive phase above), the casualty rate amounts to 1.2 million soldiers – and this is a cautious estimate. Russian historian Boris Vadimovich Sokolov, who offered some fairly accurate calculations of Soviet losses, reckons that as many as 999,300 Red Army soldiers were killed during the Battle of Kursk. By contrast, Wehrmacht and Waffen-SS suffered about 203,000 casualties according to German records.[2] Compared to the prudent estimate of 1.2 million Soviet casualties, this is a casualty ratio of 1:6.

In July and August 1943, the Red Army lost about 9,300 tanks and self-propelled guns on the entire German-Soviet front.[3] Approximately 7,000 of these were destroyed in the Battle of Kursk. In the same time period, the Wehrmacht lost about 1,570 tanks and self-propelled guns on the Eastern Front, including roughly 1,200 at Kursk.[4] The loss ratio for tanks and self-propelled guns is thus likewise 1:6. The ratio of losses with regards to aircraft is 1:5, as the Wehrmacht lost around 650 aircraft at Kursk, the Red Army (including long-range aviation) at least 3,000.[5]

Estimated Losses during the Entire Battle of Kursk

	Wehrmacht	Red Army	Loss Ratio
Men	203,000	1,200,000	1:5.9
Tanks and SP Guns	1,200	7,000	1:5.8
Aircraft	650	3,000	1:4.6

One of the main challenges when estimating the actual level of Russian casualties (not only for the Battle of Kursk but for the entire Second World War) is that even during the war, the number of casualties reported by the Red Army was usually set too low. Quite possibly the underestimated numbers served to obscure the truly horrifying number of casualties the Red Army actually suffered. Various examples illustrate this. According to the report by the Voronezh Front dating from 24 July 1943 mentioned above, the front suffered 101,000 casualties and 1,628 total losses of tanks and self-propelled guns in total from 4 to 22 July 1943. Yet, one month later, on 23 August 1943, a report drawn up by the General Staff of the Voronezh Front claimed that only 74,500 men had been lost and 1,397 tanks been destroyed. *Grif sekretnosti snyat* offers lower numbers still, listing 73,892 casualties and approximately 1,200 destroyed tanks!

The various reports about tanks losses of the Central Front during the defensive phase are just as telling. According to the list compiled by Colonel Zaev on 19 July

2 Niklas Zetterling and Anders Frankson, *Kursk 1943: A Statistical Analysis* (London, 2000), pp. 116-7.
3 Frieser, 'Schlacht', p. 201-2.
4 This estimate is based on the figures presented in: Burkhart Müller-Hillebrand, *Das Heer 1933-1945: Entwicklung des organisatorischen Aufbaues*, vol. 3 (Frankfurt/M., 1969), p. 274-5 (table); and, Fritz Hahn, *Waffen und Geheimwaffen des deutschen Heeres 1933-1945*, vol. 2 (Bonn, 2nd edn, 1992), p. 240.
5 The losses of the German Luftwaffe were estimated based on material kindly supplied by Ulf Balke. For the Soviet side, the estimate is primarily based on Gorbach, *Nad Ognennoy Dugoy*.

1943, the front lost 526 tanks. Four days later, Zaev drew up a report about the tank losses of all Soviet fronts for the time period of 5-20 July 1943; this time, revising the number of tanks lost by the Central Front down to 393. This is even more striking as Rokossovskiy's troops launched their offensive against the German Ninth Army on 15 July. Their losses should therefore have been even higher, certainly not lower, than the first report. Zaev's compilation of 23 July obviously cannot be correct; according to it, the Central Front had 1,654 tanks at its disposal on 5 July 1943 and was sent another 109 tanks as reinforcements. So, in total, the Central Front had 1,763 tanks (not counting the self-propelled guns). On 20 July, Zaev claims, only 672 tanks were still operational, while 415 more were undergoing repair. Subtracting these 1,087 tanks still available to the Central Front on 20 July from the 1,763 it had at the beginning of the battles makes a difference of 676 tanks, not 393. In fact, 676 total losses for the time period of 5-20 July seems much more realistic. Of these, 526 tanks were lost during the defensive phase, 150 during the first days of the *Kutuzov* counteroffensive.

The number of Soviet tanks losses was remarkably high during other counterattacks as well. This is surprising, as an attacking formation usually did not lose as many tanks as the defenders. The reason for this is that after a successful advance, damaged tanks remained with the attackers, while withdrawing troops often could not recover their knocked out tanks, having to leave them to the advancing enemy. This can be illustrated through the following examples of Soviet tank losses at Kursk: according to Zaev's 19 July summary, the Central Front lost 651 tanks during the defensive phase, including 526, or 80 percent totally destroyed. The Voronezh Front reported a total number of 2,405 tanks lost until 22 July; 1,571 of these, or 65 percent, were beyond repair. By contrast, the percentage of total losses decreased significantly during the ensuing counteroffensives. By the end of July 1943, the Soviet 3rd Guards Tank Army, for instance, wrote off 669 tanks in Operation *Kutuzov*, but only 309 of these (i.e. 46 percent) were complete losses. The Soviet 4th Tank Army lost 534 tanks and self-propelled guns within just a few days at the end of July; but only 249, or 47 percent of these were 'irretrievable' losses, as the Russians used to call their AFVs which had been completely destroyed.

Hence, the Soviets wrote off relatively fewer tanks as 'irretrievable' losses during the counteroffensive. Still, the Red Army had no less than 2,586 total losses of tanks and self-propelled guns during Operation *Kutuzov*, and 1,864 during Operation *Polkovodets Rumyantsev* – and this is according to the official numbers published in *Grif sekretnosti snyat*. In total, this is 4,450 tanks and self-propelled guns, though the actual losses were most probably even higher, amounting to approximately 4,800 tanks and self-propelled guns. Measured against the average daily losses, the Battle of Kursk was one of the costliest engagements for the Red Army during the Second World War. During July and August 1943, its total losses on the entire Eastern Front amounted to more than 9,000 tanks (*not* including self-propelled guns), the same number of tanks that the Wehrmacht had lost on the same front in the two years since the summer of 1941. And, of course, it was not just about destroyed vehicles: tens of thousands of Soviet soldiers died in these tanks. Of the roughly 400,000 tank soldiers the Red Army trained during the entire duration of the Second World War, more than 300,000 were killed in action.[6]

So why did the Red Army suffer such horrific losses? In fact, the Battle of Kursk offers an eloquent case study. As already shown, the German panzer forces and the Luftwaffe were clearly superior in terms of both tactics and weapons technology, while the firepower of the German infantry was greatly enhanced when the MG 42 was introduced. The MG 42 was an extremely reliable weapon with a rate of fire of 25 rounds per second. Many German units taking part in Operation Citadel were equipped with this machine-gun in the spring of 1943. But there are many more important factors. The German Army placed particular importance on an optimum cooperation between the different branches in combined-arms combat (*Gefecht der verbundenen Waffen*), as well as on leading troops from the front (*Führen von vorn*), and on mission-type tactics (*Führen mit Auftrag*). Thanks to these tactical concepts, the Wehrmacht was able, time and again, to achieve surprising success even against far superior opponents; they will not be described in detail here, however, since they have already been amply recounted by a number of historians.[7] But what has often been neglected is the fact that the Wehrmacht's artillery, too, was very accurate, playing a pivotal role in the 1943 summer battles. On 14 July 1943, for instance, strong Soviet forces attacked the front of the German XXXXVIII Panzer Corps. The war diary of the Fourth Panzer Army Headquarters recorded: 'Masses of infantry keep rushing towards us yet falling in the perfectly accurate fire of the very skilfully commanded corps artillery.'[8] On 17 July, the war diary of the 7th Infantry Division noted: '[The] artillery regiment's observed fire dominates every enemy movement.'[9]

The self-propelled guns of the 'armoured artillery', in particular, proved themselves in combat. An after-action report by the commander of the II Battalion of the 103rd Panzer Artillery Regiment (4th Panzer Division) from 20 August 1943 gave the following account of the previous battles: 'The advantages of the nearly invulnerable (*unempfindlich*) self-propelled artillery were of crucial importance especially in the past battle of materiel in the east. While the emplacements of other battalions of the regiment suffered considerable losses due to constant air strikes and artillery fire, this was not case with the [II] Battalion – thanks to the armour [of its self-propelled artillery pieces], and because they could simply drive away from heavily concentrated fire,

6 Showalter, *Armor and Blood,* p. 22.

7 See, for example: Karl-Heinz Frieser, *Blitzkrieg-Legende: Der Westfeldzug 1940* (Munich, 2nd edn, 1996), pp. 412-32; Marco Sigg, *Der Unterführer als Feldherr im Taschenformat: Theorie und Praxis der Auftragstaktik im deutschen Heer 1869 bis 1945* (Paderborn, 2014), passim; and, Adrian E. Wettstein, *Die Wehrmacht im Stadtkampf 1939-1942* (Paderborn, 2014), pp. 102-8.

8 BA-MA, RH 21-4/104, Kriegstagebuch des Oberkommandos der 4. Panzerarmee, Ia, 25.3.-31.7.1943, fol. 162.

9 BA-MA, RH 26-7/40, Kampfgruppe 7. Division, Ia, Kriegstagebuch Nr. 5 des Kommandos der 7. Infanterie-Division 'Russland' für die Zeit vom 1.1.-30.9.1943, pt. B, p. 1509.

even though, according to the situation, they often had to be in firing positions which were exposed [to enemy fire].'[10] The Soviets, by contrast, did not have any 'armoured artillery' at their disposal; instead, they focused on the development of assault guns and self-propelled tank destroyers.

Moreover, the ammunition expenditure of German artillery in July and August 1943 was higher than ever before during the Second World War. The commander of the 200th Assault Gun *Ersatz- und Ausbildungsabteilung* (Replacement and Training Battalion), Lieutenant-Colonel Hellmut Christ, visited the Eastern Front from 30 August to 22 September 1943 to document the troop's experiences. In his report he stated that 'the German artillery is unfailingly excellent. It is the backbone of the front. When there is no more infantry, there is always the forward observer. One division commander said: 'The artillery is my last resort."[11]

Another important reason for the heavy Soviet losses were the remarkably efficient air strikes by German bombers and dive-bombers. The famous Junkers Ju 87 *Stukas* in particular were much feared by the enemy. One reason for this was that many *Stuka* pilots were not only well trained but had gained considerable combat experience. The other reason was the aircraft itself. Even though the Ju 87 was outdated and required air superiority for effective employment, it usually fulfilled its task with deadly accuracy in the battles at Kursk. A British test pilot, who had the opportunity to fly a captured Ju 87 shortly after the war, stated 'that the feeling of being on a runaway roller-coaster experienced with most other dive bombers was missing ... Somehow the [Ju 87] did not appear to find its natural element until it was diving steeply. It seemed quite normal to stand this aircraft on its nose in a vertical dive because its acceleration had none of that uncontrollable runaway feeling associated with a 90 degree inclination in an aircraft like the *Stuka*.'[12]

The efficacy of the German tactical air strikes was increased by air liaison officers (*Fliegerverbindungsoffiziere*), who were assigned to major formations of the Army and the Waffen-SS to facilitate the cooperation between the ground forces and the Luftwaffe, and who relayed ground targets to be engaged by the pilots. Additionally, *Stuka* or *Schlachtflieger-Leitoffiziere* (control officers) and *Fliegerfunker* (aerial radio operators) were sent to the forward area of the ground troops, maintaining constant direct radio contact with the formations of the Luftwaffe. The effect this could have on the cooperation between the ground troops and the Luftwaffe is highlighted in one of the daily reports from the Panzer Regiment *Großdeutschland* of 9 July 1943: 'In the

10 BA-MA, RH 10/58, Panzer-Artillerie-Regiment 103, II. Abteilung, Kommandeur, Taktische und artilleristische Erfahrungen in den Angriffs- und Abwehrkämpfen südlich Orel vom 5.7.-18.8.1943, fol. 278-302, quote, fol. 284 [emphasis in original, RT].

11 BA-MA, RH 10/58, Bericht über die Ostfrontreise des Kommandeurs der Sturmgeschütz-Ersatz- und Ausbildungsabteilung 200 vom 30.8.-22.9.1943, Abschrift, fol. 383-9, quote, fol. 385.

12 Eric Brown, *Wings of the Luftwaffe: Flying the Captured German Aircraft of World War II* (Manchester, 2010), pp. 180-1.

course of the afternoon, our Luftwaffe was very active. While the enemy air forces limited themselves to attacks against targets in the rear, our Luftwaffe, above all the *Stuka*, offered absolutely outstanding support to the panzer spearhead, combating enemy tanks, anti-tank guns and artillery autonomously and with notable success.'[13] The daily report of the Ninth Army from 11 July 1943 commented on the battle of the XXXXI Panzer Corps as follows: 'Around 1800 an enemy attack on Hill 253.5 supported by 6-8 tanks and lorry-mounted infantry, was destroyed by *Stukas* during its deployment.'[14] A Soviet soldier who was taken prisoner in the Sixth Army's sector at the Mius on 31 July 1943 told his interrogators that an assault his unit was to carry out two days earlier had to be called off because they lacked artillery support – *Stukas* had completely wiped out an artillery regiment brought up to the frontline. As for the Germans, there are no known cases where entire units or formations were destroyed by Soviet air strikes during the summer battles of 1943.

The *Stukas* were not only deadly accurate, they also had a dramatic psychological effect on the Red Army soldiers, particularly inexperienced ones, when they dived at a target with their screaming sirens. These sirens, often incorrectly called 'Jericho trumpets', were small propellers mounted on the fixed landing gear, which were turned on before the dive.[15] The 'Jericho trumpets', by contrast, were another invention which also served to demoralise the enemy: small whistles attached on the fins of bombs which made a nerve-wracking noise once the bomb was dropped. As disheartening as these devices were for the opposing troops, they greatly encouraged the German soldiers: 'The howling of the *Stukas* is music to our ears', a soldier of the 7th Infantry Division wrote in his diary on 5 July 1943.[16]

Quite apart from the Wehrmacht's superior tactics and weapons technology and the better training of its soldiers, there were other reasons for the high losses suffered by the Red Army in the Battle of Kursk. It became clear during the Soviet defensive phase that the Red Army was very capable when it came to building and fortifying defensive positions and tenaciously holding them as part of a relatively inflexible defence. This notwithstanding, Soviet commanders again and again made fatal mistakes, especially when it came to counterattacks. They kept dividing their own forces, parcelling them out or, worse, using their soldiers as cannon fodder. Naturally, both the Soviet military and Soviet historiography sought to conceal these inglorious occurrences. But, there are numerous reports of such incidents in German military

13 BA-MA, RH 39/631, Panzerregiment 'Großdeutschland', Ia-Tagesmeldung, 9.7.1943, no pagination.

14 BA-MA, RH 20-9/144, Anlage zum Kriegstagebuch Nr. 8 des Armee-Oberkommandos 9, Ia, vol. II, Tagesmeldungen, Berichtszeit: 1.7.-17.8.1943, no pagination.

15 The official name of the *Stuka* siren was 'Lärmgerät' (noise-making device), see D. (Luft) T. 2087 D-1 trop, *Ju 87 D-1 trop: Flugzeug-Handbuch*, Teil 12D: *Sondereinbauten*, Heft 1: *Lärmgerät*, Mai 1942.

16 Rudolf A. Haag (ed.), *So war es: Berichte von und über Soldaten der Aufklärungsabteilung 7 der 7. Bayerischen Infanterie-Division* (Munich, 1985), p. 81.

records, as well as reminiscences from former combatants. The Soviet 3rd Tank Corps and the 307th Rifle Division, for instance, carried out no less than 11 unsuccessful attacks at Ponyri on 8 July 1943, splitting their troops into smaller units rather than making a concentrated thrust; such a thrust would likely have been fatal for the weakened German defenders. On 8 July, Anton Bumüller, a radio operator in the 18th Panzer Division, witnessed close-up how a Soviet attack at Ponyri was repelled by a single *Ferdinand* tank destroyer:

> About 600-700 metres away there was a hollow in the terrain, running parallel to the frontline, which was deep enough to hide any tank. The Russian tank commander sent up the first T-34. It crept up and, just as it stuck out its nose and gun, it received a hit immediately in the hull from below. There was a flash and the tank rolled back down. It went on like this until the [final] fourteenth tank; all of them were knocked out. Only then did two tanks drive up at the same time, almost side by side. The first had just put its nose up when it was hit. The second nearly got as far as the plain but then it was hit, too, and burst into flames. After that the Russian commander gave up.[17]

Two days later, on 10 July 1943, the war diary of the XXXXVIII Panzer Corps noted: 'An exchange of experiences of the chief [of the corps general staff] with the chief of staff [of the] SS Panzer Corps gives a consistent picture: the numerous and strong armoured enemy formations in front of both corps were never employed in a coordinated major attack. Usually the enemy attacks in individual groups of 20-30 tanks. The reason for this is probably the poor fighting qualities of the Russian infantry, which mainly consists of very old and very young soldiers, whereas the mid-age range is nearly absent. The enemy is thereby forced to spread his tanks to bolster the morale of the infantry.'[18]

Many more similar statements could be listed here – and not just for the defensive phase, but for the Soviet counteroffensives *Kutuzov* and *Polkovodets Rumyantsev* as well. With regards to defence against Soviet tank attacks in the sector of the XXXXVI Panzer Corps during Operation *Kutuzov*, an experience report of the I Battalion of the 35th Panzer Regiment (4th Panzer Division) from 21 August 1943 stated the following: 'The continuous losses eventually prompted the enemy to remain at a considerable distance in open terrain. When attacking, he advanced into ravines and villages with infantry support only; he did achieve successes against our own infantry this way, but then he was knocked out by our tanks lying in wait on the reverse slope. The flexibility in choosing a better position to attack was lost; even where several tanks had already been knocked out he stubbornly kept attacking. Apart from using his

17 Interview with Anton Bumüller, 18 February 2013.

18 BA-MA, RH 24-48/115, Kriegstagebuch des Generalkommandos XXXXVIII. Panzerkorps, Ia, 1.7.-31.7.1943, fol. 54.

tanks as infantry support, the enemy attempts to use them – like the Germans do – by brigade to achieve a breakthrough. But the Russian tank commanders are not trained well enough yet to keep attacking with their tanks once they have penetrated the enemy lines. Instead, their vehicles just stand still and observe until they are knocked out.'[19]

One last example, this time illustrating the Soviet infantry losses during the summer battles in 1943, can be found in the aforementioned report by Lieutenant-Colonel Christ: 'Russian infantry is generally very poor and will usually only attack when supported by tanks. They suffered incredibly high losses, hardly received any training, advance without a fight and are basically all but leaderless. A lieutenant was captured who was actually a filing clerk, without any training, who was given command of 30 men and supposed to lead an attack against the German positions with this so-called platoon.'[20] What must be noted here is that these accounts were not propaganda reports but, in fact, secret documents drawn up for the military command in order to draw lessons from them.

Apart from the insufficient training of its soldiers and the lack of experience of Soviet lower and middle echelon commanders, command mistakes in the upper echelon were another reason for the enormous losses of the Red Army. Time and again the Soviet command ordered frontal attacks against the strongest sectors of the German frontline, for instance at Novosil' and Prokhorovka on 12 July 1943, at Ponyri and Tëploe on 15 July, or, two days later, at Dmitrievka and Kuybyshevo. For many Soviet commanders losses simply did not matter, so they kept sending their soldiers into 'senseless and bloody attacks' even later in the war.[21] It is clear that the sheer scale of losses could not be completely concealed. Soviet commanders therefore found themselves forced to justify them in a manner which would not expose themselves to accusations of incompetence. After all, Stalin had given enough warnings, with unsuccessful commanders arrested or even executed. The easiest way to justify failures or high losses suffered by one's own units was to exaggerate the opponent's strength and, at the same time, report huge enemy losses. However, this could backfire. In view of the constant exaggerated reports of successes by the Red Army, the Soviet leadership was bound to believe eventually that their troops were by now facing only weak and beaten German formations. This might be one reason why Stalin again and again ordered his armies to launch frontal attacks against the most powerful German formations.

19 NARA, T315/220/149, Kriegstagebuch der 4. Panzerdivision, Führungsabteilung, 1.7.-31.7.1943, Anlage d, Gefechts- und Erfahrungsberichte.

20 BA-MA, RH 10/58, Bericht über die Ostfrontreise des Kommandeurs der Sturmgeschütz-Ersatz- und Ausbildungsabteilung 200 vom 30.8.1943 bis 22.9.1943, Abschrift, fol. 383-9, quote, fol. 384.

21 Boris V. Sokolov, 'The Cost of War: Human Losses for the USSR and Germany, 1939-1945', *The Journal of Slavic Military Studies*, 9 (1996), pp. 152-93, here, 181.

Compared to the Soviet losses, the number of German casualties at the Battle of Kursk seems almost low. But this conclusion would be wrong, as for the Germans the losses were very high, and by the end of summer 1943 the combat strength of the *Ostheer* was severely reduced. These losses, however, were not the cause of the failure of Operation Citadel, as the material losses sustained during the second phase of the battle were even higher than during the offensive against Kursk. Even if the Wehrmacht had not attacked in early July, the Red Army would still have launched its summer offensives as planned. According to Guderian's memoirs, the panzer formations which had been replenished in spring could have been kept in reserve and allowed some rest by avoiding major battles on the Eastern Front.[22] In reality, this was never an option. The Wehrmacht would have been involved in fierce fighting and suffered heavy casualties regardless – and, the losses would almost certainly not have been lower than during Operation Citadel. Various examples can help to substantiate this hypothesis. On 9 August 1943, the headquarters of Army Group Centre presented the Army General Staff a list of the number of tanks the panzer formations assigned to Army Group Centre had lost between 5 July and 1 August 1943. This period included both the offensive and the defensive fighting during Operation Citadel and Operation *Kutuzov*, respectively, which began on 12 July. Of the eight panzer divisions listed, it was the 5th Panzer Division which suffered the highest losses, having to write off 55 tanks as not recoverable – and this division did not even take part in Operation Citadel. It was followed by the 2nd Panzer Division, which had 45 completely destroyed, and the 8th Panzer Division, which lost 41 tanks, although the latter did not participate in the attack on Kursk. The other panzer divisions, all of which took part in the defensive actions at Orël after Citadel had been abandoned, lost between 14 and 27 tanks.

The two SS Divisions *Das Reich* and *Totenkopf* lost 23 tanks and assault guns in their counterattack at the Mius on 30-31 July 1943. This was exactly the same number they had lost in the period of 5-18 July, that is, during the entire duration of Operation Citadel. This is particularly noteworthy as both divisions had considerably fewer operational tanks available at the Mius, so their losses were relatively higher.

In comparison to the Soviet casualty levels, the personnel losses suffered by German units during Operation Citadel were higher than during the ensuing defensive battles. The ratio of losses during the offensive at Kursk was, as calculated above, about 1:4; for the entire Battle of Kursk, however, it was 1:6. This is not really surprising, though, considering the fact that while the strong Soviet defensive positions in the Kursk salient had to be breached by the infantry of the attacking divisions, the Red Army relied less on infantry than on mines, tanks and artillery to defend against the German attacks, especially in the northern sector of the Kursk salient. In fact, Field-Marshal von Kluge was probably right when he observed on 11 July that the attack by

22 Heinz Guderian, *Panzer Leader* (New York, 2nd edn, 2002), p. 307.

Model's Ninth Army had failed 'only due to the impact of the enemy artillery, rocket and mortar fire.'[23]

Formations tend to suffer higher casualties in the attack rather than defence, as the defenders can take cover in defensive positions and bunkers, whereas the attackers are in the open. Despite what was repeatedly claimed in post-war memoirs by former German generals and in the Soviet historiography, the German attack formations were not completely burnt out. This can for instance be proved by the weekly reports, in which the division commanders had to give an assessment of their division's combat strength. On 18 July 1943, the commanders of the 3rd and 11th Panzer Division as well as of the Panzergrenadier Divisions *Das Reich*, *Totenkopf* and *Großdeutschland*, reported to the Fourth Panzer Army Headquarters that their units were still 'capable of any offensive action',[24] which was the highest assessment a commander could offer. The combat strength of the 255th Infantry Division, too, was still considered the same as on 5 July, that is as 'partly capable of offensive action.'

Only two divisions of the Fourth Panzer Army – the *Leibstandarte SS Adolf Hitler* and the 332nd Infantry Division – suffered such casualties during Operation Citadel as to markedly reduce their combat strength. On 5 July, both divisions were given the highest ranking assessment of 'capable of any offensive action.' Yet, a fortnight later, on 18 July, the *Leibstandarte*'s weekly report stated: '[The] division is fully capable of offensive action [but] only partly capable of defensive action due to a lack of infantry.' It is indeed true that the *Leibstandarte* had taken very heavy casualties among the Waffen-SS panzergrenadiers during Operation Citadel. On the first day of battle, the division suffered 636 casualties when it broke through the main Soviet army defence line. On 6 July, the division successfully penetrated the second defence line, but again it suffered heavy casualties, losing 487 soldiers in total. After that, the number of casualties declined. The third highest casualty rate suffered by the division was 374 men on 12 July 1943, when the *Leibstandarte* was taken by surprise by the attack of the 5th Guards Tank Army. However, these losses occurred in defensive not offensive combat. The 332nd Infantry Division was only 'partly capable of offensive action', as was reported on 18 July; its combat strength had been dramatically reduced over the course of Operation Citadel.

In the sector of Army Detachment Kempf, the 106th, 168th and the 320th Infantry Division, as well as the 19th Panzer Division, had also suffered heavy casualties, as did the infantry divisions of Model's Ninth Army. The 78th Assault Division lost 912 men on the first day of Operation Citadel, the 216th Infantry Division suffered 862

23 BA-MA, RH 24-46/91, Generalkommando XXXXVI. Panzerkorps, Ia, Kriegstagebuch Nr. 7 vom 1.6.-15.8.1943, fol. 90.

24 For this and the following quotes about the assessments of the divisions' combat strength see: BA-MA, RH 21-4/111, Anlagen zum Kriegstagebuch des Panzerarmee-Oberkommandos 4, Ia, Operationen vom 25.4.-31.7.1943, pt. 2, fol. 135-7; and, BA-MA, RH 21-4/112, Anlagen 3 zum Kriegstagebuch (C 2 Operationen II) vom 1.1.-31.7.1943, Panzerarmee-Oberkommando 4, Ia, fol. 300-2.

casualties. Two days later, the war diary of the 292nd Infantry Division remarked: 'The division took very heavy casualties on 7 [July]; the division's combat strength has therefore already declined after just 3 days of combat. The main reason for the high rate of casualties is the very heavy enemy artillery fire which cannot be countered.'[25]

There can be no doubt that some of the German assault divisions were decimated during Operation Citadel; in fact, some formations, for instance the 73rd Panzergrenadier Regiment of the 19th Panzer Division, were all but destroyed. Still, it also has to be taken into consideration that during the defensive battles in summer 1943, a number of units were 'burned out' within a few days. The 16th Panzergrenadier Division, for example, was in the thick of the fighting at the Mius from 17 July 1943, that is, during the Soviet Donbas offensive. It proved itself particularly well, and General Zeitzler suggested to Hitler on 25 July that the division be named in the Wehrmacht report. On the same day, the Army High Command announced: 'In the past battles at the Mius, the Rhenish-Westphalian 16th Panzergrenadier Division in particular distinguished itself.'[26] But this prestige came at a price – the division had nearly been wiped out at the Mius River. On 21 July 1943, the war diary of the Sixth Army remarked: 'Our own losses due to exceptionally heavy enemy artillery fire and massed air strikes (including phosphorous attacks) are substantial; the combat strength of the troops, who have been in fierce combat for five days now, has declined significantly, particularly [the] 16th Panzergrenadier Division, the 294th and the 306th Infantry Division.'[27] Of the 53 tanks the 16th Panzergrenadier Division had at its disposal, only four were still operational at the end of that day. The following day the Sixth Army's war diary stated: '[The] 16th Panzergrenadier Division, which had to carry the brunt of the defensive combat over the past few days, is very exhausted due to heavy personnel losses as well as the oppressive heat.'[28] On the morning of 23 July, the division reported that the combat strength of its grenadier battalions had in some cases decreased to 50 men and that the infantry's total strength was only 550 men – in a panzergrenadier division it normally amounted to more than 6,000 men.

There is still further evidence that the Germans did not suffer unusually heavy casualties during Operation Citadel compared to the ensuing defensive battles in summer 1943: the reports issued every ten days by the Wehrmacht Casualty Department (*Abteilung Wehrmachtverlustwesen*) of the Army High Command. During the 20 days between 11 and 31 July 1943, the Sixth Army lost 18,673 men in total in the Donets Basin – more than Army Detachment Kempf and the Fourth Panzer Army had respectively lost in as many days from 1-20 July 1943 (17,769 and 15,702 men),

25 BA-MA, RH 26-292/43, Kriegstagebuch Nr. 6 der 292. Infanterie-Division, Ia, für die Zeit vom 11.6.-30.9.1943, no pagination.

26 *Die Wehrmachtberichte 1939-1945*, p. 524.

27 BA-MA, RH 20-6/303, Kriegstagebuch des Armee-Oberkommandos 6, Nr. 5, 17.7.-17.8.1943, fol. 75.

28 BA-MA, RH 20-6/303, Kriegstagebuch des Armee-Oberkommandos 6, Nr. 5, 17.7.-17.8.1943, fol. 81.

that is, during Operation Citadel. Only Model's Ninth Army suffered even heavier casualties (28,447 men). In the 10 days from 21-31 August 1943, the Fourth Panzer Army had nearly as many casualties – 14,545 men – as during Operation Citadel (15,702 casualties from 1-20 July 1943). Army Detachment Kempf (Eighth Army) lost 23,470 men in the 20 days from 11-31 August 1943; again, this casualty rate exceeded that of the attack on Kursk from 1-20 July 1943 (17,769 casualties). And the Second Panzer Army reportedly had more losses (34,749 men) in the 10 days from 21-31 July 1943 than any other German Army suffered in a period of 10 or 20 days in summer 1943. Even the number of casualties of the Ninth Army during the twenty days of Operation Citadel was not as high (28,447), whereas the Fourth Army lost nearly as many soldiers (21,453) during the defensive combat from 11-20 August 1943 as the Ninth Army during the attack on Kursk (22,201).[29]

These examples clearly show that the offensive against Kursk by no means had as devastating an effect on the combat strength of the German *Ostheer*, as Generals Heinz Guderian, Friedrich-Wilhelm von Mellenthin or Walter Warlimont claimed in their memoirs after the war. Rather, it was the summer battles of 1943 on the Eastern Front in general, not Operation Citadel specifically which greatly reduced German fighting power. In fact, the months of July and August 1943 proved to be the bloodiest for the German field army since the beginning of the war. However, the Red Army also suffered horrific losses: in July 1943, its personnel losses were 44 percent higher than the monthly average for the entire 'Great Patriotic War'; in August 1943 they were 73 percent higher. This confirms that the summer battles of 1943 were among the fiercest for both sides during the entire war, regardless of which side was on the offensive or defensive. Still, there was one major difference: the Soviet Union was better able to absorb the horrendous casualty rate, not least because it had more than twice as many inhabitants as the German Reich. Unlike the Soviet Union, Germany was moreover facing a coalition of opponents, which by this time spanned half the globe and had by far more resources at their disposal than the Axis powers. Even though the German Reich managed to increase weapons production in the months that followed, its human losses could no longer be replaced. From July to October 1943 alone the German *Ostheer* lost 911,000 soldiers in total, whilst receiving only 421,700 replacements. This meant that weakened divisions could be replenished less and less. On 27 August, Manstein wrote in his private war diary that beyond any doubt the situation was grave and the troops were at the end of their tether. Two weeks later, on 9 September 1943, Goebbels noted in his diary: 'Our soldiers are worn out, our divisions bled-out.'[30]

29 Zetterling and Frankson, *Kursk 1943*, p. 200.
30 Goebbels, *Tagebücher*, pt. II, vol. 9, p. 452.

The Significance of the Battle of Kursk for German Reich and USSR

For the Germans, the failure of their summer offensive at Kursk came as a heavy blow to morale. In an order of the day issued in early July 1943, Hitler had still assured his commanders of the 'outstanding importance of the first strike of the year.' The 'success of this first major strike of the year 1943', Hitler continued, was of greater significance than 'an ordinary victory.' He issued another order of the day to the troops of the attack formations, which began as follows: 'Today you are going to launch a grand attack whose outcome may decide the war.' Towards the end of this order, Hitler reiterated: 'You must know that everything could depend on the success of this battle.'[31] In fact, he deliberately overstated the significance of the coming battles so as to motivate the soldiers – this was one of his propaganda principles. As early as 1924, Hitler had written in *Mein Kampf*:

> In every case where there are exigencies or tasks that seem impossible to deal with successfully, public opinion must be concentrated on the one problem, under the conviction that the solution of this problem alone is a matter of life or death. Only in this way can public interest be aroused to such a pitch as it will urge people to combine in a great voluntary effort and achieve important results … Therefore, the most essential preliminary condition necessary for an attack on such a difficult stage of the human road is that the authorities should succeed in convincing the masses that the immediate objective which is now being fought for is the only one that deserves to be considered and the only one on which everything depends.[32]

In summer 1943, however, this propaganda tactic backfired. When the supposedly decisive offensive had to be cancelled after just one week in the north of Kursk and after barely two weeks in the south, many soldiers were aghast. On 16 July 1943, Lieutenant Karl Freygang, member of the 7th Infantry Division, wrote in his diary: 'We have to retreat!!! All sacrifices were in vain, all effort for nothing, I cried of anger and sadness.'[33] A month later, on 17 August 1943, Major Markus von Busse drew up an account on a visit to the front he had undertaken by order of the General Staff's organisational division from 12-15 August. Busse not only visited the Headquarters of Army Group Centre but also numerous army, corps and division headquarters to hear about their experiences first-hand. His conclusion about the mood prevailing at the front was that 'the confidence in the command threatens to be shaken … The Citadel attack was supposed to bring about *the decision* – but what followed were fierce battles

31 Klink, *Gesetz*, p. 329-30.
32 Adolf Hitler, *My Struggle* ('Stalag Edition', Munich, n.d.), p. 261.
33 Haag, *Berichte*, p. 86.

and retreat. The commanders lack up-to-date information; as it is, they are unable to answer at the moment the multitudinous questions from the soldiers.'[34]

From the point of view of operational history, the Battle of Kursk heralded the beginning of the major German retreats. Contrary to what the German command had hoped, the German-Soviet front did not settle down. On 7 August, the Soviets launched their offensive against Smolensk. Six days later the Red Army renewed the attack against the Donets Basin, then mounted an offensive against Poltava on 26 August, with another against Bryansk on 1 September. Hitler now realized that the Wehrmacht would not be able to force a decision on the Eastern Front, so he decided to shift the strategic focus to Western Europe in autumn 1943. He believed that if their expected landing in France could be turned into a devastating defeat for the Western Allies, then the war could still be won.

But was Kursk really a decisive battle from the strategic point of view – or even *the* deciding battle of the Second World War, as is sometimes claimed?[35] Certainly not! There were other events which had a much greater impact on the course of the war, such as the entry of the United States of America into the war, the failure of the two major German campaigns on the Eastern Front in 1941 and 1942, or the Battle of Midway in June 1942, after which the Japanese lost the initiative in the Pacific theatre. Nonetheless, the Battle of Kursk marked a turning point; no longer could the reversal of fortunes on the Eastern Front simply be ignored. The development leading to this change had begun earlier, and the defeat of the German Reich had been looming since the Battle of Stalingrad. Yet, the victories of the German *Ostheer* in March 1943, as well as the ensuing long period of rest on the Eastern Front kindled the Germans' hopes that there was still a chance to defeat the Soviet Union militarily. The shock was therefore all the greater when the German summer offensive failed, making it painfully obvious that the war in the East could not be won so long as Germany was opposed by the Anti-Hitler coalition and forced to wage war on multiple fronts. On 2 September 1943, the SS Security Service reported the following on the mood of the German population: 'The situation at the *Eastern Front* gives rise to the greatest concerns. Even if the Soviets had not achieved a decisive breakthrough yet, it was nevertheless downright alarming that they were still at all capable of conducting such an offensive, which has been going for almost two months.'[36] Four days later the Security Service detected that a 'growing number of *soldiers on leave from the Eastern Front* come home with pessimistic views, while just a few months ago nearly all of them were still inspired with an unwavering faith and full confidence in the victory of

34 BA-MA, RH 10/54, Reisebericht des Majors i. G. von Busse zur Heeresgruppe Mitte, fol. 92 [emphasis in original, RT].

35 See, for example: Dmitriy B. Khazanov, *Air War over Kursk: Turning Point in the East* (Bedford, 2010), p. 125; Zamulin, *The Battle of Kursk: Controversial and Neglected Aspects*, p. xiii; and, Tucker-Jones, *Kursk 1943*, p. 217.

36 Boberach, *Meldungen*, vol. 14, p. 5700 [emphasis in original, RT].

our arms.'[37] Furthermore, Karl-Friedrich Kolbow, the governor of Westphalia, wrote in his diary on 18 September 1943: 'The threat to Germany from the east is becoming a huge danger; it is only with horror that I think about the coming winter. If our front in the east breaks, the war will be lost – and all of us with it. Let's keep hoping for a miracle and German fortitude!'[38] The summer battles of 1943 obviously had a profound impact both on the combat strength of the German *Ostheer* as well as on the morale on the frontline and at home, as these statements demonstrate.

For the Soviets, too, the Battle of Kursk had far-reaching consequences. Not only did the Red Army fail to destroy the German forces in the Orël salient and in the area of Khar'kov, as had been the goal of Operations *Kutuzov* and *Polkovodets Rumyantsev*, the objectives set by the *Stavka* for 1943 could not be achieved either. Lieutenant-General Sergey Matveevich Shtemenko, at that time Deputy Chief of the Red Army General Staff, recalled in his memoirs published in 1968 that the operations plan for *Kutuzov* had envisaged 'an attack by the combined forces of the Western and the Bryansk Front directly to the west, whose objectives were the destruction of the enemy groups at Orël, the liberation of Belorussia and then the invasion of East Prussia and Eastern Poland.'[39] The Red Army achieved these goals only one year later.

Moreover, the casualties suffered by the Red Army during the Battle of Kursk were so high that to this day many Russian historians struggle to acknowledge the true scale of the losses. Many have become so used to the long-standing official interpretation that the battle had ended with a glorious victory for the Red Army and that it had, above all, been characterized by the horrible losses inflicted on the German formations. In truth, the victory at Kursk came at a heavy cost, which the Russian historian Boris Vadimovich Sokolov even twenty years ago called 'catastrophic.'[40] But what mattered most for the Soviet Union was the fact that the Red Army had been victorious – in the Battle of Kursk and the Second World War. According to the communist ideology, the Red Army's victories 'bore the character of a law', since they demonstrated the supposed superiority of the Soviet social system.[41] Or, as a common propaganda phrase in the German Democratic Republic would have it: 'Learning from the Soviet Union means learning to prevail.'[42] The numerous shortcomings of the Soviet high command, their tactical inferiority to the Wehrmacht, as well as the horrific number of casualties suffered by the Red Army, did not fit with the image

37 Ibid., p. 5715 [emphasis in original, RT].

38 Kolbow, *Tagebücher*, p. 598.

39 Sergei M. Schtemenko, *Im Generalstab* (East Berlin, 1969), pp. 170-1.

40 Boris V. Sokolov, 'The Battle of Kursk, Orel, and Char'kov [sic!]: Strategic Intentions and Results. A Critical View of the Soviet Historiography', in Foerster, *Gezeitenwechsel*, pp. 69-88, quote, 86.

41 Boris G. Solowjow, *Wendepunkt des Zweiten Weltkrieges: Die Schlacht bei Kursk* (Cologne, 1984), p. 13.

42 Peter Jahn, et al. (ed.), *Unsere Russen, unsere Deutschen: Bilder vom Anderen 1800 bis 2000* (Berlin, 2007), p. 147.

of their own ingenuity. As a result, they were subjected to obfuscation in Soviet historiography.

The former Wehrmacht generals, who had a considerable influence on German post-war historiography, too, were likewise intent on drawing a veil over discreditable events and developments as well as over their own mistakes. Both sides were less committed to the truth than they were in establishing exculpatory myths. They were both able to perpetuate myths with remarkable success.

4

Lost Memories: The Battle of Kursk in Post-War Historiography

The Battle of Kursk in the Memoirs of German Military Leaders

After the war, the majority of the former German military leaders attempted to depict the Battle of Kursk in a manner which left no doubt that Hitler was to blame for everything. Allegedly, according to the Chief of the Army General Staff Kurt Zeitzler, Operation Citadel had been Hitler's idea, and nobody could dissuade him from it. Zeitzler, who during the Second World War had been a loyal follower of Hitler, and had received the Golden Party Badge on 30 January 1944, pulled his *Führer* metaphorically to pieces in his post-war historical accounts.

Just like Zeitzler, Hermann Teske, Army Group Centre's Chief of Transportation in 1943, also claimed that Hitler had been the originator of Citadel. In his memoirs, published in 1952, Teske wrote: 'In retrospect it is inexplicable how the High Commands of the Wehrmacht, the Army and of Army Group Centre could ever have agreed to Hitler's plan, which from the very start bore the seeds of failure.'[1] The former Inspector General of the Panzer Troops, Heinz Guderian, contacted Teske on 3 November 1952, disagreeing with that statement: 'The offensive against Kursk did not correspond to any of Hitler's plans. In fact, he had the greatest doubts about it. Unfortunately, he yielded to the urgings of Zeitzler (Chief of the Army General Staff), who hoped to reclaim the lost initiative in the east with an attack.'[2] Even though Guderian's statement was closer to the truth than Teske's claim, its one-sidedness still obscured the facts. Additionally, Guderian's remarks about Zeitzler must be viewed against the backdrop of the tensions between the two generals which arose during the war and, according to Guderian himself, did not cease after it was over. Guderian

1 Hermann Teske, *Die silbernen Spiegel: Generalstabsdienst unter der Lupe* (Heidelberg, 1952), p. 188.

2 Hermann Teske, 'Die Bedeutung der Eisenbahn bei Aufmarsch, Verteidigung und Rückzug einer Heeresgruppe: Dargestellt an der deutschen Operation "Zitadelle" gegen Kursk und ihre Auswirkungen im Sommer 1943', *Allgemeine Schweizerische Militärzeitschrift*, 121 (1955), pp. 120-35, here, 121, fn 1.

also took liberties with the truth in his memoirs published in 1950. His unsupportable claim that the German panzer formations had suffered such heavy casualties during Operation Citadel that they 'could not be employed for a long time to come' has been discussed in detail earlier in this study.[3]

Another persistent claim is the myth propagated by Guderian that the *Ferdinand* tank destroyers, whose deployment had been so important to Hitler, did not prove successful at Kursk. However, this assessment is entirely contradicted by the contemporary experience of the frontline troops. The war diary of the Ninth Army, for instance, contained the following passage on 9 July 1943: 'Particularly noteworthy is a successful partial attack by the XXXXI Panzer Corps, during which the *Ferdinand* tanks, as usual, proved their worth as the driving force behind the attack.'[4] Two days later, the XXIII Army Corps reported: 'The deployment of 7 *Ferdinands*, which followed the infantry and which were escorted by assault guns, proved themselves well for both the penetration of the enemy's defensive positions and the defence against repeated counterattacks.'[5] On 7 October 1943, the commander of the 16th Panzergrenadier Division wrote: '*Ferdinand* and *Sturmpanzer* are currently the strongest and best attack weapons of the German Army.'[6] The list of such examples could easily be extended.

Guderian also claimed in his memoirs that after a meeting on 10 May 1943, he had tried to talk Hitler out of Operation Citadel, to which the latter had replied: 'You are quite right. Whenever I think of this attack my stomach turns over.'[7] There are only a handful of accounts of the Battle of Kursk where this exchange between Guderian and Hitler is not quoted. Whether it took place is anyone's guess. It is certain, though, that during the conference in Munich on 4 May 1943, where the postponement of Citadel was being discussed, Guderian did not speak out against the attack in broad terms. Instead, he favoured postponing the operation and suggested 'concentrating all panzer forces in one area, either of [Army Group] South or Centre, and piling on with overwhelming force.'[8]

3 Guderian, *Panzer Leader*, p. 312.
4 NARA, T312/317/7886159, Kriegstagebuch Nr. 8, Armee-Oberkommando 9, Führungsabteilung, 26.3.-18.8.1943.
5 BA-MA, RH 24-23/123, Kriegstagebuch Nr. 15, XXIII. Armeekorps, Abteilung Ia, 22.3.-22.7.1943, fol. 197.
6 BA-MA, RH 10/56, 16. Panzer-Grenadier-Division, Kommandeur, Zusammenarbeit mit Panzern 'Ferdinand' und Sturmpanzern, 7.10.1943, fol. 90-2, quote, fol. 92.
7 Guderian, *Panzer Leader*, p. 309.
8 BA-MA, RH 19 VI/45, Kriegstagebuch Ia der Heeresgruppe Don/Süd, März bis Juli 1943, fol. 78-82, quote, fol. 81-2. These proceedings have so far been largely ignored in research. They were brought to the author's attention by Dr Karl-Heinz Frieser in 2000. In 2003, the author provided the military historian Dr Marcel Stein with a copy of the document; Stein quotes it in his biography of Manstein, published in 2004. See Marcel Stein, *Der Januskopf: Feldmarschall von Manstein – eine Neubewertung* (Bissendorf, 2004), pp. 199-202.

An alternative to the pincer attack planned for Operation Citadel was also mentioned by Hermann Teske in his memoirs:

> On 19 April 1943, the Chief of Transportation of Army Group [Centre] had to report whether it would be possible to transfer the formations of the attack army assembling south of Orel to the area of Vorozhba and west within a short time. This way, the bulge in the Russian front west of Kursk was to be pushed in by a frontal, non-flanked attack, which would economize forces, rather than with a thrust from Orel towards the south, which would be in danger of a Russian flanking [movement].... It can unfortunately not be determined anymore where this sound solution came from. Technically, this task could easily have been carried out with regards to transportation, as the area of Vorozhba offered favourable conditions both in terms of distance and unloading. This is exactly what was reported. It is not known why this suggestion was not taken up. Its advantages lay in the immediate cooperation with the strong panzer formations of Army Group South; in the opportunity to advance to the gates of Kursk against almost no opposition due to lack of Russian troops in the salient west of the city; as well as in avoiding a possible flanking of the attacking forces, which was likely to happen if the attack was carried out from Orel towards the south.[9]

In the aforementioned letter, in which Guderian pointed out to Teske that it had been Zeitzler not Hitler who had wanted the attack against Kursk, the Inspector General of the Panzer Troops wrote: 'Solving the Kursk question with a frontal attack was Hitler's idea, but it was rejected by the Chief of the General Staff (Zeitzler) and by the commanders of the army groups.'[10] This was actually true but it did not fit the bias of most memoirists, who wanted to blame Hitler alone for any poor decisions. Once Teske learned from Guderian that the suggestion for a frontal attack had been put forth by Hitler, he became considerably less enthusiastic about this alternative operational plan. In an article published in 1955, Teske only said the following about it: 'The material provisioning was obviously in the wrong place. This must have been the reason why this basically reasonable plan was not carried out.'[11]

Guderian's influence was considerable not only on Teske's views but also on the viewpoints of other memoirists. Friedrich Wilhelm von Mellenthin, in 1943 Chief of Staff of the XXXXVIII Panzer Corps, for instance, used many of Guderian's recollections of the preparation phase of Operation Citadel in his own memoirs. These were first published in London in 1955, a year later in the USA, and even in the Soviet Union in 1957. In 1963, they were printed in the Federal Republic of Germany under the title *Panzerschlachten* (Tank Battles). While this remained the only edition

9 Teske, *Spiegel*, p. 186.
10 Teske, *Bedeutung*, p. 127, fn 1.
11 Ibid., p. 127.

in Germany, the book was reprinted six times in the USA, the last edition appearing in 1982. It had a lasting effect on how the Americans perceived the Red Army and the battles on the German-Soviet front during the Second World War – despite the fact Mellenthin made many absurd claims in his memoirs. He wrote, for example, that 'if Citadel had been launched in April or May [1943], it might have yielded a valuable harvest, but by June the conditions were totally different.'[12] In reality, an attack in April 1943 was never a possibility, and Operation Citadel could not have been carried out in May either, as has been demonstrated above. Rather than an attack on Kursk, Mellenthin speculated, the German High Command should instead have conducted 'strategic withdrawals or surprise attacks in quiet sectors.'[13] Such a point of view seems downright naive, as in summer 1943 the Wehrmacht was no longer in a position to play cat-and-mouse games with the Red Army – indeed, the opposite was the case. Thanks to its effective reconnaissance and its enormous resources, the Soviet high command could react to any larger assembly or regrouping of German troops. In turn, the Red Army was in a position to concentrate major formations behind the frontlines largely unnoticed by the Germans.

According to Mellenthin, Operation Citadel had a catastrophic outcome for the Germans. He wrote that after the operation was cancelled, the panzer divisions which had taken part in it 'had been bled white.'[14] As has been shown in the previous chapter, this was not the case. It is true that the units of the XXXXVIII Panzer Corps, whose Chief of General Staff Mellenthin had been, had suffered heavy casualties. But the weekly reports dating from 18 July 1943 prove that the corps' three panzer and panzergrenadier divisions in particular were still 'capable of any offensive action.'[15] And, just like the other German memoirists, Mellenthin was careful not to mention the fact that many casualties during Citadel were the direct result of operational and tactical mistakes committed by their own troop commanders.

Of all the myths cultivated by German memoirists, there is one which stubbornly persists even today; Hitler 'had thrown away' the victory at Kursk because he broke off the attack 'before a decision had been reached', the reason for which had first and foremost been the Allied landing on Sicily. These claims were raised in Manstein's memoirs entitled *Lost Victories*, quite possibly the most influential of German post-war writings.[16] First published in 1955, they were reprinted in 2011 in their 19th edition and have been translated into many languages. Manstein's account of the Battle of

12 Friedrich von Mellenthin, *Panzer Battles 1939-1945: A Study of the Employment of Armour in the Second World War* (London, 1955), p. 213.

13 Ibid., p. 213.

14 Ibid., p. 225.

15 BA-MA, RH 21-4/111, Anlagen zum Kriegstagebuch des Panzerarmee-Oberkommandos 4, Ia, Operationen vom 25.4.-31.7.1943, pt. 2, fol. 136-7.

16 Erich von Manstein, *Verlorene Siege: Erinnerungen 1939-1944* (Bonn, 13th/14th edn, 1993), pp. 502, 504. A critical view of Manstein's claim has already been offered in Roman Töppel, 'Legendenbildung in der Geschichtsschreibung – Die Schlacht bei Kursk',

Kursk is far more accurate than what other German military commanders wrote after the war; this is because he relied heavily on the records preserved in his personal papers. Nevertheless, his memoirs also suffer from certain weaknesses. With regards to the Battle of Kursk one can find fault with the fact that even 10 years after the war Manstein still believed in the reasons Hitler had given him for cancelling Operation Citadel; the point is that he was the only one to whom these explanations were offered as they were Hitler's attempt to assuage Manstein's disagreement. While it is true that unlike many other memoirists Manstein did not make anything up in his account of the Battle of Kursk, he did omit whatever contradicted his arguments. He also ignored the friction and command mistakes on the German side during Operation Citadel. In doing so, he helped establish the myth that the Wehrmacht had been defeated in the east only because of Hitler's mistakes, the Allies' overwhelming material superiority and harsh weather.

In view of such heavily skewed post-war accounts, it seems as if the generals had suffered from memory loss after the war. In 1958, Hermann Breith, the former Commanding General of the III Panzer Corps, wrote about his corps' crossing of the Donets River on 5 July 1943: 'The enemy, as had to be expected, reacted to the attack of the corps with heavy artillery fire on the crossing sites and the approach routes leading to the river. The enemy air forces, too, were very active on that first day of the attack. Thanks to a Luftwaffe concentration the crossing could be carried out without any serious trouble.'[17] Yet, as described above, the III Panzer Corps actually faced massive problems when crossing the Donets, not least because of poor tactical planning, and there can be no talk of a Luftwaffe concentration over the corps' sector, either.

It would nevertheless be wrong to conclude that the shortcomings of the troops and commanders involved in the attack were the prime cause for the failure of the German offensive against Kursk. This was not the case at all. Yet one still cannot ignore the errors committed on the German side, the more so as they did not go by unnoticed by contemporary observers. A telling example for this is a statement by Lieutenant-Colonel Georg Ernst von Grundherr, the panzer officer with the Chief of the Army General Staff, who on 14 July 1943 was at the command post of Hoth's Fourth Panzer Army. Grundherr had already visited several attack corps and divisions of Army Group South in the previous days. The memories of the recent fighting were still fresh when he wrote the following to the First General Staff Officer of the Operations Section of the Army General Staff, Colonel Heinz Brandt:

Militärgeschichtliche Zeitschrift, 61 (2002), pp. 369-401, here, 387-92; idem, 'Kursk – Mythen und Wirklichkeit einer Schlacht', pp. 378-84.

17 Hermann Breith, 'Der Angriff des III. Pz.Korps bei "Zitadelle" im Juli 1943', *Wehrkunde*, 7 (1958), pp. 543-8, here, 544.

> Without being able to prove it at the moment, I am under the impression that the majority of units do not adhere to the principle of objectivity when writing reports. Trying to keep all options open and cover up one's own shortcomings and mistakes often takes away the leading figures' opportunity to see [the situation] as clearly as they could with an honest report. It is perfectly obvious that in such a case both the clarity of missions and the absolute will to reach the objective must suffer. In the past few days I have often been thinking about the proverb that a young horseman must first throw his heart over an obstacle. If everybody had unconditionally thrown their hearts at Kursk, many things might have turned out differently. In the first two days one was honestly convinced of a quick success and of the operation in general. Yet when the colleague in the north and the northwest did not do a thing, when the fierce advance was hindered by both enemy positions and the worries and trouble at the flanks, one began making a virtue out of necessity and forming small and smaller pockets. It is quite obvious that this way the forces must become too weak for the operational objective.[18]

Grundherr did not have the chance to write his memoirs after the war. In September 1944, Guderian had him transferred from the panzer troops because of 'political unreliability'; in December 1944, he assumed command of a grenadier regiment.[19] He was seriously wounded in spring 1945 and died on 1 May 1945 in a field hospital in Tyrol. By then the recipient of his letter of 14 July 1943 was no longer alive, either: Colonel Brandt was fatally injured during the attempt on Hitler's life on 20 July 1944 and died the following day. Whether Grundherr and Brandt would have contributed to the myth-making or opposed it is hence impossible to say.

The Battle of Kursk in Soviet/Russian Historiography

Soviet post-war historiography was as heavily influenced by high-ranking military commanders who had been involved in the events as it was on the German side. At first, however, Kursk only played a minor role in Soviet historiography. This changed in the second half of the 1950s when the first monographs about the battle began appearing in the USSR, above all Il'ya Ivanovich Markin's book *Kurskaya bitva* (The Kursk Battle).[20] From then on, the glorification of the Battle of Kursk gained momentum. In Soviet history books, it soon took the third place among the pivotal

18 BA-MA, RH 10/54, letter from Lieutenant-Colonel Grundherr to Brand [sic!], 14.7.1943, fol. 50-7, quote, fol. 54-5.

19 I would like to thank Professor Jürgen Förster (Freiburg im Breisgau), who provided me with this information on 16 August 2010.

20 Markin's book, published in Russian in 1958, was soon translated to German and published in the GDR as, Ilja I. Markin, *Die Kursker Schlacht* (East Berlin, 1960).

battles of the Second World War – right after the battles of Moscow and Stalingrad. Briefly the Soviet interpretation ran as follows: 'The crushing destruction of the fascist troops in the Kursk salient brought about the turning point in the war. In the Battle of Kursk, Soviet troops broke the fascist Wehrmacht's backbone, thwarted any attempts to take revenge for the defeat at Stalingrad and finally forced the fascists onto the strategic defensive … The outstanding victory of the Soviet troops at Kursk was achieved through the superiority of the Soviet social and political order and the socialist economy, the wise leadership of the CPSU [the Communist Party of the Soviet Union], the strength of the Soviet armed forces, the fine military mastery and the mass heroism of the Soviet soldiers.'[21] Most Soviet historians made recourse to the memoirs of former Red Army commanders, which were published in the Soviet Union in large print-runs. Since only selected researchers were granted access to Soviet archives – and the interpretation of the Second World War was determined by the official historical works anyway – most Soviet accounts largely resemble each other.

With the dissolution of the Soviet Union in 1991, the entire basis for historical research changed. For the first time, researchers were now granted genuine access to many archives, including the Central Archive of the Russian Ministry of Defense (TsAMO). However, not all Russian historians welcomed the new political and social climate. The Great Patriotic War was and is a key narrative in Russian identity, and many historians of the former Soviet Union were reluctant to question the myths surrounding the war. An impressive example is provided by the two historians Grigoriy Avtonomovich Koltunov and Boris Grigor'evich Solov'ëv. In 1970 they wrote possibly the most influential account of the battle that was published during the Soviet era. Owing to the numerous tables of organization and statistics, their book *Kurskaya bitva* (The Kursk Battle) is today still frequently used as a source. After the breakup of the Soviet Union, the two authors went separate ways. At an international meeting of military experts in July 1996, Koltunov freely admitted to having 'falsified and lied' during the Soviet era.[22] He had been ordered to give higher numbers for German losses and lower ones for the Red Army, so his works were not to be taken seriously. His colleague Boris Solov'ëv, by contrast, remained a proponent of the old legends. In an article written about the Battle of Kursk in 1998, he suspected that the number of 1,500 destroyed German tanks – that is the figure given by most Soviet historians – was too low. Entirely contrary to the truth, Solov'ëv implied that the German government denied researchers access to the relevant archive material.

Still, the historians who had made their mark in the old Soviet Union were not the only ones to cling to these myths. The established legends have also been passed on by researchers of the younger generation, such as Valeriy Nikolaevich Zamulin, one of the most prolific authors on the subject of the Battle of Kursk. Zamulin was born in

21 Bagramjan, *Geschichte*, pp. 278–9.
22 Wolfgang Will, 'Wo Panzer Geschichte schrieben', *Berliner Morgenpost*, 20/21 July 1996, Supplement, p. 2.

1968 and graduated with a history degree from Belgorod State Pedagogical Institute in 1992. In 2005 he published his first comprehensive monograph about the tank battle at Prokhorovka, which was published in translation in English in 2011. Since the 1990s, scholarship has deconstructed the myth of Prokhorovka piece by piece and shown that this legendary battle did not end in a victory for the Soviet troops but rather in a bitter tactical defeat for the Red Army. Zamulin, however, has a different interpretation and writes of the tank battle at Prokhorovka as follows: 'Even though the [Soviet] counterattack failed to reach its assigned goal, so much damage was inflicted on the enemy that he was forced to abandon his intentions to continue the offensive [Citadel].'[23] As this claim cannot be substantiated by contemporary German records, Zamulin declares that the II SS Panzer Corps had only 131 of its originally 422 tanks and assault guns left after the tank battle at Prokhorovka. His source for this statement is a popular historical study by Joachim Engelmann published in 1980, which has no scholarly references; it is therefore rather questionable as a source. A verification of the quoted reference shows, moreover, that Engelmann does not mention the figure given by Zamulin at all – so Zamulin must have simply invented it. In another instance, where Zamulin writes about the total German losses sustained in the Battle of Kursk, he refers to the book *Waffen und Geheimwaffen des deutschen Heeres 1933-1945* by Fritz Hahn, which is based mainly on records from the German Army High Command and is reliable despite missing references. Again, none of the figures given by Zamulin can be found in Hahn's work. Indeed, in his description of the battle, Zamulin occasionally uses falsified sources.[24]

Zamulin's work is therefore a good example of the fact that 'falsifying and lying' in order to uphold the myths of the Great Patriotic War has not only occurred in the Soviet era. Fortunately, there are some Russian historians who resist the myths surrounding the Battle of Kursk, such as Nikolay Mikhaylovich Ramanichev, a military historian born in 1938. In 1996, he commented on the heavy casualties that the Red Army suffered during the Battle of Kursk as follows: 'Even before the war Stalin's repressions created an atmosphere which made it quite impossible for commanders to act independently … In cases of insubordination, open opposition and wilful infractions of discipline and order, the commander was forced to take many coercive measures including force of arms … At the front, these regulations turned to open terror.'[25] Ramanichev also criticized the Red Army's command performance: 'A number of German historians, among them Paul Carell and Werner Haupt, tend to think that the Soviet command quickly learned from its negative experiences and rapidly adapted in the course of the war. Unfortunately, this was not the case. Despite two

23 Valeriy N. Zamulin, *Demolishing the Myth: The Tank Battle at Prokhorovka, Kursk, July 1943: An Operational Narrative* (Solihull, 2011), p. 530.

24 See Roman Töppel, review of Zamulin, *Demolishing the Myth*, *sehepunkte*, 12 (2012), No. 1 [15 January 2012] (available online).

25 Nikolaj N. Ramaničev, 'Die Schlachten bei Kursk: Vorgeschichte, Verlauf und Ausgang', in Foerster, *Gezeitenwechsel*, pp. 57-67, quote, 62.

years of war experience, the Soviet commanders, staffs and troops had not managed to acquire adequate military combat experience. Even the highest military command had not learned from these experiences but instead remained stuck in their old thought patterns.'[26]

Possibly the harshest critic of the myths of the Great Patriotic War is the Russian humanities scholar Boris Vadimovich Sokolov, who was born in 1957. From 1993 to 1995 Sokolov was a professor at the State Academy of Slavic Culture in Moscow; from 2002 to 2008, he was Professor of Social Anthropology at the Russian State Social University. According to his own account, he was forced to resign from his job by the government after publishing a critical article about the war in the Caucasus in 2008. Since then he has been working as a freelance historian and literary theorist.

When the Soviet Union collapsed, Sokolov was one of the first scholars to criticize the official version of the Great Patriotic War. In his book *Tsena pobedy* (The Price of Victory), published in 1991, Sokolov presented his findings on the Red Army's losses during the Second World War. He estimated the personnel losses in the Battle of Kursk to be 2.25 million soldiers in total, the losses of tanks and self-propelled guns at 8,700 and of planes at 5,000. These figures proved to be too high, so he revised his estimates in the years that followed. In 1996, Sokolov published new calculations, in which the losses of the Red Army at Kursk now amounted to 1,677,000 soldiers and 3,300 planes. He adopted the number of 6,064 tanks lost from the (seemingly) credible figures given in the official compilation, *Grif sekretnosti snyat*. Again and again Sokolov has been strongly criticized by other Russian historians because his calculations of Soviet losses are always the highest of all the published figures. However, it has repeatedly been proved in the past that his numbers are by no means far-fetched. His 1996 estimate of 3,300 aircraft lost, for instance, is very close to the figure which can be calculated from the more recent publications. Another of Sokolov's assessments has also proven to be surprisingly accurate, namely the number of tanks lost by the Soviet Central Front during the defensive phase of the Battle of Kursk. Sokolov estimated the number of total losses of Rokossovksiy's units to be 530 tanks; and, according to the aforementioned unpublished report by Colonel Zaev dating from 19 July 1943, the Central Front did lose 526 tanks. It is likely that of all the calculations of the personnel losses suffered by the Red Army, Sokolov's estimate of 1.68 million casualties also comes closest to the truth.

Deviating from the official Russian historiography has made Sokolov an outsider. Other scholars, too, had to experience first-hand that Russia officially prefers to adhere to the myth of the Great Patriotic War, regarding critical historians with suspicion or even hostility. One example for this is the German historian Sebastian Stopper, born in 1982. In his doctoral thesis, submitted to the Humboldt University Berlin in 2012, in addition to various articles, Stopper ventured to question the myth of the partisan movement in the area of Bryansk. Based on his research in German and Eastern

26 Ramaničev, 'Die Schlachten bei Kursk', p. 64.

European archives, he came to the conclusion that 'the military efficiency of partisan warfare, praised in Soviet propagandist historiography, was actually minimal.'[27] With regards to the Battle of Kursk, Stopper has written: 'The fact remains that the German attack against Kursk was not notably disrupted by the partisans in the Bryansk forests, in spite of all the casualties.'[28] Stopper thus confirms what Ernst Klink wrote in his standard work on Operation Citadel in 1966: 'For the area of Army Group Centre it can be concluded that the attacks against railway lines and bridges had no decisive impairing effect on the supply traffic.'[29] In Russia, however, Stopper's research findings sparked an outcry. In June 2014, the German news magazine *Der Spiegel* reported that Russian authorities had put Stopper's works on the list of 'extremist materials', just behind the writings of the Italian dictator Benito Mussolini.[30] Since then, Stopper has been considered *persona non grata* in Russia and has even been defamed as a 'neo-Nazi' – without doubt, a rather alarming development.

The struggle over Kursk thus continues; now it is no longer a material fight for the city, but another type of struggle over how Kursk is portrayed in books, films and other media.

27 Sebastian Stopper, '"Die Straße ist deutsch": Der sowjetische Partisanenkrieg und seine militärische Effizienz: Eine Fallstudie zur Logistik der Wehrmacht im Brjansker Gebiet April bis Juli 1943', *Vierteljahrshefte für Zeitgeschichte*, 59 (2011), pp. 385-411, here, 409.

28 Ibid., p. 411.

29 Klink, *Gesetz*, p. 128.

30 Benjamin Bidder, 'Streit über Partisanen-Propaganda: Moskau stuft deutschen Historiker als Extremisten ein', *Spiegel Online*, 16 June 2014 (accessed 31 July 2016).

Epilogue: The Place of the Battle of Kursk in History

While Kursk has been the object of continual dispute, with both separate Russian and German versions emerging since 1945, there is one final aspect which requires consideration. That is the question: 'Was the Battle of Kursk really the biggest tank battle of World War II?' What about the Battle of Brody in 1941? And was Kursk indeed the greatest battle of the Second World War? What about Operations *Overlord* and *Bagration* in 1944?

There are indeed a few authors who claim that the Battle of Brody (also known as Battle of Dubno) rather than Kursk was the biggest tank battle of the Second Word War, first and foremost Russian military historian Aleksei Isaev.[1] But this claim is not convincing. According to Isaev, a total of 3,647 tanks (2,973 Soviet and 674 German) operated in the area of Brody, Dubno, Lutsk and Rovno at the end of June 1941.[2] Indeed, the Battle of Brody is in many ways comparable with the first phase of Operation Citadel in the Southern sector of the Kursk salient, in the area of Belgorod, Oboyan and Prokhorovka. There, the main attacks of Hoth's Fourth Panzer Army and Army Detachment Kempf towards the north continued for nine days, from 5-13 July 1943. The Battle of Brody lasted nine days, too, from 23 June to 1 July 1941. Both battles took place over an area which was roughly the same size, about 3,500 square kilometres in 1941, roughly 3,000 in 1943. But in the Southern sector of the Kursk salient both sides deployed no less than 4,768 tanks and self-propelled guns, the Russians 2,889, the Germans 1,879.[3]

1 Aleksei Isaev, *Dubno 1941: The Greatest Tank Battle of the Second World War* (Solihull, 2017); and, see also Robert A. Forczyk, *Tank Warfare on the Eastern Front, 1941-1945*, vol. 1 (Barnsley, 2016), p. 64.

2 Isaev, *Dubno 1941*, pp. 35-7. For the strengths of the German panzer formations see Thomas L. Jentz, *Panzertruppen: The Complete Guide to the Creation & Combat Employment of Germany's Tank Force*, vol. 1 (Atglen, PA, 1996), pp. 191-2.

3 For the Soviet side, see: Spravka o poteryakh tankovykh po deystvuyushchim frontam v boyach s 5.7.43 g. po 20.7.43 g., copy from the document collection ('Materialsammlung') of the ZMSBw; Koltunov, 'Kurskaya bitva v tsifrakh', p. 61; and, Valeriy N. Zamulin, *Zasekrechennaya Kurskaya bitva: Neizvestnye dokumenty svidetelstvuyut* (Moscow, 2007), pp. 766-7. For the German figures, see Töppel, *Die Offensive gegen Kursk 1943*, Appendix 4.

Moreover, it has to be taken into account that in summer 1941 a high number of the Soviets tanks fell victim to mechanical failures before they could even reach the Brody battlefield. And, even if one considers Isaev's figures for the Soviet side too low and agrees with the numbers given by David Glantz – 'on paper' 3,800 Soviet versus 800 German tanks[4] – Brody 1941 still does not match Kursk 1943 in terms of the sheer quantity of material, artillery, aircraft, and all the other munitions which were thrown into the maelstrom, and even less so since given that half the Soviet tanks available did not take part.[5]

The next question is usually: 'but apart from the tanks, was Kursk really the greatest battle of the Second World War?' Here again, the figures speak for themselves. At the beginning of July, the five German armies which in the following weeks would be involved in the Battle of Kursk (2nd Panzer Army, 9th Army, 2nd Army, 4th Panzer Army and Army Detachment Kempf) had about 900,000 soldiers, 3,500 tanks and self-propelled guns (not including the non-combat-ready vehicles), and almost 9,500 guns and mortars at their disposal. The Soviet forces (Western Front, Bryansk Front, Central Front, Voronezh Front and Steppe Front) had more than 2.6 million soldiers, about 8,500 tanks and self-propelled guns as well as 47,400 guns and mortars available. In sum, 3.5 million soldiers, 12,000 tanks and self-propelled guns and almost 57,000 guns and mortars were assembled at Kursk and Orël. Furthermore, this is only for the beginning of the Battle of Kursk and does not include the reserves which were brought up in the course of the fifty-day-long battle.

By comparison, at the end of July 1944, there were 380,000 German, 812,000 American and 640,000 British and Canadian soldiers deployed in Normandy, i.e. 1,832,000 men in total.[6] Even considering the fact that both sides had suffered a significant amount of casualties in the weeks of fighting since the Allied invasion on 6 June 1944, and adding the replacements arriving in the weeks to follow, the total number of soldiers involved in the Battle of Normandy never came close to the masses of troops –3.5 million– at Kursk. The same is true for the number of tanks. At the end of July 1944, Wehrmacht and Waffen-SS had committed about 2,000 tanks and self-propelled guns to battle; the Allies on the other hand had shipped almost 7,000 tanks to Normandy in the same period of time.[7] Thereby, many of these armoured fighting vehicles had already been destroyed by the end of July, so neither side ever had the quantity of tanks which were available at Kursk at any specific moment.

4 David M. Glantz and Jonathan M. House, *When Titans Clashed: How the Red Army Stopped Hitler* (Lawrence, KS, 2nd edn, 2015), p. 62.

5 Another account of the Battle of Brody is given by Victor Kamenir, using far more modest figures. See Victor J. Kamenir, *The Bloody Triangle: The Defeat of Soviet Armor in the Ukraine, June 1941* (Minneapolis, 2008).

6 Niklas Zetterling, *Normandy 1944: German Military Organization, Combat Power and Organizational Effectiveness* (Winnipeg, Manitoba, 2000), pp. 32, 408.

7 Ibid., pp. 408-26.

But this still leaves the gigantic clash of forces in Belarus in the summer of 1944, which lasted two months and ended as one of the harshest military defeats the German Reich suffered during World War II. On 22 June, when the Red Army launched Operation *Bagration* against the German Army Group Centre, the Soviets had 1,254,300 soldiers, 4,070 tanks and self-propelled guns as well as 34,000 guns and mortars available.[8] The Germans could only muster about 336,600 soldiers, 500 tanks and assault guns, and 2,600 artillery pieces.[9] Even though these figures were probably higher in reality at least for the German side,[10] the total quantity of forces on both sides hardly exceeded 2 million soldiers, 5,000 tanks and self-propelled guns as well as 40,000 guns and mortars. At Kursk, however, no less than 3.5 million soldiers, 12,000 tanks and self-propelled guns and 57,000 guns and mortars were ready for battle.

Thus, defined by the number of men and material involved, the Battle of Kursk was without doubt not only the biggest tank clash of the Second World War, but indeed at the same time the largest battle of the Second World War. It remains then a paradox that the largest battle cannot be considered a decisive one. Even if the Germans had succeeded in cutting off the Kursk salient and destroying all the Soviet forces assembled there, the Red Army would not have been fatally weakened. Although the quantity of Soviet troops at Kursk was considerable, the Red Army had twice as many tanks on the entire Eastern Front as well as three times as many soldiers, guns and aeroplanes in summer 1943. A German victory at Kursk would have lengthened the war on the German-Soviet front, but not decided it. On the other hand, if the Soviet Operations *Kutuzov* and *Polkovodets Rumyantsev* had reached the goals set by the *Stavka*, the war could possibly have been considerably shortened. But this is a hypothetical point, one which can only distract from the actual historical facts after the decades of legend-making.

The lack of a decisive result at Kursk should not distract, however, from its significance in the wider history of armoured warfare. The Battle of Cambrai (November-December 1917) was not a decisive victory, either. It became a key moment in history because it was the first combined-arms attack using tanks *en masse* with operational goals, a bloody stalemate, but one which pointed to the future possibilities of the tank. The French Campaign in May-June 1940 did not win the Second World War for Nazi

8 Glantz and House, *When Titans Clashed*, p. 265.

9 Karl-Heinz Frieser, 'Der Zusammenbruch der Heeresgruppe Mitte im Sommer 1944', in Militärgeschichtliches Forschungsamt (ed.), *Das Deutsche Reich und der Zweite Weltkrieg*, vol. 8: *Die Ostfront 1943/44: Der Krieg im Osten und an den Nebenfronten* (Munich, 2007), pp. 526-603, here, 526-35.

10 Frieser's comparison of strengths appears erroneous. On the Soviet side, he takes all self-propelled guns into consideration, while excluding self-propelled tank destroyers and self-propelled artillery from the German table of strengths. Furthermore, the number of artillery pieces he calculates for the German side apparently does not include mortars, whereas the corresponding figure for the Red Army comprises guns and mortars.

Germany, but it showed how devastating a rapid attack with tanks and aircraft could be if both smaller units and frontline commanders were willing to take risks. The fighting on the Golan Heights in October 1973 between units of the Israeli Armoured Corps and Syrian tank divisions took place over a relatively small strip of terrain. Yet if the IDF armour had failed to prevent a Syrian breakthrough, it is possible that the Middle East could have been engulfed in a nuclear conflagration.[11]

Like these three examples, Kursk will remain as one of the key tank battles of the twentieth century for a number of very specific reasons. It has been explained in this book what those reasons are; but also which reasons have been cited in the past, but which should now be recognised as legends.

11 For the wider history of armour in the twentieth century, and these examples, see Alaric Searle, *Armoured Warfare: A Military, Political and Global History* (London, 2017), esp. pp. 18-24, 57-64, 161-7.

Bibliography

Unpublished Material

I. Bundesarchiv-Militärarchiv, Freiburg im Breisgau

M 823-1053: Microfilmed files from the former 'Kriegsarchiv der Waffen-SS'
MSG 2/13924: Fritz Farnbacher, Tagebuch 1943
MSG 3/281/1: Franz Weber, Auszug aus meinem Kriegstagebuch
N 53: Nachlass Hellmuth von Wienskowski
N 63: Nachlass Kurt Zeitzler
N 460: Nachlass Gerlach von Gaudecker
RH 2: OKH/Generalstab des Heeres
Kart RH 2 Ost: OKH/Generalstab des Heeres/Lagekarten Ostfront
RH 8: OKH/Heereswaffenamt
RH 10: OKH/Generalinspekteur der Panzertruppen
RH 19 II: Heeresgruppe Mitte
RH 19 VI: Heeresgruppe Don/Süd
RH 20-2: 2. Armee
RH 20-6: 6. Armee
RH 20-8: Armeeabteilung Kempf/8. Armee
RH 20-9: 9. Armee
RH 21-1: 1. Panzerarmee
RH 21-2: 2. Panzerarmee
RH 21-4: 4. Panzerarmee
RH 24-3: III. Panzerkorps
RH 24-11: Korps Raus z. b. V./XI. Armeekorps
RH 24-23: XXIII. Armeekorps
RH 24-24: XXIV. Panzerkorps
RH 24-41: XXXXI. Panzerkorps
RH 24-46: XXXXVI. Panzerkorps
RH 24-48: XXXXVIII. Panzerkorps
RH 24-52: LII. Armeekorps
RH 26-6: 6. Infanteriedivision
RH 26-7: 7. Infanteriedivision
RH 26-10: 10. Panzergrenadierdivision

RH 26-167: 167. Infanteriedivision
RH 26-292: 292. Infanteriedivision
RH 27-4: 4. Panzerdivision
RH 27-9: 9. Panzerdivision
RH 27-18: 18. Panzerdivision
RH 27-19: 19. Panzerdivision
RH 27-20: 20. Panzerdivision
RH 39: Stäbe, Verbände und Einheiten der Schnellen Truppen und Panzertruppen
RL 2 III: Generalstab der Luftwaffe/Generalquartiermeister
RS 2-2: II. SS-Panzerkorps
RS 3-1: SS-Panzergrenadierdivision 'Leibstandarte SS Adolf Hitler'
RW 6: OKW/Allgemeines Wehrmachtamt
ZA 1/62: Günther Reichhelm, Nachträglicher Bericht über die Schlacht der 2. Panzer-Armee u. 9. Armee im Orel-Bogen vom 5.7.-18.8.1943.
ZA 1/1234: Oldwig von Natzmer, Der Einsatz der deutschen Panzerwaffe 1943-1945.
ZA 1/1569: Rolf Möbius, Die schwere deutsche Panzerwaffe.
ZA 1/1601: Hermann Breith, Durchbruch eines Panzerkorps durch ein tief gegliedertes feindliches Stellungssystem in der Schlacht bei Charkow im Juli 1943.
ZA 1/1700: Hermann Teske, Die Bedeutung des Eisenbahn-Transportwesens einer Heeresgruppe (H.Gr. Mitte) bei Aufmarsch, Verteidigung und Rückzug, März bis Sept. 1943.
ZA 1/1734: Kurt Zeitzler, Das Ringen um die großen Entscheidungen im zweiten Welkriege: Abwehrschlachten in Russland nach dem Wendepunkt im Kriege.
ZA 1/1902: Burkhart Müller-Hillebrand, et al., Das Panzerinstandsetzungswesen im Deutschen Heer.
ZA 1/1944: Walter Warlimont, Die Strategie der deutschen obersten Führung im zweiten Vierteljahr 1943.
ZA 1/1958: Burkhart Müller-Hillebrand, Statistik über Zahl, Verluste und Ersatz der deutschen Panzerkampfwagen.
ZA 1/2373: Theodor Busse, et al., Der Angriff 'Zitadelle' im Osten 1943.
ZA 1/2661: Hellmuth Reinhardt & Alfred Zerbel, Die Abwehrschlacht der 6. Armee am Mius im Juli/August 1943.

II. Archive of the Institut für Zeitgeschichte, Munich

ZS/A 31: Sammlung Bodo Scheurig
ZS 74: Friedrich Hoßbach

III. National Archives and Records Administration, Archives II, College Park, Maryland

A3343, SSO: SS Officers' Service Records
T-312/54-9: Armee-Abteilung Kempf/8. Armee
T-312/317-20: 9. Armee
T-312/1242: 2. Armee

T-313/153-72: 2. Panzerarmee
T-313/365-73: 4. Panzerarmee
T-314/200: III. Panzerkorps
T-314/864: XXXV. Armeekorps
T-315/94-7: 2. Panzer-Division
T-315/220: 4. Panzer-Division
T-315/277: 5. Panzer-Division
T-315/315: 6. Infanterie-Division
T-315/543-5: 9. Panzer-Division
T-315/599-603: 11. Panzer-Division
T-315/636: 12. Panzer-Division
T-315/724: 19. Panzer-Division
T-315/746-7: 20. Panzer-Division
T-315/902: 36. Infanterie-Division
T-315/1481: 167. Infanterie-Division
T-315/2076: 332. Infanterie-Division
T-315/2290: Panzer-Grenadier-Division 'Großdeutschland'
T-354/605-6: II. SS-Panzerkorps

IV. Österreichisches Staatsarchiv, Vienna

NLS, B/186: Nachlass Erhard Raus

V. Private Archive of Rüdiger von Manstein, Icking

Estate of Erich von Manstein

VI. Privately Owned Diaries and Manuscripts (Copies in Author's Possession)

Bergner, Harry W., Tagebuch, 8.11.1942-1.10.1943.

Diercks, Rolf, Lebenserinnerungen – überschattet vom Irrweg im 'Dritten Reich': Autobiographische Schilderungen von den Anfängen der Weimarer Republik bis zum Beginn des 21. Jahrhunderts (MS, 2009).

Fuchs, Fritz, Am Vormittag (MS, 1991).

Gührs, Erhard, In der Mitte des Infernos (MS, n.d.).

——., Kriegstagebuch: von 1939-1945.

Hupfeld, Carl, Bericht zum Unternehmen 'Zitadelle' vom 5.-12. Juli 1943 (MS, 2003).

Mulzer, Rainer, Tagebuch: 22.6.1942-18.7.1943.

Pilz, Wolfgang, Erinnerungen an meine Dienstzeit bei der 6./SS-Panzer-Regiment 1 LSSAH (MS, 1997).

Schüle, Walter (ed.), Panzerschlacht bei Prochorowka, 12. Juli 1943: Erinnerungen ehemaliger Angehöriger der 6./SS Pz.Rgt. 1 LSSAH (MS, 1997).

VII. The National Archives of the United Kingdom, Kew, London

WO 208/3573: War Office, British Military Intelligence, Section 14 (MI14), weekly summaries for the Chief of the Imperial General Staff (CIGS), 1941-1944.

VIII. Archive of the Verein Garnisongeschichte Jüterbog 'St. Barbara' e. V.

Beitrag zur Geschichte der Sturmgeschütz-Brigade 909. 3 Teile: Tagebuchaufzeichnungen, Ergänzungen zu den Tagebuchaufzeichnungen und Zusammenstellung aus Briefen des damaligen Lt. d. R. Ludwig Schön.

Geschichte der Sturmgeschützbrigade 911, ergänzt und neu zusammengestellt von Brigadeleiter Hans L. Mayer, Haunsheim.

Geschichte der Sturmgeschütz-Brigade 911 FGD – GD, zusammengestellt im Dezember 1985 von Karl-Heinz Stahmann, Bokel.

Geschichte der Sturmgeschützbrigade 911 von Febr. 1943 bis Mai 1945 (Stand: 31.7.1975).

Kriegstagebuch Nr. 1 der Sturmgeschütz-Abteilung 244, 27.3.1943-31.12.1943.

Sturmgeschütz-Brigade Großdeutschland. 2 Jahre Einsatz im Osten, 28.6.1942-23.6.1944.

Sturmgeschütz-Brigade 911. Erfahrungsbericht Juli 1943-Juni 1944.

Verlustlisten der StuGAbt. 905, zusammengestellt 1966 von Heinz Borisch nach den Erkennungsmarkenlisten der Deutschen Dienststelle (WASt) in Berlin.

IX. Zentrum für Militärgeschichte und Sozialwissenschaften der Bundeswehr, Potsdam

Held in Library:

Der Ostfeldzug der 86. rhein.-westf. Inf.-Division, dargestellt aufgrund von Tagebuchnotizen, Karten, Fotos, Briefen und unvergessenen und unvergesslichen Eindrücken und Erlebnissen (MS, 1962, ref. F.500.2373).

'Materialsammlung':

Copies of documents from the Central Archive of the Russian Ministry of Defence (Tsentral'nyy Arkhiv Ministerstva Oborony Rossiskoy Federatsii, Podolsk).

Published Material

Bagramjan, Iwan C. (ed.), *Geschichte der Kriegskunst* (East Berlin: Militärverlag der DDR, 1973).

Barbas, Bernd, *Geschichte der I. Gruppe des Jagdgeschwaders 52* (Eutin: Struve, 2006).

——., *Geschichte der III. Gruppe des Jagdgeschwaders 52* (Eutin: Struve, 2010).

Bauermeister, Christian & Jason Mark (eds.), *Iron Cross Brigade: The Story of Werner Gösel and Sturmgeschütz-Abteilung 244* (Sydney: Leaping Horseman, 2016).

Bergström, Christer, *Kursk. The Air Battle: July 1943* (Hersham: Classic, 2007).

Boberach, Heinz (ed.), *Meldungen aus dem Reich 1938-1945: Die geheimen Lageberichte des Sicherheitsdienstes der SS*, 17 vols. (Herrsching: Pawlak, 1984).

Boelcke, Willi A. (ed.), *Deutschlands Rüstung im Zweiten Weltkrieg: Hitlers Konferenzen mit Albert Speer 1942-1945* (Frankfurt/M.: Athenaion, 1969).

Breith, Hermann, 'Der Angriff des III. Pz.Korps bei "Zitadelle" im Juli 1943', *Wehrkunde*, 7 (1958), pp. 543-8.

Brown, Eric, *Wings of the Luftwaffe: Flying the captured German aircraft of World War II* (Manchester: Crécy, rev. edn, 2010).

Buchheit, Gert, 'Verrat der "Kursker Offensive"? Eine Abwehrmeldung gibt Aufschluss', *Die Nachhut*, 1 (1967), pp. 1-3.

Bukeikhanov, Pyotr E., *Kurskaya bitva*, 3 vols. (Moscow: Izdatel'stvo Tsentrpoligraf, 2011-2013).

Caidin, Martin, *The Tigers are burning* (New York: Hawthorn, 1974).

Carell, Paul, *Verbrannte Erde: Schlacht zwischen Wolga und Weichsel* (Berlin: Ullstein, 1966).

Chamberlain, Peter & Hilary L. Doyle, *Encyclopedia of German Tanks of World War Two: A Complete Illustrated Directory of German Battle Tanks, Armoured Cars, Self-Propelled Guns and Semi-Tracked Vehicles, 1933-1945* (London: Arms and Armour, 2nd edn, 1993).

Citino, Robert M., *The Wehrmacht retreats: Fighting a Lost War, 1943* (Lawrence, KS: University Press of Kansas, 2012).

Clark, Lloyd, *Kursk: The Greatest Battle* (London: Headline Review, 2011).

Cross, Robin, *Citadel: The Battle of Kursk* (London: Michael O'Mara, 1993).

Die Wehrmachtberichte 1939-1945, vol. 2: *1. Januar 1942 bis 31. Dezember 1943* (Cologne: Deutscher Taschenbuch Verlag, 1989).

Daynes, Vladimir O., *Tankovye voyska SSSR: 'Kavaleriya' Vtoroy Mirovoy* (Moscow: Algoritm, 2015).

Dickson, Gary A., 'Tank Repair and the Red Army in World War II', *The Journal of Slavic Military Studies*, 25 (2012), pp. 381-92.

Dörr, Manfred (ed.), *Schwere Panzerjäger-Abteilung 654: Geschrieben und aufgezeichnet noch während des Krieges durch Offiziere der Abteilung anhand der Kriegstagebücher* (Zweibrücken: VDM Heinz Nickel, 2011).

Dunn, Walter S., *Kursk: Hitler's Gamble, 1943* (Westport, CT: Praeger, 1997).

Engelmann, Joachim, *Zitadelle: Die größte Panzerschlacht im Osten 1943* (Friedberg: Podzun-Pallas, 1980).

Ershov, Aleksandr G., *Osvobozhdenie Donbassa* (Moscow: Voenizdat, 1973).

Fast, Niko, *Das Jagdgeschwader 52*, vol. 4: *Die Verluste des Jagdgeschwaders 52 sowie Nachträge für die ersten 3 Bände* (Bergisch Gladbach: Bensberger, 2nd edn, 1992).

Feuersenger, Marianne, *Im Vorzimmer der Macht: Aufzeichnungen aus dem Wehrmachtführungsstab und Führerhauptquartier 1940-1945* (Munich: F.A. Herbig, 5th edn, 1999).

Fleischer, Wolfgang, *Die größte Panzerschlacht des Zweiten Weltkrieges: Operation 'Zitadelle'* (Wölfersheim-Berstadt: Podzun-Pallas, 1997).

Fletcher, David (ed.), *Tiger! The Tiger Tank: A British View* (London: Her Majesty's Stationery Office, 1986).

Foerster, Roland G. (ed.), *Gezeitenwechsel im Zweiten Weltkrieg? Die Schlachten von Char'kov und Kursk im Frühjahr und Sommer 1943 in operativer Anlage, Verlauf und politischer Bedeutung* (Hamburg: E.S. Mittler, 1996).

Forczyk, Robert A., *Panther vs T-34: Ukraine 1943* (Oxford: Osprey, 2007).

——., *Kursk 1943: The Northern Front* (Oxford: Osprey, 2014).
——., *Tank Warfare on the Eastern Front, 1941-1945*, 2 vols. (Barnsley: Pen & Sword, 2016).
——., *Kursk 1943: The Southern Front* (Oxford: Osprey, 2017).
Friedli, Lukas, *Repairing the Panzers: German Tank Maintenance in World War 2*, 2 vols. (Heathfield: Panzerwrecks, 2011).
Frieser, Karl-Heinz, *Blitzkrieg-Legende: Der Westfeldzug 1940* (Munich: R. Oldenbourg, 2nd edn, 1996).
——., 'Die Schlacht im Kursker Bogen', in Militärgeschichtliches Forschungsamt (ed.), *Das Deutsche Reich und der Zweite Weltkrieg*, vol. 8: *Die Ostfront 1943/44: Der Krieg im Osten und an den Nebenfronten* (Munich: Deutsche Verlags-Anstalt, 2007), pp. 81-208.
——., 'Der Zusammenbruch der Heeresgruppe Mitte im Sommer 1944', in Militärgeschichtliches Forschungsamt (ed.), *Das Deutsche Reich und der Zweite Weltkrieg*, vol. 8: *Die Ostfront 1943/44: Der Krieg im Osten und an den Nebenfronten* (Munich: Deutsche Verlags-Anstalt, 2007), pp. 526-603.
Gehlen, Reinhard, *Der Dienst: Erinnerungen 1942-1971* (Mainz: Hase & Koehler, 1971).
Glantz, David M., *Soviet Military Intelligence in War* (London: Frank Cass, 1990).
——., *From the Don to the Dnepr: Soviet Offensive Operations, December 1942 – August 1943* (London: Frank Cass, 1991).
——. & Jonathan M. House, *The Battle of Kursk* (Lawrence, KS: University Press of Kansas, 1999).
——. & Harold S. Orenstein (eds.), *The Battle for Kursk 1943: The Soviet General Staff Study* (London: Frank Cass, 1999).
——., *When Titans Clashed: How the Red Army Stopped Hitler* (Lawrence, KS: University Press of Kansas, 2nd edn, 2015).
Goebbels, Joseph, *Die Tagebücher von Joseph Goebbels*, ed. Elke Fröhlich, pt. II: Diktate 1941-1945, 15 vols. (Munich: K.G. Saur, 1993-1996).
Goncharov, Vladislav L. et al. (eds.), *Bitva pod Kurskom: Ot oborony k nastupleniyu* (Moscow: Ast, 2006).
Gorbach, Vitaly G., *Nad Ognennoy Dugoy: Sovyetskaya aviatsiya v Kurskoy bitve* (Moscow: Yauza/Eksmo, 2007).
Grenkevich, Leonid D., *The Soviet Partisan Movement 1941-1944: A Critical Historiographical Analysis* (London: Frank Cass, 1999).
Groehler, Olaf, *Kampf um die Luftherrschaft: Beiträge zur Luftkriegsgeschichte des zweiten Weltkrieges* (East Berlin: Militärverlag der DDR, 2nd edn, 1989).
Großmann, Horst, *Geschichte der rheinisch-westfälischen 6. Infanterie-Division 1939-1945* (Bad Nauheim: Hans-Henning Podzun, 1958).
Guderian, Heinz, *Panzer Leader* (New York: Da Capo, 2nd edn, 2002).
Haag, Rudolf A. (ed.), *So war es: Berichte von und über Soldaten der Aufklärungsabteilung 7 der 7. Bayerischen Infanterie-Division* (Munich: Verlag für Wehrwissenschaften, 1985).

Hahn, Fritz, *Waffen und Geheimwaffen des deutschen Heeres 1933-1945*, 2 vols. (Bonn: Bernard & Graefe, 2nd edn, 1992).

Harrison, Richard W. (ed.), *The Battle of Kursk: The Red Army's Defensive Operations and Counter-Offensive, July-August 1943* (Solihull: Helion & Company, 2016).

Healy, Mark, *Zitadelle: The German Offensive against the Kursk Salient 4-17 July 1943* (Stroud: The History Press, 2008).

Heiber, Helmut et al. (eds.), *Hitler and His Generals: Military Conferences 1942-1945* (London: Greenhill, 2002).

Heinlein, Walter, *Vom Fahnenjunker zum Abteilungsführer*, ed. Ingo Möbius (Chemnitz: I. Möbius, 2nd edn, 2007).

Hitler, Adolf, *My Struggle* (Munich: Franz Eher Nachfolger, 'Stalag Edition', n.d.).

Hubatsch, Walter (ed.), *Hitlers Weisungen für die Kriegführung 1939-1945: Dokumente des Oberkommandos der Wehrmacht* (Erlangen: K. Müller, 4th edn, 1999).

Isaev, Aleksei, *Dubno 1941: The Greatest Tank Battle of the Second World War* (Solihull: Helion & Company, 2017).

Jahn, Peter et al. (eds.), *Unsere Russen, unsere Deutschen: Bilder vom Anderen 1800 bis 2000* (Berlin: C.H. Links, 2007).

Jähnert, Erhard, *Mal oben – mal unten: Einer, der immer dabei war* (Bad Kissingen: Remer-Heipke, 1992).

Jaugitz, Markus, *Funklenkpanzer: A History of German Army Remote- and Radio-Controlled Armor Units* (Winnipeg, Manitoba: J.J. Fedorowicz, 2001).

Jentz, Thomas L., *Germany's Panther Tank: The Quest for Combat Supremacy* (Atglen, PA: Schiffer, 1995).

——., *Panzertruppen: The Complete Guide to the Creation & Combat Employment of Germany's Tank Force*, 2 vols. (Atglen, PA: Schiffer, 1996).

——. & Hilary L. Doyle, *Germany's Tiger Tanks*, 3 vols. (Atglen, PA: Schiffer, 1997-2000).

——., *Panzer Production from 1933 to 1945* (Boyds, MD: Panzer Tracts, 2011).

Josten, Günther, *Gefechtsbericht: Kriegstagebücher 1939-1945*, ed. Kurt Braatz und Wilhelm Göbel (Moosburg: NeunundzwanzigSechs, 2011).

Kamenir, Victor J., *The Bloody Triangle: The Defeat of Soviet Armor in the Ukraine, June 1941* (Minneapolis: Zenith Press, 2008).

Karpenko, Alexander W., *Sowjetisch-russische Panzer 1905-2003* (Klitzschen: Elbe-Dnjepr, 2004).

Kavalerchik, Boris, 'Once again about the T-34', *The Journal of Slavic Military Studies*, 28 (2015), pp. 186-214.

Khazanov, Dmitriy B., *Air War over Kursk: Turning Point in the East* (Bedford: SAM, 2010).

——., *Aviaciya v Kurskoi bitve: Proval operacii 'Citadel'* (Moscow: Yauza/Eksmo, 2013).

Khazanov Dmitriy B./Gorbach Vitaly G., *Aviatsiya v bitve nad orlovsko-kurskoy dugoy: Oboronitel'nyy period* (Moscow: Pervaya Obraztsovaya, 2004).

Kielmansegg, Johann Adolf Graf von, 'Bemerkungen eines Zeitzeugen zu den Schlachten von Char'kov und Kursk aus der Sicht des damaligen Generalstabsoffiziers Ia in der Operationsabteilung des Generalstabs des Heeres', in Roland G. Foerster (ed.), *Gezeitenwechsel im Zweiten Weltkrieg? Die Schlachten von Char'kov und Kursk im Frühjahr und Sommer 1943 in operativer Anlage, Verlauf und politischer Bedeutung* (Hamburg, 1996), pp. 137-48

Kindel, Richard (ed.), *Die 8. Panzer-Division der Deutschen Wehrmacht 1939-1945: Bilder, Texte, Dokumente*, vol. 2 (Wuppertal: Sammlung Alte Armee und Deutsche Wehrmacht, 2nd edn, 2007).

Klink, Ernst, *Das Gesetz des Handelns: Die Operation 'Zitadelle' 1943* (Stuttgart: Deutsche Verlags-Anstalt, 1966).

Knittel, Hartmut H., *Panzerfertigung im Zweiten Weltkrieg: Industrieproduktion für die deutsche Wehrmacht* (Herford: E.S. Mittler & Sohn, 1988).

Kolbow, Karl Friedrich, *Die Tagebücher Karl Friedrich Kolbows (1899-1945): Nationalsozialist der ersten Stunde und Landeshauptmann der Provinz Westfalen*, ed. Martin Dröge (Paderborn: Ferdinand Schöningh, 2009).

Kolomiec, Maksim, *'Pantery' v Kurskoy bitve* (Moscow: Yauza/Eksmo, 2013).

Koltunov, Grigori A., 'Kurskaya bitva v tsifrakh', *Voenno-istoricheskii Zhurnal,* 6 (1968), pp. 58-68; and, 7 (1968), pp. 77-92.

Konew, Iwan S., *Aufzeichnungen eines Frontoberbefehlshabers 1943/44* (East Berlin: Militärverlag der DDR, 1978).

Kosar, Franz, *Panzerabwehrkanonen: 1916-1977* (Stuttgart: Motorbuch, 1978).

Kozhevnikov, Michail N., *The Command and Staff of the Soviet Army Air Force in the Great Patriotic War 1941-1945: A Soviet View* (Washington, D.C.: U.S. Government Printing Office, 1977).

Krausnick, Helmut, 'Zu Hitlers Ostpolitik im Sommer 1943', *Vierteljahrshefte für Zeitgeschichte*, 2 (1954), pp. 305-12.

Kregel, Heiko, *Geschichte des Panzer-Regiments 10 und der Panzer-Abteilung 67 1938-1945 und seiner Kriegsformationen Stab/Panzer-Brigade 10, Panzer-Kompanie 10 und Panzer-Ersatz-Abteilung 10* (Berlin: H. Kregel, 2010).

Krivosheev, Grigori F., *Soviet Casualties and Combat Losses in the Twentieth Century* (London: Greenhill, 1997).

——., *Rossiya i SSSR v voynach XX veka: Poteri vooruzhennykh sil: Statisticheskoe issledovanie* (Moscow: Olma-Press, 2001).

——., *Velikaya Otechestvennaya bez grifa sekretnosti: Kniga poter* (Moscow: Veche, 2009).

Krull, Albert, *Das Hannoversche Regiment 73: Geschichte des Panzer-Grenadier-Regiments 73 (vorm. Inf.Rgt. 73) 1939-1945* (Hanover: Regimentskameradschaft 73, 1967).

Lawrence, Christopher A., *Kursk: The Battle of Prokhorovka* (Sheridan, CO: Aberdeen, 2015).

Lehmann, Rudolf, *Die Leibstandarte*, vol. 3 (Osnabrück: Munin, 1982).

Lehweß-Litzmann, Walter, *Absturz ins Leben*, ed. Jörn Lehweß-Litzmann (Querfurt: Dingsda, 1994).

Léonard, Herbert, *Les avions de chasse russes et soviétiques 1915-1950* (Bayeux: Heimdal, 1995).

Lerche, Hans-Werner, *Testpilot auf Beuteflugzeugen* (Oberhaching: Aviatic, 7th edn, 1999).

Liedtke, Gregory, 'Furor Teutonicus: German Offensives and Counter-Attacks on the Eastern Front, August 1943 to March 1945', *The Journal of Slavic Military Studies*, 21 (2008), pp. 563-87.

Litvinenko, Vladimir V., *Lyudskie poteri na frontakh Velikoy Otechestvennoy: Krasnaya armiya protiv vermakhta* (Moscow: Veche, 2015).

Lochmann, Franz-Wilhelm et al. (eds.), *Erinnerungen an die Tiger-Abteilung 503 1942-1945* (Bassum: A. Rubbel, 1990).

Lodieu, Didier, *III. Pz. Korps at Kursk: The Part played by 6. Pz. Div., 7. Pz., 19. Pz. Div. and s. Pz. Abt. 503 during Operation 'Zitadelle' (Citadel)* (Paris: Histoire & Collections, 2007).

Lopez, Jean, *Koursk: Les quarante jours qui ont ruiné la Wehrmacht (5 juillet – 20 août 1943)* (Paris: Economica, 2008).

Lopukhovskiy, Lev N., *Prokhorovka: Bez grifa sekretnosti* (Moscow: Yauza/Eksmo, 2007).

——. & Boris Kavalerchik, *The Price of Victory: The Red Army's Casualties in the Great Patriotic War* (Barnsley: Pen & Sword, 2017).

Manstein, Erich von, *Verlorene Siege: Erinnerungen 1939-1944* (Bonn, 13th/14th edn, 1993).

Markin, Ilja I., *Die Kursker Schlacht* (East Berlin: Verlag des Ministeriums für Nationale Verteidigung, 1960).

Mehner, Kurt (ed.), *Die geheimen Tagesberichte der Deutschen Wehrmachtführung im Zweiten Weltkrieg 1939-1945: Die gegenseitige Lageunterrichtung der Wehrmacht-, Heeres- und Luftwaffenführung über alle Haupt- und Nebenkriegsschauplätze: 'Lage West' (OKW-Kriegsschauplätze Nord, West, Italien, Balkan), 'Lage Ost' (OKH) und 'Luftlage Reich'. Vol. 7: 1. Juni 1943-31. August 1943* (Osnabrück: Biblio, 1988).

Mel'chin, Sergej A.,'"Obespechit' prevoskhodstvo sovetskikh tankov": Dokladnye zapiski I. V. Stalinu', *Istoricheskiy Arkhiv*, 1 (1993), pp. 105-15.

Mellenthin, Friedrich Wilhelm von, *Panzer Battles 1939-1945: A Study of the Employment of Armour in the Second World War* (London: Cassell & Company, 1955)

Mostowenko, Wladimir D., *Panzer gestern und heute: Abriss der Entstehung und Entwicklung der Panzertechnik* (East Berlin: Deutscher Militärverlag, 1961).

Müller-Hillebrand, Burkhart, *Das Heer 1933-1945: Entwicklung des organisatorischen Aufbaues*, vol. 3: *Der Zweifrontenkrieg: Das Heer vom Beginn des Feldzuges gegen die Sowjetunion bis zum Kriegsende* (Frankfurt/M.: E.S. Mittler & Sohn, 1969).

Müller, Peter & Wolfgang Zimmermann, *Sturmgeschütz III: Rückgrat der Infanterie*, 2 vols. (Andelfingen: History Facts, 2007/2008).

Mulligan, Timothy P., 'Spies, Ciphers and "Zitadelle": Intelligence and the Battle of Kursk, 1943', *Journal of Contemporary History*, 22 (1987), pp. 235-60.

Münch, Karlheinz, *Combat History of schwere Panzerjäger Abteilung 653, formerly the Sturmgeschütz Abteilung 197* (Winnipeg, Manitoba: J.J. Fedorowicz, 1997).

——., *Combat History of schwere Panzer-Jäger-Abteilung 654: In Action in the East and West with the Ferdinand and the Jagdpanther* (Winnipeg, Manitoba: J.J. Fedorowicz, 2002).

——., *StuG.Abt./Brig. 210* (Katowice: Model Hobby, 2007).

Mund, Ernst (ed.), *Grenadiere, Jäger: Quellen und Darstellungen zu einer Geschichte des Infanterieregiments 17* (Osterode: Giebel & Oehlschlägel, 1959).

Murray, Williamson, *Strategy for Defeat: The Luftwaffe 1933-1945* (Montgomery, AL: Air University Press, 1983).

Nehring, Walther K., *Die Geschichte der deutschen Panzerwaffe 1916-1945* (Stuttgart: Motorbuch, 1974).

Neumann, Joachim, *Die 4. Panzerdivision 1938-1945*, 2 vols. (Bonn: J. Neumann, 2nd edn, 1989).

Nevshemal, Martin, *Objective Ponyri! The Defeat of XXXXI. Panzerkorps at Ponyri Train Station* (Sydney: Leaping Horseman, 2015).

Newton, Steven H. (ed.), *Kursk: The German View* (New York: Da Capo, 2002).

Nipe, George M., *Decision in the Ukraine, Summer 1943: II. SS and III. Panzerkorps* (Winnipeg, Manitoba: J.J. Fedorowicz, 1996).

——., *Last Victory in Russia: The SS-Panzerkorps and Manstein's Kharkov Counteroffensive, February-March 1943* (Atglen, PA: Schiffer, 2000).

——., *Blood, Steel, and Myth: The II. SS-Panzer-Korps and the Road to Prochorowka, July 1943* (Stamford, CT: RZM, 2011).

Nowarra, Heinz J., *Die deutsche Luftrüstung 1933-1945*, 4 vols. (Koblenz: Bernard & Graefe, 1993).

Piekalkiewicz, Janusz, *Unternehmen Zitadelle. Kursk und Orel: Die größte Panzerschlacht des 2. Weltkrieges* (Herrsching: Pawlak, licensed edn, 1989).

Plato, Anton D. von, *Die Geschichte der 5. Panzerdivision 1938-1945* (Regensburg: Walhalla & Praetoria, 1978).

Pöhlmann, Markus, *Der Panzer und die Mechanisierung des Krieges: Eine deutsche Geschichte 1890 bis 1945* (Paderborn: Ferdinand Schöningh, 2016).

Popjel, Nikolai N., *Panzer greifen an* (East Berlin: Deutscher Militärverlag, 1964).

Prien, Jochen & Gerhard Stemmer, *Messerschmitt Bf 109 im Einsatz bei der II./Jagdgeschwader 3, 1940-1945* (Eutin: J. Prien, 1996).

——., *Messerschmitt Bf 109 im Einsatz bei der III./Jagdgeschwader 3, 1940-1945* (Eutin: J. Prien, 1996).

Rahn, Werner & Gerhard Schreiber (eds.), *Kriegstagebuch der Seekriegsleitung 1939-1945*, pt. A, 68 vols. (Herford: E.S. Mittler, 1988-1997).

Reichhelm, Günther, *Verantwortung und Gewissensnot: Erinnerungen* (Würzburg: Wilhelm Gottlieb Korn, 2003).

Restayn, Jean & Nicole Moller, *Operation Citadel: A Text and Photo Album*, 2 vols. (Winnipeg, Manitoba: J.J. Fedorowicz, 2004/2006).

Ribbentrop, Rudolf von, *Mein Vater Joachim von Ribbentrop: Erlebnisse und Erinnerungen* (Graz: Ares, 2008).

Roes, Wilhelm, *Freiwillig in den Krieg: Auf den Spuren einer verlorenen Jugend*, ed. Jörn Roes (Berlin: Edition q, 2005).

Rogmann, Willi, *Meine Kriegserlebnisse* (Bad Lobenstein: Bethge, 2009).

Rokossowski, Konstantin K., *Soldatenpflicht: Erinnerungen eines Frontoberbefehlshabers* (East Berlin: Deutscher Militärverlag, 1971).

Rosen, Richard von, *Als Panzeroffizier in Ost und West: Im Panzer III, Tiger und Königstiger in Russland, Frankreich und Ungarn* (Würzburg: Flechsig, 2013).

Rotmistrov, Pavel A., *Tankovoe srazhenie pod Prokhorovkoy* (Moscow: Voennoe izdatel'stvo, 1960).

——., *Stalnaya gvardiya* (Moscow: Voennoe izdatel'stvo, 1984).

Sadarananda, Dana V., *Beyond Stalingrad: Manstein and the Operations of Army Group Don* (New York: Praeger, 1990).

Schlabrendorff, Fabian von, *Begegnungen in fünf Jahrzehnten* (Tübingen: Wunderlich, 1979).

Schadewitz, Michael, *Panzerregiment 11/Panzerabteilung 65 1937-1945, Panzerersatz- und Ausbildungsabteilung 11 1939-1945: Auszüge aus Kriegstagebüchern und anderen Quellen sowie Berichten von Soldaten eines Westfälischen Panzerregiments* (Lünen: Schmidt, 1987).

Schäufler, Hans (ed.), *So lebten und so starben sie: Das Buch vom Panzer-Regiment 35* (Bamberg: Kameradschaft ehem. Panzer-Regiment 35, 1968).

——., *Der Weg war weit: Panzer zwischen Weichsel und Wolga* (Neckargemünd: Kurt Vowinckel, 1973).

Schleicher, Karl-Theo & Wolfgang Schneider, 'Gedanken zur Weiterentwicklung des Kampfpanzers', *Das schwarze Barett*, 14 (1995), pp. 8-14.

Schmidt, August, *Geschichte der 10. Division: 10. Infanterie-Division (mot), 10. Panzer-Grenadier-Division, 1933-1945* (Bad Nauheim: Podzun, 1963).

Schneider, Wolfgang, *Tigers in Combat*, 2 vols. (Winnipeg, Manitoba: J.J. Fedorowicz, 1994/1998).

——., *Tiger der Division 'Das Reich'* (Uelzen: W. Schneider, 2005).

——., *Tiger der Division Totenkopf* (Uelzen: W. Schneider, 2009).

——., & Frank Köhler, *Tiger im Kampf*, vol. 3 (Uelzen: W. Schneider, 2013).

Schramm, Percy E. (ed.), *Kriegstagebuch des Oberkommandos der Wehrmacht (Wehrmachtführungsstab) 1940-1945*, kept by Helmuth Greiner and Percy E. Schramm, 4 vols. (Bonn: Bernard & Graefe, 1990).

Schramm, Wilhelm von, *Verrat im Zweiten Weltkrieg: Vom Kampf der Geheimdienste in Europa* (Düsseldorf: Econ, 1967).

——., *Geheimdienste im Zweiten Weltkrieg: Nach Öffnung der alliierten Geheimarchive fortgeführt, ergänzt und erweitert von Hans Büchler* (Munich: F.A. Herbig, 6th edn, 2002).

Schranck, David, *Thunder at Prokhorovka: A Combat History of Operation Citadel, Kursk, July 1943* (Solihull: Helion & Company, 2013).
Schtemenko, Sergei M., *Im Generalstab* (East Berlin: Deutscher Militärverlag, 1969).
Schwarz, Eberhard, *Die Stabilisierung der Ostfront nach Stalingrad: Mansteins Gegenschlag zwischen Donez und Dnjepr im Frühjahr 1943* (Göttingen: Muster-Schmidt, 1986).
Searle, Alaric, *Armoured Warfare: A Military, Political and Global History* (London: Bloomsbury Academic, 2017).
Shchekotikhin, Egor E., *Krupneyshee tankovoe srazhenie Velikoy Otechestvennoy: Bitva za Orël* (Moscow: Yauza/Eksmo, 2009).
Shirokorad, Aleksandr B., *Entsiklopediya otechestvennoy artillerii* (Minsk: Kharvest, 2000).
Showalter, Dennis E., *Armor and Blood: The Battle of Kursk* (New York: Random House, 2013).
Shukow, Georgi K., *Erinnerungen und Gedanken*, vol. 2 (East Berlin: Deutscher Militärverlag, 1969).
Sigg, Marco, *Der Unterführer als Feldherr im Taschenformat: Theorie und Praxis der Auftragstaktik im deutschen Heer 1869 bis 1945* (Paderborn: Ferdinand Schöningh, 2014).
Sokolov, Boris V., *Tsena Pobedy: Velikaya Otechestvennaya: Neizvestnoe ob izvestnom* (Moscow: Moskovskii Rabochii, 1991).
——., 'The Cost of War: Human Losses for the USSR and Germany, 1939-1945', *The Journal of Slavic Military Studies*, 9 (1996), pp. 152-93.
——., *Georgy Zhukov: Polkovodec, despot, lichnost* (Moscow: Zebra E, 2013).
——., *The Role of the Soviet Union in the Second World War: A Re-Examination* (Solihull: Helion & Company, 2013).
———., *Marshal K.K. Rokossovsky: The Red Army's Gentleman Commander* (Solihull: Helion & Company, 2015).
——., *Tsena voiny: Lyudskie poteri Rossii/SSSR v XX –XXI vv.* (Moscow: Airo-XXI, 2017).
Solowjow, Boris G., *Wendepunkt des Zweiten Weltkrieges: Die Schlacht bei Kursk* (Cologne: Pahl-Rugenstein, 1984).
——., '"Kutuzov" i "Rumyantsev" protiv "Tsitadeli"', *Voenno-istoricheskii Zhurnal*, 4 (1998), pp. 2-13.
Spielberger, Walter J.: *Der Panzerkampfwagen Panther und seine Abarten* (Stuttgart: Motorbuch, 4th edn, 1994).
——., *Der Panzerkampfwagen Tiger und seine Abarten* (Stuttgart: Motorbuch, 5th edn, 1994).
——., *Sturmgeschütze: Entwicklung und Fertigung der sPak* (Stuttgart: Motorbuch, 3rd edn, 1997).
——., Hilary L. Doyle & Thomas L. Jentz, *Schwere Jagdpanzer: Entwicklung, Fertigung, Einsatz* (Stuttgart: Motorbuch, 2nd edn, 1996).
——., *Begleitwagen, Panzerkampfwagen IV* (Stuttgart: Motorbuch, 1998).

Stadler, Silvester (ed.), *Die Offensive gegen Kursk 1943: II. SS-Panzerkorps als Stoßkeil im Großkampf* (Osnabrück: Munin, 1980).

Stein, Marcel, *Der Januskopf: Feldmarschall von Manstein – eine Neubewertung* (Bissendorf: Biblio, 2004).

Stopper, Sebastian, '"Die Straße ist deutsch." Der sowjetische Partisanenkrieg und seine militärische Effizienz: Eine Fallstudie zur Logistik der Wehrmacht im Brjansker Gebiet April bis Juli 1943', *Vierteljahrshefte für Zeitgeschichte*, 59 (2011), pp. 385-411.

Stoves, Rolf, *Die gepanzerten und motorisierten deutschen Großverbände 1935-1945: Divisionen und selbständige Brigaden* (Wölfersheim-Berstadt: Podzun-Pallas, 1994).

Strauß, Franz J., *Geschichte der 2. (Wiener) Panzer-Division* (Eggolsheim: Dörfler, 2005).

Suld'in, Andrey V., *Kurskaya bitva: Polnaya khronika – 50 dnei i nochei* (Moscow: Ast, 2014).

Svirin, Mikhail N., *Panther: Pz.Kpfw V* (Armada, No. 5, Moscow: Eksprint, 2000).

——., *Das Schwere Sturmgeschütz Ferdinand* (Armada, No. 12, Moscow: Eksprint, 2002).

Teske, Hermann, *Die silbernen Spiegel: Generalstabsdienst unter der Lupe* (Heidelberg: Kurt Vowinckel, 1952).

——., 'Die Bedeutung der Eisenbahn bei Aufmarsch, Verteidigung und Rückzug einer Heeresgruppe: Dargestellt an der deutschen Operation "Zitadelle" gegen Kursk und ihre Auswirkungen im Sommer 1943', *Allgemeine Schweizerische Militärzeitschrift*, 121 (1955), pp. 120-135.

Tiemann, Ralf (ed.), *7. Panzerkompanie: Chronik der siebenten Panzerkompanie der 1. SS-Panzerdivision 'Leibstandarte'* (Neustadt an der Aisch: R. Tiemann, 1992).

Töppel, Roman, *Die Offensive gegen Kursk 1943: Legenden, Mythen und Propaganda* (MA thesis, Dresden University of Technology, 2001), available online at: https://independent.academia.edu/RomanToeppel.

——., 'Legendenbildung in der Geschichtsschreibung: Die Schlacht bei Kursk', *Militärgeschichtliche Zeitschrift*, 61 (2002), pp. 369-401.

——., 'Kursk: Mythen und Wirklichkeit einer Schlacht', *Vierteljahrshefte für Zeitgeschichte*, 57 (2009), pp. 349-84.

——., 'Das Ritterkreuz des Eisernen Kreuzes und der Kampfwert militärischer Verbände', *Zeitschrift für Heereskunde*, 76 (2012), pp. 180-90.

——., 'Waffen-SS und Wehrmacht in der Schlacht bei Kursk: Ein Vergleich im operativen Einsatz', in Jan Erik Schulte, Peter Lieb & Bernd Wegner (eds.), *Die Waffen-SS: Neue Forschungen* (Paderborn: Ferdinand Schöningh, 2014), pp. 317-35.

Tucker-Jones, Anthony, *Kursk 1943: Hitler's Bitter Harvest* (Stroud: The History Press, 2018).

Venohr, Wolfgang, *Die Abwehrschlacht: Jugenderinnerungen 1940-1955* (Berlin: Junge Freiheit, 2nd edn, 2003).

Vopersal, Wolfgang, *Soldaten, Kämpfer, Kameraden: Marsch und Kämpfe der SS-Totenkopfdivision*, vol. 3 (Bielefeld: Biblio, 1987).

Wagner, Gerhard (ed.), *Lagevorträge des Oberbefehlshabers der Kriegsmarine vor Hitler 1939-1945* (Munich: J.F. Lehmann, 1972).

Waiss, Walter, *Chronik Kampfgeschwader Nr. 27 Boelcke. pt. 4: 01.01.1943-31.12.1943* (Aachen: Helios, 2007).

Warlimont, Walter, *Inside Hitler's Headquarters 1939-1945* (London: Weidenfeld and Nicolson, 1964).

Warnick, Rüdiger & Stephan Cazenave, *Tiger! Von schwere Kompanie/SS-Pz.Rgt. 2 bis s.SS-Panzerabteilung 102/502* (Bayeux: Heimdal, 2008).

Wasner, Adalbert, *Inf.- und Pz.-Gren.-Regiment 74: Erinnerungen an den Weg des Regiments durch Polen, Holland, Belgien, Frankreich und Russland 1939-1945* (Hanover: Regimentskameradschaft 74, 1970).

Wassilewski, Alexander M., *Sache des ganzen Lebens* (East Berlin: Militärverlag der DDR, 1977).

Weidinger, Otto, *Division Das Reich: Der Weg der 2. SS-Panzer-Division 'Das Reich'*, vol. 4 (Osnabrück: 2nd edn, Munin, 1986).

Wettstein, Adrian E., *Die Wehrmacht im Stadtkampf 1939-1942* (Paderborn: Ferdinand Schöningh, 2014).

Wilbeck, Christopher W., *Sledgehammers: Strengths and Flaws of Tiger Tank Battalions in World War II* (Bedford, PA: The Aberjona Press, 2004).

Woche, Klaus-Rainer, *Zwischen Pflicht und Gehorsam: Generaloberst Rudolf Schmidt 1886-1957* (Berlin: K.-R. Woche, 2002).

Wood, Ian M., *Tigers of the Death's Head: SS Totenkopf Division's Tiger Company* (Mechanicsburg, PA: Stackpole, 2013).

Woroshejkin, Arseni W., *Jagdflieger*, vol. 2 (Berlin: Militärverlag der DDR, 3rd edn, 1985).

Zährl, Hugo, *Vier Jahre in vorderster Front: Kriegstagebuch eines Trägers der Ehrenblattspange in der 3. SS-Panzerdivision 'Totenkopf'* (Trier: Munin, 2007).

Zaloga, Steven J. & James Grandsen, *Soviet Tanks and Combat Vehicles of World War Two* (London: Arms and Armour, 1984).

——., 'Technological Surprise and the Initial Period of War: The Case of the T-34 Tank in 1941', *The Journal of Slavic Military Studies*, 6 (1993), pp. 634-646.

Zamulin, Valeriy N.: *Zasekrechennaya Kurskaya bitva: Neizvestnye dokumenty svidetelstvuyut* (Moscow: Yauza/Eksmo, 2007).

——., *Kurskii izlom: Reshayushchaya bitva Velikoi Otechestvennoi* (Moscow: Yauza/Eksmo, 2008).

——., *Zabytoe srazhenie Ognennoy Dugi: Krushenie operatsii 'Citadel'* (Moscow: Yauza/Eksmo, 2009).

——., *Demolishing the Myth: The Tank Battle at Prokhorovka, Kursk, July 1943: An Operational Narrative* (Solihull: Helion, 2011).

——., 'The Battle of Kursk: New Findings', *The Journal of Slavic Military Studies*, 25 (2012), pp. 409-17.

——., *The Battle of Kursk 1943: The View through the Camera Lens* (Solihull: Helion & Company, 2014).

——., *The Battle of Kursk: Controversial and Neglected Aspects* (Solihull, 2017: Helion & Company).

Zavizion, Gavriil T. et al., *Boevoy sostav Sovetskoy Armii*, pt. III: yanvar – dekabr 1943 g. (Moscow: Voennoe izdatel'stvo, 1972).

Zetterling, Niklas, *Normandy 1944: German Military Organization, Combat Power and Organizational Effectiveness* (Winnipeg, Manitoba: J.J. Fedorowicz, 2000).

——., & Anders Frankson, *Kursk 1943: A Statistical Analysis* (London: Frank Cass, 2000).

Zhilin, Vitaly A. et al. (eds.), *Kurskaya bitva: Khronika, fakty, lyudi*, 2 vols. (Moscow: Olma-Press, 2003).

Zhukov, Vasily I., *Kurskaya bitva: Vzglyad iz XXI veka* (Moscow: Russkii Renessans, 2008).

Zins, Alfred, *Die Operation Zitadelle: Die militärgeschichtliche Diskussion und ihr Niederschlag im öffentlichen Bewusstsein als didaktisches Problem* (Frankfurt/M.: Peter Lang, 1986).

Zolotaryov, Vladimir A. et al. (eds.), *Russkii arkhiv: Velikaya Otechestvennaya*, vol. 15 (4-4): *Kurskaya bitva: Dokumenty i materialy 27 marta – 23 avgusta 1943 goda* (Moscow: Terra, 1997).

Index

People

Places

Military Units: German

Military Units: Soviet